More praise for
Climate change and human development

'Whilst there is a clear moral and ethical dilemma that the
world's poorest, and least responsible for carbon production,
are bearing and will continue to bear the brunt of climate
change, this positive and timely book uses case studies that
remind us there are new models of human development
coming from those most impacted, which can guide us
in both our adaptation and our mitigation efforts.'

JULIAN AGYEMAN,
TUFTS UNIVERSITY

'This is an important book for several reasons. It shows that
across all sectors and all countries, the livelihoods of the
poorest are today being undermined by climate change.
Yet at the same time the capacity not only to cope, but
to build improved lives, resides within these communities,
sometimes catalysed by the work of NGOs such as those in
the Up in Smoke coalition. The central conclusion, that both
development and adaptation must focus on strengthening
communities from the bottom up and build opportunities
for participation in policy-making, is an urgent message.'

JONATHAN ENSOR,
STOCKHOLM ENVIRONMENT INSTITUTE

About the author

DR HANNAH REID is a researcher currently working with the Climate Change Group and the Biodiversity Team at the International Institute for Environment and Development in London. She has a PhD in Biodiversity Management and over twelve years' experience working on climate change, with particular focus on how best to help those who are most vulnerable to its impacts. She was one of the founding members of the Up in Smoke group in 2003. She is a co-editor of *Reducing Poverty and Sustaining the Environment: The Politics of Local Engagement* (2005) and of *Community Based Adaptation to Climate Change: Scaling it Up* (2014).

Climate change
and human development

HANNAH REID

Zed Books | LONDON

Climate Change and Human Development was first published in 2014 by Zed Books Ltd, 7 Cynthia Street, London N1 9JF, UK

www.zedbooks.co.uk

Copyright © Hannah Reid 2014
Cover images Tarawa, Kiribati © Jocelyn Carlin/Panos

The right of Hannah Reid to be identified as the author of this work has been asserted by her in accordance with the Copyright, Designs and Patents Act, 1988

Designed and typeset in Calluna by illuminati, Grosmont
Index by John Barker
Cover designed by www.roguefour.co.uk

A catalogue record for this book is available from the British Library
Library of Congress Cataloging in Publication Data available

ISBN 978-1-78032-441-8 hb
ISBN 978-1-78032-440-1 pb

Printed and bound by CPI Group (UK) Ltd, Croydon, CR0 4YY

MIX
Paper from
responsible sources
FSC
www.fsc.org   FSC® C013604

Contents

Acknowledgements

Thanks are due to all individual and institutional members of the Up in Smoke coalition for their energy, time and commitment to help the world's poorest in the context of the transformations that climate change will bring, and for providing much of the raw material for this book. Andrew Simms deserves special thanks for his invaluable inputs, writing and time spent collating material for the many original Up in Smoke reports on which this book is based; for his critical thinking, which provides much of the direction for this book, particularly the final chapter; and also for providing inspirational leadership, along with Saleemul Huq, to the Up in Smoke coalition when it started in 2003. John Magrath, Victoria Johnson and Michael Edwards also helped write some of the original Up in Smoke reports on which this book draws. Victoria Johnson, Hannah Morrill and Arjen Bouwmeester provided writing, editorial and fact-checking assistance in the final stages of this book, and Kim Walker at Zed Books provided valuable editorial assistance. Thanks are due to the New Economics Foundation and the International Institute for Environment and Development for providing resources (mostly staff time but also office space and limited financial support) for enabling Up in Smoke coalition meetings to take place, and for the reports and this book to be published.

Preface

In recognition of the need to think of climate change as a development issue and not just an environmental one, the International Institute for Environment and Development (IIED) and NEF (the New Economics Foundation) decided to establish a coalition to bring development organisations into the climate debate.

The Working Group on Climate Change and Development, otherwise known as the Up in Smoke group, first met in 2003. It met regularly, organised numerous events and media outreach activities, and wrote a number of Up in Smoke reports to raise awareness about the issue.

These reports showed that whilst the world's poor are clearly hit hardest by climate change, so too do they hold many of the solutions for how best to cope with its effects, and at times reduce greenhouse gas emissions to boot. Resources are always limited; it is important that a focus on increasing scientific capacity or debating how to reduce greenhouse gas emissions does not happen to the exclusion of investment in helping communities cope with climate change at the grassroots level. Many already have no choice but to adapt to change, and need additional support now to strengthen their resilience. This book outlines what several of those approaches could be.

> I am delighted that such a broad group of environment and development organizations, many of which are faith based, have come together to speak with a common voice, drawing attention

to climate change in the African context. It is well known that climate change will have particularly devastating effects on Africa. Indeed, case studies in this report suggest that this is already happening. But this report also shows the strength and creativity of African people in times of stress. What is needed most now is that Africans are supported in their efforts to build on these strengths. (Archbishop Desmond Tutu)

Although this book cannot be viewed as representing the views of all Up in Smoke coalition members, it pulls together stories and material from the Up in Smoke reports, all of which were provided by coalition members and their partner organisations. For more detailed information on where material in the book comes from, readers should refer back to the original Up in Smoke reports.[1] Some of the data in the original reports has, however, been updated in this book to reflect advances in knowledge since the reports were published.

Up in Smoke coalition members

ActionAid
Birdlife International
CARE
Catholic Agency for Overseas Development
Christian Aid
Churches Together in Britain and Ireland
Columban Faith and Justice
The Energy and Resources Institute, Europe
Friends of the Earth
Greenpeace
Institute of Development Studies
International Institute for Environment and Development
Medact
New Economics Foundation

Operation Noah
Oxfam
Panos
People and Planet
Practical Action
Progressio
Royal Society for the Protection of Birds
Tearfund
Water Aid
World Vision
WWF

Introduction

The celebrated Swedish chemist Svante Arrhenius was the first to attempt to quantify the relationship between the most common man-made greenhouse gas, carbon dioxide (CO_2) and global surface temperatures. Arrhenius is often reported to have said 'we are evaporating our coal mines into the air.' While this is now known to have been incorrectly attributed to Arrhenius, and propagated for the past twenty years due to some slapdash referencing,[1] the essence of this statement remains true.

While Arrhenius's predictions of the relationship between global average surface temperature and atmospheric CO_2 was remarkably accurate given the simplicity of his calculations compared to today's global climate models, his assessment of the impact of climate change on mankind couldn't have been more wrong. In fact, Arrhenius had actually celebrated the 'hot house theory' as he called it, believing that

> we may hope to enjoy ages with more equable and better climates, ... ages when the earth will bring forth much more abundant crops than at present, for the benefit of a rapidly propagating mankind.

Arrhenius had not understood, however, that his 'hot house theory', or global warming as it is commonly known now, would lead to increasingly volatile and unpredictable weather and climate, such as extreme rainfall events or the failure of monsoon rains. Neither had he considered that the amplitude and direction of change would vary across various geographical scales and would affect people in different ways, depending on their age, income or overall health.

Just over 110 years have passed since Arrhenius estimated that a doubling of CO_2 would cause a global temperature rise of 5–6°c – remarkably close to the current predictions of the Intergovernmental Panel on Climate Change (IPCC). Over that time, scientists have travelled to the far reaches of the planet to try to understand the relationship between CO_2 and global surface temperatures over several hundred millennia.

Reliable global surface temperature records collected from thermometers have existed only since widespread reliable measurements began in the late nineteenth century. As a result, climate scientists have had to rely on biological and geological records – tree rings, ice cores, ocean sediment cores, stalagmites and stalactites – to reconstruct a record of atmospheric concentrations of CO_2 and methane (another greenhouse gas), and surface and ocean temperatures. This record now reaches as far back as 570 million years. Past variations in the earth's climate and in the composition of the atmosphere provide a long-term perspective against which the human-induced changes in the atmosphere, and projected changes in the atmosphere and climate, can be compared.

Ice cores have been particularly important, as the ice preserved in the Antarctic and Greenland ice caps contains air bubbles that were sealed off within a few hundred years of the accumulation of snow. These tiny, almost microscopic bubbles provide a means to analyse the composition of the earth's atmosphere for the past 800,000 years.[2]

Gradually, from multiple ice cores from the northern and southern hemispheres, scientists have been able to piece together a chronology of atmospheric levels of the key greenhouse gases. They are now in agreement that the relationship between Antarctic temperatures and CO_2 concentrations over the last

650,000 years has been very close, and that current atmospheric concentrations of carbon dioxide and methane exceed any natural variation in these concentrations experienced over the same period.[3]

This is the result of humankind's activities: the burning of fossil fuels such as coal, oil and natural gas; land use change such as the felling of forests and the growth of cities; and industrial agricultural practice. And while the human race has changed the composition of the atmosphere for at least the past five millennia, it is only in the wake of the Industrial Revolution that concentrations began to grow exponentially. The result is global climate change.

The primary source of the increased concentration of CO_2 is unequivocally the burning of fossil fuels, although land-use changes have also contributed significantly to increasing rates of CO_2 emissions. Annual fossil fuel CO_2 emissions have increased year on year since the 1990s, and in May 2013 measurements from the 'Keeling Lab' on the Mauna Loa Volcano in Hawaii, which has the longest continuous records of atmospheric CO_2 concentrations, registered more than 400 parts per million of CO_2. The last time CO_2 was regularly above 400 parts per million was 3–5 million years ago – before modern humans existed. The climate back then was also much warmer than it is today.

While the media occasionally present global warming as an issue open for debate, and some politicians still dispute the facts because they do not suit their agenda (or their funders' or advisers' agendas), few reputable scientists these days deny the realities of global warming and climate change. There is, in fact, remarkably strong consensus among scientists such as those involved in the IPCC and more than forty scientific societies and academies of science, including all of the national academies of science of the major industrialized countries, that the earth's climate is being modified by human activities.[4] One recent study of peer-reviewed scientific literature showed that this consensus is increasing and that 'the number of papers rejecting the consensus on anthropogenic global warming is a vanishingly small proportion of the published research.'[5]

Many have worked hard to refute or undermine this consensus. For example, between 2002 and 2010 anonymous conservative billionaires donated nearly US$120 million to more than a hundred anti-climate groups casting doubt on the science behind climate change[6] in a campaign that has been likened to previous efforts by the tobacco industry to undermine the now widely accepted science regarding the influence of tobacco on health.[7] Along with a weariness of disaster narratives, an unwillingness to take the bitter pill that many believe acting on global warming will require, and a focus on economic issues in recent years, this has helped influence public opinion. Many still doubt the realities of global warming despite the scientific consensus and despite increasingly visible signs all around us of its impacts.[8]

As each year passes, more frequent and more severe extreme weather events, such as hurricanes and droughts, and gradual changes to local weather patterns are making it harder and harder for the poor to survive, stay healthy and earn a living. Ironically it is these same poor people and countries that produce the lowest greenhouse gas emissions and have done least to cause the problem of climate change. At roughly midday on the third day in January, an average American is already responsible for emitting the same amount of greenhouse gases from burning fossil fuels as the average Tanzanian uses the entire year.[9] Food production, water supplies, public health and people's livelihoods are all being damaged and undermined.

Until roughly 2000, climate change was seen principally as an 'environmental' problem. The main agenda of scientists working on climate change and those who determine climate change policy responses in industrialised countries was one of monitoring and measuring the changing climate, then predicting future changes. At international climate change negotiations these countries focused their arguments around the issue of reducing greenhouse gas emissions to deal with climate change, otherwise known as 'mitigation' in climate change circles. They argued that all countries should have the responsibility to do this. Poorer countries, by contrast, tended to be more concerned with the immediate impact climate change was having on their citizens. These countries have minimal responsibility for climate change due to their historically very low levels of greenhouse gas emissions, so they rightly argued that it was unfair that the burden of climate change should fall so heavily on their citizens. Instead, they argued that more attention should be given to the issue of how people living with climate change should be helped to cope with its effects. Thus the emphasis on 'adaptation' to climate change as opposed to just 'mitigation' grew.

More recently, climate change debates have entered a new 'era' whereby the issue is no longer just about tackling an environmental or development problem, but about addressing climate change in the context of global justice. With the gap between what scientists say is necessary – in terms of action on mitigation and adaptation – and the trajectory we are travelling on widening every year[10] the question now is how to compensate those who we knowingly acknowledge are worst affected.[11]

Energy and economic growth

Since the first commercial oil well was opened in Titusville, Pennsylvania, in the late 1850s, the world has experienced a period of rapid economic growth. Over 97 per cent of humanity's financial wealth has been created in just 0.01 per cent of human history, with the global use of fossil fuels increasing by at least 800-fold since the Industrial Revolution.[12] And, while still a contentious issue among conventional economists, compelling evidence suggests that this rapid period of growth can be attributed almost entirely to the availability of ever-cheaper energy from coal, oil and gas.[13]

Yet growth as a means of ending poverty has been failing on its own terms too, with a shrinking share of benefits reaching those who need it the most. In the 1990s, to achieve a single dollar of poverty reduction, for those living on less than US$1 per day, it took US$166 of extra global production and consumption, generating enormous environmental impacts which counterproductively hurt the poorest the most. Global economic growth is thus an extremely inefficient way of achieving poverty reduction.[14]

But the great narrative of the twenty-first century so far, and likely to continue to be, is the unintended consequence of this energy-driven growth – the release of vast quantities of carbon dioxide (CO_2) into the earth's lower atmosphere.

In 1958, American chemist Charles Keeling set up the first CO_2 monitoring site at Mauna Loa Observatory in Hawaii. At the time, the atmospheric concentration of CO_2 was between 312 and 313 parts per million by volume (ppmv).[15] It has now climbed to over 400 ppmv, 40 per cent above the concentration at the start of the Industrial Revolution, and rising at a rate of approximately 2.1 ppmv per year since 2000.[16]

Between 1990 and 2000, CO_2 emissions from fossil fuel combustion and cement production grew at an average rate of 1 per cent a year. However, this rose to an annual average growth rate of 3.1 per cent after 2000. Although the global financial and economic crisis led to a negative CO_2 growth rate of 1.4 per cent in 2009, figures from the Global Carbon Project, an international collaboration between leading climate researchers, suggests CO_2 emissions jumped to 5.9 per cent as the global economy began to recover after 2008–09.[17] The authors argue that the dynamics of the emissions growth rates over this period can be explained by:

- rapid easing of energy prices removing pressure for structural changes in energy consumption;
- large government investment in many countries to promote a rapid return to economic recovery;
- the effect of a decade of high economic growth (around 7 per cent a year) in the developing world providing a strong foundation for a return to high emissions after the global financial crisis.

In addition to rising CO_2 and other greenhouse gases, falling freshwater availability, widespread loss of terrestrial and marine biodiversity, disruption of the nitrogen and carbon cycles, stratospheric ozone depletion, land-use change, soil erosion and ocean acidity are just a handful of the observed human-induced changes to the earth system. Whether single or aggregated, these indicators illustrate that humanity may already be close to irreversibly disrupting the patterns and process within the earth system, or even perturbing the entire system itself.

The 1972 report *Limits to Growth* raised concerns over what would happen to the global system under conditions of unchecked economic and population growth with finite resource supplies.[18] These were revisited in discussions around 'planetary boundaries' in 2009, where Professor Johan Rockström and colleagues argued that a new way to define human development was needed because crossing certain biophysical thresholds that should not be overstepped could have disastrous consequences for humanity. He identified three of these nine thresholds – relating to climate change, biodiversity loss and the nitrogen cycle – which have already been crossed.[19] Some argue that the ultimate problem is not that the earth doesn't have enough resources to support a global population that could peak at 9 billion, but rather the inability of humanity to share these resources fairly.[20] But what is clear is that we are moving into uncharted and potentially catastrophic territory where climate change is concerned.

The body of scientific evidence showing that the climate is changing due to human activity is so overwhelming that you might expect the facts to speak for themselves. Unfortunately they do not, and many people still do not accept the reality or seriousness of climate change. For some, climate change is seen as something that the future holds; it need not concern them because they and their children will not be around to see or have to cope with the consequences. For others the impacts of climate change are 'acts of God' which they can do nothing about. Climate change is also seen as an issue of importance to environmentalists and people working in the physical sciences, and not those concerned with the welfare of humankind. Other issues such as health care, education and employment are seen as more pressing. It is becoming increasingly clear that these preconceptions are wrong. Climate change is happening here and now; it is human-induced; it will multiply threats to health, education, livelihoods and food security; and it is making life particularly difficult for the world's poorest communities and countries.

Living with climate change in South Africa and Mozambique

Climate data for Africa for the last thirty to forty years shows global warming has taken a firm hold. If current trends continue, climate models predict that by 2050 sub-Saharan Africa will be warmer by 0.5°c to 2°c and drier, with 10 per cent less rainfall in the interior and with water loss exacerbated by higher evaporation rates. There will be more extreme events such as drought and floods, and seasonal patterns will shift.

These changes are happening right now, and already people are having to learn to live with the consequences across the whole of the Sahel, the Horn of Africa and Southern Africa. Food security may become increasingly difficult to achieve and humanitarian crises may be exacerbated. Research supported by Oxfam and Save the Children looking at what strategies people are using to cope with changing environments is taking an in-depth look at life in three districts in South Africa and one in neighbouring Mozambique. Research is focusing on areas that have already experienced significant changes in climate over the last thirty years, within many people's lifetimes. In Lehurutshe, people are seeing an increase in regular periodic droughts; in Dzanani, farmers are experiencing a more general, significant drying trend with more pervasive drought; in Uthukela, rural households have experienced increasing intensity and variability in rainfall and seasonality; and in Manjacaze, Mozambique, extreme weather patterns with floods and droughts are having a severe impact on people's lives.

One of the researchers, Professor David Thomas said: 'What we're seeing is that people's responses are complex and dynamic – they are not helpless in the face of these major changes. It looks as though the communities that are most able to cope are those which are most cooperative and with the strongest social institutions. They are able to innovate and experiment in the face of change, as well as drawing on traditional knowledge and networks.' Dr Chasca Twyman added: 'But other communities are doing much less well, and even with those that are more successful, we don't know whether they will continue to be able to cope with such serious stresses.' The research aims to help local and regional governments, policymakers and non-governmental organisations like Oxfam and Save the Children understand how communities cope with climate change and what kinds of assistance will be most effective in the face of current and predicted climate changes.

Progress on the MDGs

In September 2000, several nations met at the United Nations Millennium Summit and declared: 'We will spare no effort to free our fellow men, women and children from the abject and dehumanizing conditions of extreme poverty.'

They agreed eight Millennium Development Goals (MDGs), to which nearly 190 countries have subsequently signed up. Meeting some of these goals is already proving challenging, and climate change threatens to make this even less likely, and indeed may well undo the advances made in development in recent years. As the deadline for meeting these ambitious goals approaches – 2015 – climate change threatens to undermine progress made so far on the goals relating to levels of poverty, hunger and environmental sustainability.

The Millennium Development Goals

1. Eradicate extreme poverty and hunger
2. Achieve universal primary education
3. Promote gender equality and empower women
4. Reduce child mortality
5. Improve maternal health
6. Combat HIV and AIDS, malaria and other diseases
7. Ensure environmental sustainability
8. Develop a global partnership for development

In India alone, over 400 million people (32.7 per cent of the population) already survive on less than US$1 per day.[21] As the impacts of climate change increasingly materialise, their lives will not get any easier. The ambitious targets for reducing child and maternal mortality will be hampered by the unpredictable spread of diseases, destruction of property and contamination of water supplies that go hand in hand with the impacts of climate change.[22] Achieving universal primary education will also be undermined. Time spent finding and fetching (often unsafe) water is already a major reason why girls in particular fail to go to school. The pressures of poverty that keep children away from the classroom will be reinforced by the impacts of climate change. Furthermore, the number of environmental refugees and displaced people will grow and infrastructure like schools be damaged by weather extremes.

Developing countries are particularly vulnerable to climate change, as are the poor and marginalised within both developing and developed countries. Many poor countries already have to cope with issues like high population density, few resources, poor governance and a high incidence of disasters. All these factors limit economic growth and exacerbate poverty. Bangladesh, for example, has over 158 million people.[23] Of them, nearly 50 million live below the national poverty line, without enough income and food.[24] Many are extremely poor and have no employment or income and suffer from continuous food insecurity, malnutrition and social vulnerability. These people cannot access civic amenities such as basic health services, sanitation, safe drinking water and education for their children.

Changing weather conditions threaten the livelihoods of the poor, who more often than not depend on their environment more than do the wealthy. Poor people suffer most when the natural resources they need, such as land, water, fisheries and forests, become degraded, and they are at greater risk of losing their jobs. Climate change threatens their food sources and nutrition, as well as reducing the number of livelihood options available to them. They often live in fragile ecosystems that are prone to cyclones, floods or droughts. And poor people are particularly at risk from disasters because they are usually unprepared and lack adequate shelter. They also struggle more to recover from disasters when they occur. Whilst poor people have a wealth of understanding and knowledge regarding how to cope with climate change, their ability to do so is constrained by a lack of resources and information and weak institutions. So when disaster strikes, many are pushed beyond their capacity to cope and have no choice but to migrate, often to overcrowded slums, which are themselves incredibly vulnerable to climate change.

'We are experiencing a major change in both weather and climate over the last 10 to 15 years. These changes, like almost all changes, affect and impact the lives of the poor... Crop failures, loss of capital investment, failure to replenish the inputs essential for recovery not only increases food insecurity, but also loss of household assets. These events increase not only vulnerability but push more people into the vicious cycle of poverty.'[25]

Health, Education and Economic Development, Bangladesh

Climate change through the eyes of a Sherani tribal community elder

In the Sulaiman Ranges and Balochistan in Pakistan, Sherani tribal community elder Mr Azam Khan explains his observations of climate change: 'Large numbers of Urial herds and flocks of Chukkar partridges have not been swept away by the bullets of hunters. It is the climatic change which means that now we seldom find and see wild ungulate through binoculars, while about forty years ago they could be found in our agriculture fields during night. In fact, in the past we were helpless in protecting our agricultural fields from Chukkar partridges.'

He added: 'Even the mosquitoes are reduced in the valley bottom and now they have shifted to our uphill summer huts ... the summer season flash floods are now more common than in the past. The Lahar streamed which was just 12 feet wide during our grandfather's time is now about 300 feet at the same point. These floods have eroded our irrigation channels and agricultural fields. The decline in arable area has reduced our agricultural produce. Now we have to purchase most of our staple food from market. Those families who have no remittance from abroad are forced to cut Chilghoza pine [Pinus gerardiana] forests and sell as timber to get money for their survival, which is of course considered unwise activity according to our cultural values, but what should they do? Our options for survival are shrinking day by day.'

1

Climate change:
what to expect

For the next two decades we can expect global warming of about 0.2°c per decade. After this time, what happens to changes in temperature depends a great deal on how much we keep filling the atmosphere with greenhouse gases. The best estimates from a range of models predict temperature increases of between 2 and 4°c by 2100 compared to 1980–99 levels. As a result of this global warming, scientists expect the following regional climate change impacts over the coming years:[1]

- Observed warming will be greatest over land areas and at high northern latitudes, and least over the Southern Ocean and parts of the North Atlantic Ocean.
- Contraction of areas covered by snow, increases in the depths of thaw experienced over most permafrost regions, and decreases in the extent of sea ice. Some scientists expect Arctic late-summer sea ice to disappear almost entirely by the latter part of the twenty-first century.
- Very likely increase in the frequency of hot extremes, heatwaves and heavy precipitation.
- Likely increase in the intensity of tropical cyclones, but possible decreases in their number.
- Poleward shifts of extra-tropical storm tracks, with consequent changes in wind, precipitation and temperature patterns.
- Very likely precipitation increases in high latitudes and likely decreases in most subtropical land regions.

Estimates of sea-level rise have concluded that this will most likely be 50–140 cm above 1990 levels by the year 2100,[2] and that even 200 cm is theoretically possible,[3] particularly in view of the fact that ice sheets in Greenland and Antarctica are melting at ever-increasing rates.

Climate change is an uncertain science. Although scientists are getting better at predicting long-term regional trends, it is difficult to predict accurately what to expect over short time-scales and in specific locations. Some areas of climate science have more uncertainty associated with them than others. For example, the properties and roles of clouds in limiting global warming, and the extent to which CO_2 uptake by land and oceans will change future atmospheric greenhouse gas concentrations, are poorly understood.[4] Scientists are in agreement, however, that greenhouse gas emissions are warming the planet, and will continue to do so for many years. Complete certainty about the detailed mechanisms for this and its implications are not needed before we take action. If 98 per cent of doctors say your son is sick and needs treatment, and 2 per cent say he is fine, wouldn't you take precautions and go with the majority view, especially if the consequences of ignoring the majority view could be dreadful? It is the same with climate change.

Developing countries are the most susceptible to these climate change impacts, which, as the box on Uzbekistan below shows, are already being felt. Their economies are heavily dependent on sectors vulnerable to the climate, such as agriculture, fishing, forestry and hydropower. Many poor countries are also located in vulnerable areas such as drought-prone sub-Saharan Africa, flood-prone Bangladesh and low-lying islands such as Tuvalu. But developing countries are also the least able to cope with the impacts of extreme weather conditions, because they have limited financial resources, few skills and technologies, and high levels of poverty.

The effects that these droughts, cyclones, temperature changes and rises in sea level will have, particularly on the world's poorest, are described in the following chapters, alongside many of the creative ways in which they are learning to cope.

Projected climate change impacts at the regional level[5]

AFRICA

- By 2020, between 75 and 250 million people are projected to be exposed to increased water stress due to climate change.
- By 2020, in some countries, yields from rain-fed agriculture could be reduced by up to 50 per cent. Agricultural production, including access to food, in many African countries is projected to be severely compromised. This would further adversely affect food security and exacerbate malnutrition.
- Towards the end of the twenty-first century, projected sea-level rise will affect low-lying coastal areas with large populations. The cost of adaptation could amount to at least 5–10 per cent of gross domestic product (GDP).
- By 2080, an increase of 5–8 per cent of arid and semi-arid land in Africa is projected under a range of climate scenarios.

ASIA

- By the 2050s, freshwater availability in Central, South, East and South-east Asia, particularly in large river basins, is projected to decrease.
- Coastal areas, especially heavily populated mega-delta regions in South, East and Southeast Asia, will be at greatest risk due to increased flooding from the sea and, in some mega-deltas, from the rivers.
- Climate change is projected to compound the pressures on natural resources and the environment associated with rapid urbanisation, industrialisation and economic development.
- Endemic morbidity and mortality due to diarrhoeal disease, primarily associated with floods and droughts, are expected to rise in East, South and Southeast Asia due to projected changes in the hydro-logical cycle.

LATIN AMERICA

- By mid-century, increases in temperature and associated decreases in soil water are projected to lead to gradual replacement of tropical forest by savanna in eastern Amazonia. Semi-arid vegetation will tend to be replaced by arid-land vegetation.

- There is a risk of significant biodiversity loss through species extinction in many areas of tropical Latin America.
- Productivity of some important crops is projected to decrease and livestock productivity to decline, with adverse consequences for food security. In temperate zones, soybean yields are projected to increase. Overall, the number of people at risk of hunger is projected to increase.
- Changes in precipitation patterns and the disappearance of glaciers are projected to significantly affect water availability for human consumption, agriculture and energy generation.

SMALL ISLANDS

- Sea level rise is expected to exacerbate inundation, storm surge, erosion and other coastal hazards, thus threatening vital infrastructure, settlements and facilities that support the livelihood of island communities.
- Deterioration in coastal conditions, for example through erosion of beaches and coral bleaching, is expected to affect local resources.
- By mid-century, climate change is expected to reduce water resources in many small islands, for example in the Caribbean and Pacific, to the point where they become insufficient to meet demand during low-rainfall periods.
- With higher temperatures, increased invasion by non-native species is expected to occur, particularly on mid- and high-latitude islands.

Observed changes in Uzbekistan

'In recent years, the change in climatic conditions in all seasons of the year has been sharply felt. Changes in climate often influence agricultural yield; for example, many kinds of grain crops do not have time to ripen. From 2000 to 2003, because of a drought, none of the districts of Karakalpakstan could obtain productivity in grain.'

'The problem of water facilities, especially drinking water and water for irrigating agriculture, has recently become one of the largest problems ... because of the drying of the Aral Sea; on its former coasts the influence of dust storms and sand drifts is strongly felt. Almost in the whole territory of the Republic of Karakalpakstan it is possible to see salt on the ground left over from evaporation. Salinity of the soil negatively affects vegetative cover. In many places, trees and other vegetations are drying out. Huge tracts of land and agricultural fields are covered by copious saline deposits. As a result, productivity drops and quality worsens.'

'In recent years, as a result of the change in climatic conditions and pollution, the frequency of allergic and bronchial diseases has sharply increased.'

'Little by little the extinction of not only many kinds of vegetation, animals and rare varieties of fauna fade away.'

Joint Development Associates, Uzbekistan, a partner organisation of Tearfund

2

Food and farming

There are now at least 815 million chronically malnourished people in the world, 95 per cent of them in developing countries.[1] Inequitable access to food is a major factor in fuelling world hunger, but global warming is also undermining food security. The World Food Programme estimates that by 2050 the number of people at risk of hunger as a result of climate change will be 10–20 per cent higher than would be expected without it, and that sub-Saharan Africa is likely to be worst affected.[2]

Poverty, conflict, disease, governance problems, an unjust international trading system, and the burden of unpayable debt hinder the ability of Africa's communities and nations to handle shocks. Africa's people and its economies are also highly vulnerable to both flood and drought, both of which are increasingly problematic. The record shows that Africa's annual rainfall has been decreasing since 1968. During the Mozambique floods in 2000 (the worst for 150 years), the lowlands of the Limpopo river were inundated for up to three months. While short-term flooding can benefit some crops, like rice, the 2000 floods lasted so long that they wiped out the plant resources that local people relied on. Stored food, seed reserves and all field crops were destroyed, forcing farmers to find fresh seeds from far away.

If not addressed, climate change could put an additional 80–120 million people at risk of hunger, 70 to 80 per cent of whom will be in Africa.[3] Livelihoods built for generations on particular patterns of farming may quickly become unviable.

Agriculture in sub-Saharan Africa – of which most is rain-fed – accounts for 60 per cent of the employment in the region (excluding South Africa) and 30 per cent of its gross domestic product.[4] This compares to 16.3 per cent of working people in Latin America being employed in the agricultural sector.[5] While many African farmers have successfully adapted to slow changes in the region's climate, the level of unpredictability which global warming introduces may overwhelm their capacity to cope.

While some agricultural areas may benefit from increased rainfall, estimates suggest climate change will significantly reduce crop yields in sub-Saharan Africa. Recent models suggest that by mid-century average falls in maize production will be 22 per cent, sorghum and millet 17 per cent, groundnuts 18 per cent and cassava 8 per cent.[6] Effects could be even greater in localised regions. Estimates predict a 33 per cent reduction in maize in Tanzania; in Sudan millet production is expected to decrease by between 20 and 76 per cent, and sorghum by between 13 and 82 per cent.[7]

'Drought is becoming more and more frequent, leading to drying out of soil and the disappearance of vegetation. The life of an entire population is on hold, waiting for clouds, which promise less and less rain and which finally destroy the hope that cattle breeders and their herds will enjoy healthy pastures. They also destroy people's hope for a better tomorrow which would usher in an abundant harvest so passionately awaited by farmers and their creditors.'

Malian development group TNT

'The change in weather has affected agriculture to the extent that some vegetables don't now grow and we yield fewer vegetables per hectare. Also, there are more plant attacks by insects than before.'

Pastor Elie Kabore, Burkina Faso

Mrs Suufee describes local changes in Ethiopia

Mrs Suufee, aged 62, is a widow living with her 31-year-old son, who has five children in Sire Baabo village, Ethiopia. Her husband died recently. Her elder son also lives nearby and has eleven children. The family culti-vates 3 hectares, on which they grow sorghum, maize, teff and wheat.

Mrs Suufee has noticed definite changes in the local climate. The amount of rainfall has been reduced and it tends to be erratic. In particu-lar, the sorghum-growing season has been getting shorter and shorter. Sorghum does best when rainfall starts in early February and continues until October, but nowadays the earliest rain may not start until April. In her experience, they get two or three good years followed by one or two bad years. The rainfall is usually adequate for the vegetative growth stage but stops early at the heading and flowering stages in September. During those years, yields are almost halved. Hailstorms also sporadically damage crops. Villagers report increased malaria, typhus and trypanosomiasis, which claimed the lives of six oxen and several cows belonging to Mrs Suufee. In her view, the weather has not got back to normal since the severe drought of 1984–85.

Farmers in Khomele, South Africa, describe the effects of a changing climate on their lives and how they are responding[8]

OBSERVED CLIMATIC CHANGES

- Less rain
- Periods of no rain
- Unpredictable rain
- Rain comes out of season
- Late rain

IMPACT OF CLIMATE CHANGE

ON HOUSEHOLD WELFARE

- Tiredness and hunger

ON NATURAL RESOURCE-BASED LIVELIHOODS

- Seeds do not germinate
- Soil is less productive
- Effects on planning – cannot predict rainfall through flowering patterns
- Poor quality grass
- Livestock die
- Dryland crops die

- Pests proliferate
- Leaves change colour
- Less water for animals
- More thorn bushes

FARMER RESPONSES

CHANGE FARMING PRACTICES

- Grinding maize stalks as feed
- Using resistant yellow maize
- Planting late-maturing fruit trees

DIVERSIFYING ACTIVITIES

- Using irrigated land
- Eating wild fruits
- Working land in other places
- Cutting fodder from ironwood trees; collecting seeds from wild plants

COMMERCIAL RESPONSES

- Gardening projects to improve food security
- Forming groups to start new business ventures
- Selling livestock, especially at auctions
- Looking for work
- Planting winter crops
- Planting late-maturing fruit trees
- Breeding indigenous species

NETWORKS

- Asking for money from relatives
- Getting help from the government, for example with subsidised feed
- Holding a village meeting
- Local leaders decide what to do
- Getting advice from the church
- Getting medicines

Climate change and locust plagues in the Sahel

During 2004, several West African countries fell victim to the largest locust invasion in fifteen years. Millions of hectares of crops and pasture were destroyed by giant swarms of the insects. Production in the Sahel, especially of food crops, decreased drastically to reach 8,978,142 tonnes against a minimum need of 10,234,193 tonnes. This undermined poor people's livelihoods as 80 per cent of the population in the Sahel depends on seasonal staple food production to feed themselves.

West Africa is not the only region vulnerable to locust invasions. Locusts also reproduce around the Red Sea and along the Indian and Pakistani border. The total area vulnerable covers about 16 million square kilometres and includes some thirty countries. There were six major plagues of desert locusts in the 1900s, one of which lasted almost thirteen years.

Vegetation, soil structure and habitat all affect locust behaviour, all of which, in turn, are influenced by temperature and rainfall. Most climate change models predict an overall decline in rainfall in the region vulnerable to locust plagues, and more weather extremes such as droughts and heavy rainfall. Heavy rains create ideal conditions for locust reproduction. A combination of rain, vegetation and humidity can lead to rapid breeding.

Locust plagues can occur when favourable breeding conditions are present and when control operations fail to stop a series of local outbreaks from developing into an upsurge that cannot be contained. The Sahel has neither the means – in terms of equipment, products and logistics – nor the finances to avoid such disasters, much less stop the locust invasion from heading north towards the Maghreb. An invasion occurring during harvest time will lead to famine. Farmers who react quickly and save their crops before an invasion occurs suffer less, but the ability to react quickly is poor so damage can be huge.

The key to reducing impact lies in the response of governments in the region. But that means securing financial support. When poorer nations are using up to half of their revenues to pay debts it does not leave much room for any poverty-reduction measures or for action to be taken to alleviate the catastrophic consequences of locust plagues. Without money and the support of the international community it will be difficult to address the problem.

Trouble brewing: smallholder tea farmers in Kenya[9]

If temperatures rose by 2°c, large areas of Kenya currently suited to growing tea would become unsuitable. Were this to happen, the impact on Kenya's economy would be enormous. Kenya is the world's third-largest tea producer and tea is the third-biggest foreign exchange earner for the country. Three million Kenyans are directly or indirectly employed in the tea industry. But the impact on poor people would be the greatest. Over 500,000 smallholders grow 60 per cent of the country's tea, with large estates growing the rest. The large tea estates may have the capital to afford the extra irrigation and other inputs that would be needed to cope with the effects of climate change, but smallholders may not.

Elsewhere in the world evidence is also mounting about the impact that climate change will have on agricultural outputs in different regions. Stories are also increasing in number from those in poor countries who rely on the land for subsistence and for their livelihoods and have noticed that the weather is changing. In most cases, these people have not heard of global warming and they do not know what greenhouse gases are, and of course scientists are still rarely able to say with certainty that any single observed change is due to global warming as opposed to natural variation in the climate, known as 'climate variability'. But scientists can predict trends over several years with increasing confidence, and it thus comes as no surprise that many of these predictions are mirrored by observations from those who rely heavily on their environment and thus feel any changes in the climate most acutely.

According to the World Food Programme, Asia will experience up to 50 per cent declines in wheat and 17 per cent declines in rice crop yields by 2050 compared to 2000 levels due to climate change, and decreasing yields will affect 1.6 billion people in the region.[10] The Intergovernmental Panel on Climate Change estimates that an additional 49 million, 132 million and 266 million people of Asia could be at risk from hunger by 2020, 2050 and 2080 respectively.[11]

'The rain does not come at the right time. People start cultivating and there is no rain. Then it comes after a month, so the seeds die and again we have to plant.'
Latika Sagar, Evangelical Fellowship of India Commission on Relief, India

'Water is the biggest problem for me: sometimes we face floods, sometimes drought. Agriculture is my one source of income, so during floods or drought my whole livelihood is threatened.'
Kasti Bag, Evangelical Fellowship of India Commission on Relief, India

---

In India, where 60 per cent of people depend on subsistence agriculture for their livelihood, and the agricultural sector represents over one-third of the Indian economy, estimates suggest that an increase in temperature of between 2°c and 3.5°c could result in a decline in farm revenues of between 9 and 25 per cent.[12] Food insecurity is a serious threat for many, and India's large rural population, which is heavily dependent on rain- and meltwater-fed agriculture, is already beginning to experience climate change impacts. Changes to rainfall patterns driven by the monsoons will increase the risk of extreme events, for example causing flooding and destroying crops and soil quality through erosion or contamination. Melting glaciers due to rising temperatures in the Himalayas may also increase water volume in the short term. On the other hand, failure of the monsoons due to an intense El Niño event (a natural phenomenon associated with warming sea surface temperatures across the central and eastern equatorial Pacific Ocean) could cause drought.

Changes to the summer monsoon patterns in Pakistan have resulted in early or delayed monsoon rains. Unlike the usual rainfall patterns, rains come in short heavy bursts, resulting in flooding, which can affect densely populated areas and agricultural land. Floods in agricultural areas can lead to salination, chemical contamination or soil erosion, all of which affect food security.

Returning to historic livelihoods in Thal, Pakistan

Locals in the Thal region of Punjab are experiencing a longer summer season and shorter winters. A few decades ago the region was mostly grazing land, with livestock a major source of income for people. Human population density was low, and comprised nomads moving around in search of livestock fodder. Big herds of hundreds of camels, goats and sheep roamed the massive rangelands. Agriculture was practised only at a subsistence level and comprised largely the cultivation of traditional wheat varieties on small pieces of land using water from wells.

In the early 1960s, with the advent of the Green Revolution, increased land entitlement led to more irrigated agriculture and a drive to bring more land under cultivation. Big tracts of rangeland were cleared to make room for agriculture. In areas where canal irrigation water was made available, non-local tribes moved in and locals were left with no option but to abandon their traditional nomadic culture.

Where canal water was not available, gram was grown as a cash crop providing Thali farmers with a new source of income. But the gram crop depends on sufficient and timely rains, which are becoming increasingly uncertain with climate change. Locals now describe gram cultivation as a complete gamble. If rains come on time, no crop can match gram because it requires no fertilisers or pesticides. But when rains fail, everything is lost. Gram cultivation also requires the removal of natural vegetation from the land, which used to be a source of fodder for livestock throughout the year and could resist the dry climate. From 1998 to 2002, Pakistan faced one of the worst droughts in its history. Many Thalis reverted to traditional livelihood patterns comprising the use of natural vegetation, indigenous trees and livestock. Practical Action and its local partner, the Rural Development Policy Institute, are showing farmers how to adapt to climate change by helping them adopt the drought-resistant livelihood patterns that they abandoned decades ago.

In China, the latest *National Assessment Report on Climate Change* published by the Chinese government estimates that if no action is taken the gross productivity of the Chinese agricultural industry will decrease by 5–10 per cent. By the second half of this century, the production of three staple crops – wheat, rice and corn – may decrease by up to 37 per cent. This will severely affect China's food security over the next twenty to fifty years.[13]

'I've been farming in this area for the past thirty years and I've noticed that it's raining more and the temperature has changed. From October to May and March to April it's often very windy. I have also noticed that when it now hails, the hailstones are very big and damage our crops. From December to March it's very cold; this wasn't so five years ago. It's much colder than before and when it's hot it's very hot.'

Davlodmoh Inomova, 48, pumpkin farmer from Tajikistan, Oxfam interview

'We work in the field to make a living and a few weeks ago locusts attacked our fields and our entire [watermelon] crop has disappeared. I have noticed that when the temperature is above 34 degrees, when it is much hotter than usual, there is a greater chance that locusts will come to attack our crops. I will have to take a loan out to buy more seeds and spend the next two weeks working on the land to get it ready to plant. Buying one bottle of seeds is expensive and we won't have an income for the next two months that it will take the watermelons to grow.'

Umeda Ddinaeva, 19, watermelon farmer from Tajikistan,
Oxfam interview

In Bangladesh, agriculture remains the main source of livelihood for most of the population: the sector generates employment for 63 per cent of the labour force.[14] Climate change is a major threat to agricultural production and food security. Temperature and rainfall changes have already affected crop production in many parts of Bangladesh, and the area of arable land has already decreased. A shrinking winter season is resulting in decreases in winter crop production, particularly potatoes. Coastal areas of Bangladesh are very fertile and are used for growing rice, but they are prone to saltwater intrusion from storm surges or sea-level rise. One study suggests that the production of rice and wheat could fall by 8 and 32 per cent respectively by the year 2050.[15] Whilst farmers may not understand the science of climate change, they have observed changes in seasonal and rainfall patterns. They have noticed that planting seasons have shifted and that seasons are shorter than before. They have also commented that heatwaves are damaging crops, livestock and fisheries.

According to projections, national food-grain requirements in Bangladesh will be 41.6 million tonnes in the year 2030. To become self-sufficient in food-grain production by 2030, an additional 14.64 million tonnes are therefore required. But with the affects of climate change on crop production, food-grain self-sufficiency looks to remain a distant dream for Bangladesh.[16]

Md Liakat – a Bangladeshi farmer with hope

Md Liakat, a 52-year-old farmer from the village of Gidari in Gaibandha district started his farm with 19.8 acres of land, eight cows, a variety of crops and a pond with fish, but now he is completely landless. He has witnessed many changes over the last few decades such as fewer crop varieties, more floods and erosion, and many farmers becoming landless. Md Liakat feels that temperatures are steadily increasing in summer and decreasing in winter. Heavy rain and frequent floods have meant he has lost land, crops and other assets. He has shifted his homestead five times due to erosion and floods.

Md Liakat has experienced many climate-change-related disasters. The first was the flood in August/September 1978. He said that the flood came back with a vengeance in 1984 from June to September. There were also heavy hailstorms in February 1985 that damaged most of his crops. In 1988, fierce floods hit Md Liakat's village again from June to September. These washed away all of his crops, livestock and other assets. The flood was followed by severe river erosion. Md Liakat also mentioned the cold wave of 1994 and river erosion in 1996.

A study by Practical Action Bangladesh has confirmed that the temperature has been increasing over the last thirty years. Winters are becoming warmer than they were thirty years ago, which affects winter crops, particularly potatoes. The study showed that the number of days without rainfall is increasing, although total annual rainfall varies little. This indicates the occurrence of heavy rain over short time periods and more droughts.

Worried about his income, Md Liakat desperately wanted to know how to adapt to the changing climatic conditions. He received training and technological support from Practical Action and explored various activities to increase his income. After training he established a nursery in his backyard to grow vegetables. He rears ducklings and grows vegetables on floating beds during the monsoon. He has sold 3,000 tree seedlings, earning himself 12,000 taka. He has reinvested some of this money to grow more saplings in his nursery. He now meets his family's needs and is confident that soon he will be able to buy some agricultural land and livestock, making him a rich farmer in a few years, like his father was before him.

El Niño usually occurs every four to seven years, but across the Pacific climate change is altering the frequency and intensity of El Niño events and may create more permanent El Niño-type conditions. This is particularly worrying for the archipelago nations of Indonesia, the Philippines and East Timor. The strong cycle of El Niño in mid-1997 and 1998 had a major global impact. Estimates of global loss range from US$32 billion upwards. Indonesian rice yields already vary by 7 per cent each year depending on whether it was an El Niño or a La Niña (El Niño's counterpart) year.[17]

El Niño significantly affects the variability of East Timor's climate. In places like Ainaro, Lolotoe, Lore and Lospalos, annual rainfall can be reduced by up to 50 per cent in El Niño years. In others areas, such as Baucau and Oecusse, annual rainfall is higher than average. Throughout East Timor, however, El Niño causes a reduction in rainfall in the January–March wet season, with some places receiving only 25 per cent of their usual rainfall. In El Niño years, the wet season is usually delayed by two to three months, and this affects food production and security. In the year following an El Niño event, rainfall can be higher than average, which can also lead to flooding, with associated damage to crops and infrastructure, especially roads and bridges. Rainfall and water availability are already the principal constraints on agricultural production in East Timor. A drought in 2001–02 followed by the late arrival of the wet season in 2002–03 resulted in a 34 per cent decrease in maize production between 2002 and 2003.[18] This meant that over 110,000 people needed food aid. An increase in the magnitude and frequency of El Niño events is likely to make food security issues even more important.

El Niño impacts in Baucau

Marito Reis, the former district administrator of Baucau, the second-largest city of East Timor, comments that El Niño changes rainfall patterns, which in turn cause landslides that destroy fields and other infrastructure. Marito Reis explains that 'the floods bring large amount of sediments, which deposit on lowland agriculture land silting up fields, and the flash floods also destroy intake structure for irrigation system.' Denuded hillsides also increase the size and frequency of flash floods, for example in the Seixal river watershed. Marito explained that this is also linked to El Niño and climate change.

El Niño events have already led to drought and water shortages in Pacific Island nations such as Papua New Guinea, the Marshall Islands, and the Federated States of Micronesia, Samoa, Tonga, Kiribati and Fiji. More frequent El Niño events also bring an increased risk of tropical cyclones, particularly for Tuvalu, Samoa, Tonga, the Cook Islands and French Polynesia. El Niño events have already caused large decreases in rainfall in the western Pacific. For example, in 1998, forty atolls of Micronesia ran out of water during an El Niño event, resulting in the declaration of a national emergency. Outbreaks of cholera have been associated with inadequate water supplies during El Niño events in various Pacific island states.[19]

Throughout Indonesia, the Philippines and East Timor, farmers are exploring alternative ways to earn a living and feed their families under changing climatic conditions. One study suggests that by 2050 some of Indonesia's most important rice-growing areas will experience a month-long delay in the onset of monsoon rains, and that late summer rainfall could drop by as much as 25 per cent. This could make it almost impossible to plant rice and other crops during these months without irrigation. Crop diversification, drought-tolerant rice varieties, and water storage and irrigation infrastructure will be important adaptation measures.[20] David Macdonald, country programme manager of Oxfam GB in Indonesia, states that 'There are 39.05 million poor people in Indonesia, 80 per cent of which live in rural areas. They depend on the agricultural sector, a sector vulnerable to climate shock such as flood, drought and longer dry seasons.'

Indonesia's poor hit first and worst

Roz Naylor of Stanford estimates that 'Within two generations, climate change will likely cause increasing hardships for the 100 million poor and 15 million very poor in Indonesia who overwhelmingly rely on rice production for the bulk of their food and income.'[21]

Oxfam has been helping poor people in the province of East Nusa Tenggara for several years and has noted many climate anomalies in the last few years. In 2002 and 2003, for instance, the rainy seasons were late, so farmers were also late planting. In 2006 and 2007, the rainy seasons and dry seasons were so unpredictable that farmers did not know when to start planting. This resulted in many farmers failing to harvest what they planted, creating a drastic drop in income and widespread hunger and malnutrition, especially among children.

'Income level has dropped by 25 to 40 per cent while the level of malnutrition among children in East Nusa Tenggara currently has reached 36 to 50 per cent. At the beginning of 2006, over 60 per cent of families in Central North Timor and Belu, for instance, did not have enough food', said Laksmi Prasvita, spokeswoman for Oxfam GB in Indonesia.

Farming communities in Pagadian, Mindanao, the Philippines, have been affected by changing rainfall patterns over the last three years. Usually the rainy season is from March to November. However, the dry season is becoming longer and hotter, and rainfall has been arriving as late as June. Farmers' customary timing for planting and harvesting is no longer applicable, resulting in low farm productivity and reductions in income and food supply.

'Changing weather patterns are greatly affecting the lives of people in the communities we are working in. The farmers we work with are poor. They are dependent on the produce of their farms for their livelihoods, which is now being affected by increased aridity and extreme rainfall distribution.'

Mercy Delantar from local organisation JPIP, the Philippines

Subsistence agriculture is the main source of employment for at least 80 per cent of the population of the Lao People's

Democratic Republic (Lao PDR; Laos) and accounts for roughly half of its gross domestic product. Laos is landlocked, so will not suffer from sea-level rise or coastal erosion, but irregularities in the monsoon could significantly affect its agricultural sector. Agriculture is also the main source of income for many people in Thailand and Vietnam. As the Mekong region's climate changes, rice and most food crops will be more difficult to grow, yields will become more uncertain, livestock more difficult to raise, and it will be more difficult to catch fish in the region's rivers, lakes and wetlands.

'Paddy rice cultivation in our village is mainly dependent on rainfall. Increasingly we have been experiencing drought and low rice yields. We no longer are producing enough rice to eat for the full year. We are relying on initiatives, such as the community rice bank, for our survival. If not, we would have to go to private moneylenders to borrow money to buy rice to meet our families' needs. They charge very high rates of interest (around 30 per cent per month).'

Duong Soum, 58, Tareach village, Chumikiri district, Cambodia

---

Rice is the most important crop in the Mekong region and vast populations of rain-fed farms growing rice in the lower Mekong River region rely on stable climatic conditions. Changing precipitation patterns could significantly affect rice productivity, with yield reductions possibly reaching 10 to 15 per cent in various areas of Lao PDR and Thailand. Extreme weather events, particularly prolonged droughts, severe floods and more intense rainfall, between 1994 and 2004 reduced rice production by as much as 45 per cent in Thungkula-ronghai field, the heartland of the famous jasmine rice fields in the Mekong Basin in north-eastern Thailand. And from 1991 to 2000, damage to agricultural areas caused by droughts, floods and storms across Thailand cost up to 50 billion baht.[22]

In Latin America, climate change will result in a total of 6.4 million malnourished children by 2050 – with 1.4 million more suffering from hunger.[23] Research suggests that in countries like Brazil, Chile, Argentina and Uruguay global warming will lead to lower crop yields, especially in El Niño years. Production of barley, grapes, maize, potatoes, soybeans and wheat is expected to fall, even when rising concentrations of atmospheric carbon dioxide increase plant growth – known as carbon dioxide ferti-lisation – and moderate adaptation measures are implemented at the farm level. Global warming could also worsen the impacts of a range of pests and diseases affecting livestock and crops, further lowering production.

In Ecuador, a warming climate is forcing people to farm at higher altitudes to grow their staple crops. This adds to defor-estation, which in turn undermines water sources and leads to soil erosion. There is also a cultural impact. The displacement of millenary Andean cultures to higher lands means the loss of the places where their culture is rooted, putting its survival at risk. Progressio has been working with twenty-one native Kichwas communities in the Imbakucha Basin in Otavalo for ten years. These communities report unexpected frosts and long drought periods, which affect all farming activities. The older generation say they no longer know when to sow because the rains do not come as expected. Migration offers one way out but it represents a cultural nemesis with a high human and social price tag.

Mountainous regions, such as the Andes, are especially chal-lenged. There, the struggle by smallholder farmers to secure their livelihoods is accentuated by seasonal variations in climate, which can bring drought, floods, frost or hail within a single growing season and where climate change is likely to lead to more extreme cold spells.

For many farmers, the concepts of 'drought' and 'extreme rainfall' do not fully capture the dynamics of climate variability.

Factors such as the timing of the first rains (which affects when crops are planted), the distribution of rainfall within the growing season, and the effectiveness of the rains are all real criteria of farming success. Indeed, farmers often have many years of experience in dealing with drought; it is rather the confusing changes in seasons and violent, erratic and unpredictable weather conditions which cause them far greater problems. Where repeated exposure to an event such as drought has occurred, farmers may be better able to cope. In the words of one farmer from Mantsie, South Africa: 'Drought is easier to cope with because we are used to it; the heavy rains are not good because we need a little and often.'

Averages can be misleading. Whilst climate change will likely increase the average rainfall in China,[24] particularly in southern and north-western areas, water shortages in Chinese agriculture are likely to become much more severe, especially in northern regions, where droughts are already common. This is because the climate will become more irregular, and so sometimes there will be no rain when crops need it most. Higher temperatures will also increase the rate of evaporation, and the projected increases in rainfall are likely to be very unevenly distributed, with some areas receiving more water, and maybe too much, leading to floods, while other areas will experience droughts.

How farmers are coping

The International Assessment of Agricultural Knowledge, Science and Technology for Development (IAASTD) explains that agricultural yields have increased sufficiently in recent years to provide on average more than enough food for every person on the planet, but that nevertheless approximately 850 million people around the world are not able to obtain enough food to lead healthy and productive lives.[25] Addressing climate change is just one of the many ways to tackle this problem. Others include increasing investment in agricultural services, and addressing market concentrations whereby a few large companies control a disproportionate amount of the transnational trade in seeds, agrochemicals and food. Climate change is just one of many reasons why people are going hungry and struggling to earn a living from farming.

Agriculture in Africa suffers from a persistent lack of investment. It's an issue both at the national level, with African governments cutting back on farming support services, and internationally, with funding from the European Union, for example, tending to go to 'governance' and 'infrastructure'. Small-scale agriculture provides most of the food produced in Africa, but a lack of investment in drought-resistant farming stands to create serious problems for the sector's ability to adapt in a warming world.

Faced with a decline in government support, private support services have grown. But support in poor countries does not compare to the levels of support that farmers in rich countries take for granted, and few poor farmers are able to pay for private services. As a result, the emerging private sector is directed at larger commercial farmers. There are, however, a small but growing number of approaches that better complement the needs of smallholder farmers and their ability to pay. These initiatives often involve the training of farmer-to-farmer agents, information-sharing through exchange visits to working farms elsewhere, and communities coming together to share ideas and resources. Supporting small-scale farmers to develop sustainable local farming practices in this way has repeatedly been shown to increase their ability to cope with climate change impacts, as many of the examples below demonstrate.

Farmers help each other in Peru

For many communities living over 3,500 metres above sea level the most common crops are maize, potatoes and beans. Many families also have one or two head of cattle, some sheep and a number of guinea pigs (a food staple in the Andes). These communities are poorly served by government agricultural support services. Training farmer-to-farmer 'extension agents' has, therefore, become a focus of Practical Action's work in the region. Locally the agents are known as 'Kamayoq', a name associated with the Inca Empire in the sixteenth century. Kamayoq combine ancient and modern approaches. They are one of many innovations that will be needed to help the Quechua cope with the way climate change is set to alter life in the high Andes.

A Kamayoq school was established in 1996. The course covers identification and treatment of pests and diseases of crops and livestock; improved irrigation; and the breeding and rearing of guinea pigs. Since the school opened, over 140 Kamayoq have been trained, one in five of whom are women.

The Kamayoq help local smallholder farmers raise production and sales from both their plants and animals and are paid in cash or in kind for their assistance. It is the farmers' willingness to pay that makes the Kamayoq model so interesting. Apart from the initial cost of training, it is in effect an unsubsidised farmer-to-farmer service. The Kamayoq have helped farmers adopt improved guinea pig breeding techniques to raise bigger animals for their own consumption, as well as for sale. They have also provided farmers with technical advice on irrigation, improving pasture and treatment of animal diseases, which has led to increases in milk production of up to 50 per cent.

The Kamayoq also help farmers to adapt through experimentation to changing environmental, social and economic circumstances; for example, helping to work out how to treat a fungal disease of maize, to control mildew on onions, and to treat *Fasciola hepatica*, a parasitic disease of animals, with natural medicine.

Felicitas Quispe Pucho, a Kamayoq, wakes at 4.30 a.m. to feed her family before setting off to apply her skills in animal husbandry, immunisation, construction and accounting. 'The Incas were all-knowing even though they didn't use books or pens', says Felicitas. 'We're trying to recapture some of the wisdom of the Incas.' Fellow graduate Alfredo Montezinos echoes her thoughts: 'The Spanish came and fought off the Incas and some of their knowledge was lost', he says. 'They imposed their technologies and methods on us and we lost touch with our real ancestors. We're not using chemicals any more; we're trying to use natural materials. We need to get back to a better balance between nature and man.'

Dealing with extreme cold in the Andes

Whilst much of the world is warming, one possible paradox of climate change may be a new phenomenon known as *friaje* in Peru's highlands. In 2004 temperatures fell to as low as -35°C, killing fifty children and leaving an estimated 13,000 people suffering from bronchitis, pneumonia and hypothermia. There was also lasting damage to livelihoods as between 50 and 70 per cent of alpacas died, animals which the community and local economy depend on. Without alpacas, farmers cannot transport their goods to market. The animals also give nutritious milk, some of which is made into cheese, and thick wool with excellent insulation properties.

Waves of cold were felt between June and August caused by the arrival of frozen winds from the South Pole. These came with unusual storms followed by frosts that killed crops and pastures used by the alpaca. In recent years, cold winters have been followed by hot, dry summers and, recently, electric hail storms. One farmer, Huallipe, observed: 'The temperature shifts here are getting more extreme. We are peasants; we didn't know what to do about these things.'

The Quechua people responded to the *friaje* and were helped by the Kamayoq. Sheds were built to protect baby alpacas and weak animals. Forage was produced and stored, with alfalfa being grown hydroponically (in a non-soil substrate with nutrient-enriched water pumped through). Sick animals received treatment. As one newspaper reported, 'There are few climate change sceptics at this altitude.'[26]

Changing crops in Nepal

In 2005, Practical Action Nepal organised an educational tour to raise farmer awareness on crop diversification as a way of reducing the risks of climate change impacts. Pushkar Timsina, a 21-year-old farmer from in Tarai, attended the tour. He was impressed by banana growing in the area visited. He learned that bananas could fetch more money than the rice paddy from the same piece of land. In addition, bananas are more resilient to changing rain patterns than paddy. His family has a small piece of land – only 0.27 hectares – which provided little foodgrain, which erratic monsoon rainfall threatened to reduce still further. Push-kar's father was not confident that the family would benefit more from bananas, and they would also have to wait at least a year before newly planted bananas could be harvested. But Pushkar planted 250 banana trees on the land and sought alternative income sources until the banana plants produced fruit.

Pushkar purchased fresh vegetables from other farmers and took them to the market in Narayanghat by bicycle. This was possible because Practical Action trained village farmers in vegetable farming under its climate change adaptation programme, thus increasing village vegetable production. Practical Action also helped villagers collect milk from different households for sale to the Kalpana Dairy in Narayanghat. Pushkar transported more than 50 litres of milk per day to the dairy, which paid him for this service. These alternative income sources helped him feed his family while their banana plants grew.

The banana plants are now providing fruit. Pushkar hopes to harvest at least 250 bunches of bananas each year, providing an annual income of at least Rs 35,000. With the help of Practical Action he has also planted other fruit trees such as mango and lemon, as well as grapes, to further diversify his crops. He has introduced pineapple as an understorey crop, and grows fodder on the edges of his field. He grows vegetables under the banana plants for sale at the nearby market. He has also introduced beehives to his banana orchard. Although Pushkar left school after Grade 2, he is supporting his sisters, who are currently in Grades 3 and 5. Pushkar's activities have also encouraged his neighbours to diversify their activities, making them more resilient to climate change.

Using the landscape to spread risk in Mozambique

Villagers in Nwadjahane in Gaza province in southern Mozambique farm both the fertile lowlands through irrigation and the higher sandy dryland fields. Increasingly severe floods and droughts over the last two decades have increased household demand for plots of land in both areas. While the lowlands can produce good crops of rice, vegetables and potatoes, these can be destroyed during floods. Highland areas can produce good crops of maize and cassava during flood years but are less productive during drought years, when families rely on lowland production.

Households with land in just one area have developed informal farming associations to lobby those responsible for land allocation. They've gained access to new areas to farm. This is especially important for very poor households as it spreads production costs and risks, thus increasing their overall resilience to both droughts and floods.

These farming associations have also become the focus of innovative and experimental farming practices. By working in groups, villagers can spread the risk of experimenting with new practices and technologies and learning through trial and error. When successful, farmers take the lessons learnt back to their own farms. For example, 45 per cent of those interviewed had changed to more drought-resistant species of rice, maize, cassava and sweet potato in the last six years as a direct result of the information exchange within and beyond the farming associations. The associations have also been particularly popular with groups of women, strengthening their position in the farming community.

Such initiatives can strengthen livelihoods in the face of climate change and make livelihood activities more profitable and secure in the face of disturbances such as extreme climatic events and also other environmental, economic, political and cultural issues. The Mozambican government has recognised this. It sees the need to build local resilience, and national planning strategies deliberately address these issues. Some agricultural sectors are being encouraged to commercialise on a large scale, while smallholders are being encouraged to participate in local-level planning. Thus climate change in Mozambique is not being viewed in isolation; it is being dealt with within the context of wider development issues.

The Masipag Project

In the early 1960s, the 'Green Revolution' promised Filipino farmers dramatic increases in rice yields. But there was a catch! High-yielding rice varieties were part of a package that included petroleum-based fertilisers, pesticides, machinery and irrigation. Practices were tied to Western science, values and economic organisation. Increasing grain yields had other costs: soils became acidic and nutrient-poor due to intensive use of chemical fertilisers; biodiversity was lost and there was a resurgence of pests and diseases; and mono-cropping meant that many diverse sources of food were lost. The devastating effects of the Green Revolution on small farmers led a group of progressive scientists from the University of the Philippines and some NGOs to meet and explore alternative models for agricultural development. As a result, in 1987, Masipag was founded.

Masipag is now a coalition of those advocating sustainable agriculture and the empowerment of small farmers. It has 490 organisational members and serves over 30,000 farmers nationwide.

The Masipag Biodiversity Center (MBC), located in the province of Bukidnon on the island of Mindanao, opened in October 2005. The director, Bobby Pagusara, says 'the aims of MBC are: the protection and conservation of our biodiversity, a place where the organic farming technologies of our farmers can be displayed and a center for alternative and renewable energy systems.' Ten hectares of land provide a home for rice,

maize, vegetables, fruit and forest trees, fishponds and livestock. Over
a thousand native varieties of organically grown rice and forty varieties
of maize (collected by farmers from all over Mindanao) are cultivated
and conserved. Seeds are distributed to farmers all over the island and
beyond. MBC also provides training for farmers, community development
workers and university students.

For Masipag, agriculture is not just about food production; it is about
survival and a way of life. It is about restoring soil fertility, saving seeds
and protecting biodiversity. It points the way forward for agriculture in
the Philippines and provides a sound model for averting climate change
impacts and providing a secure and sustainable future.

Pooling resources in east Kenya

In east Kenya, Practical Action has been working with a farmer who has
pooled resources and shared information on farming technologies with
his neighbours. Interested in soil and water conservation, they together
built an earth pan to store floodwater. Using this water and a bucket-drip
irrigation system next to the farmer's homestead proved very successful.
The project was water-dependent, however, so the group shared the cost
of installing a well and hand pump.

The farmer and his wife also attended a workshop on different uses
of the neem tree and its products for pest control, and for animal and
human health. To reduce the damage from chafer grubs, which attack the
roots of maize seedlings, two methods involving no chemicals were used.
These reduced damage from 50 per cent to a mere 5–10 per cent, without
a biotechnologist in sight.

Applying manure increases the tolerance of maize plants to damage
from chafer grubs. The nutrients in the manure accelerate root growth
and enable the seedlings to recover after attack.

Early land preparation exposes the grubs' eggs to heat on the surface,
which kills them, thereby reducing the number of eggs that hatch.

Since the adoption of sustainable agricultural techniques, crop yields
have increased fourfold. Livestock manure increases soil water retention
and provides plants with nutrients. The farmers have discarded the previous cut, burn, plant and shift cropping system in favour of working the
same piece of land and leaving the rest for livestock pasture and environmental conservation. Currently all the farmer's cropping land is subject
to rainwater conservation. He even harvests run-off water from the
roadside. If water supplies continue he intends to grow more cash crops
like watermelons and grafted yellow passion fruit. Both have a ready
market. This will increase the productivity of his land, thereby providing

enough income to see his son through university and supply food to the local community and hotel industry.

The key to the wider adoption of sustainable agricultural techniques, however, depends on their promotion through official agricultural support, so-called 'extension services'. They in turn need to be backed by a favourable policy climate and supportive research that addresses problems identified by farmers.

Increasing climatic resilience in western Honduras

A whole range of problems face people in the Honduran province of Lempira. Securing enough food to eat is as hard as getting and holding on to the land needed to grow it. Farms produce less than they could and get little state financial or technological support. To face these challenges, producers from thirty-four rural communities joined together to increase the productivity of their farms.

After Hurricane Mitch caused regional devastation in 1998, the development organisation Asociación Popular de Desarrollo Integral (APDI) devised a new strategy to respond to environmental vulnerability with support from development organisation Progressio. Working with community groups, they chose to tackle four main problems identified by locals:

1. contamination of water sources;
2. the high cost of artificial fertilisers;
3. high household wood consumption;
4. poor soil management on farms.

Activities commenced with community and group meetings to establish how environmental and productivity problems should be discussed, and to raise awareness of the fragility of natural resources. Through consensus, this helped plan the actions to be taken, with particular focus on gender and agro-ecology. The first steps were the development and sharing of skills on the actual plot of land. Working together, people were able to capture and share local farmers' valuable knowledge of the soil, native species, plagues, diseases, rainfall patterns, and more.

They worked to reduce contamination of the community water sources. They used a range of approaches, including new management plans, declarations of sources to be protected by the municipal government, tree planting and new fruit-tree nurseries, and reforestation campaigns in areas at risk.

The majority of the communities inhabit the coffee-growing high-lands. Coffee processing produces a lot of waste pulp and water run-off (*aguas mieles*), both of which are powerful pollutants that can contaminate community water sources and negatively affect aquatic life and the health of the community. As a result of the new work, these unsustainable practices are gradually decreasing.

Organic fertilisers were developed using local resources, such as harvest waste, manure and household waste. These are mixed with low-cost materials, such as cane sugar candy and green copper, which are permitted in organic agriculture.

Instant organic *aboneras* (structures to make compost) were built using local materials. They took just two or three hours to build and could be used immediately. The compost produced can be used on everything from coffee plants to domestic vegetables and fruit trees.

Excessive fuelwood use is a burden on both the environment, due to deforestation, and on the women and children who collect and deliver it. To reduce the impact on people and ecosystems, APDI provided training for the construction and use of more efficient, improved stoves and ecological furnaces, reducing the use of fuelwood by half and consequently reducing the pressure on the forests. Even better, by cutting smoke inside households, the health of women and girls was also improved, and cooking was less arduous.

Some women built communal ovens and made bread to sell to raise their income. Distances between houses are long, so another group built individual ovens, each helping the other with materials until they all had their own.

Soil management plans helped recover the soil's natural fertility for growing staple grains and coffee. The emphasis on soil and water conservation meant an end to clearance burning, and greater use of levelling and contour lines, as well as green fertilisers. Crop residues were left with minimal tillage, and organic fertilisers were used in both communal and individual plots dedicated to growing maize, beans, coffee, sugar cane and garden vegetables. As a result, natural soil fertility improved with more meso- and micro-organisms present. The structure of soils improved, as did their capacity to retain moisture and tolerate sudden changes in temperature and rainfall.

Analysing the soil to check its nutrient balance was a novel activity for the farmers. Both women and men were trained to teach the technique to others in their communities. Use of chemical fertilisers was reduced but production actually increased. Costs fell. The soil is now treated and worked with as a live system.

Just as financial investors spread risk, it makes sense for farmers to do so as well in the face of global warming. A diversity of approaches to both cropping and the range of crops planted is the best way to achieve that. Poor farmers may need technical advice and training to help with this.

In extreme environmental conditions, such as those expected under climate change, locally adapted food crops are invaluable in producing sufficient food for survival. The conservation and development of local agricultural biodiversity are crucial in the face of climate change. Farmers need access to seeds that are adapted to drought or reduced rainfall during critical stages in the growing season. A variety of forces have led to the reduced availability of local seeds, and increased dependence on hybrid seeds and crops like maize that are not well adapted to these conditions. Maize needs rain during the development of the cobs, and therefore a gap in rainfall at a crucial time leads to crop failure. This happened in Zambia in 2005, despite plentiful rain earlier in the rainy season. Despite examples of local seed banks and seed conservation activities, the importance of farmer-led conservation of agricultural biodiversity is not appreciated in many countries. Many agricultural departments still view the cultivation of traditional varieties as backward and unproductive.

Using native potatoes in the Andes

In the high Andes of Peru and Bolivia, local potatoes, or papas, and alpacas provide the basis for survival in inhospitable conditions. Family incomes are typically less than US$500 a year, and the mortality rate among children is higher than one in ten. Over 60 per cent of small children are chronically undernourished.

Communities living at altitudes above 3,800 metres get help from Practical Action to commercialise native potatoes as niche products in local markets. Native potato varieties are consumed by the people who grow them, who like their taste and find them easy to cook. Potato varieties that have been introduced to the area, which are bigger but of poorer quality, tend to be sold at markets. To improve alpaca production, training is provided on how to improve local pastures and treat common animal diseases.

Work in the area set out to increase native potato availability for both local consumption and commercial sale in order to raise incomes. Work aimed to directly benefit 600 peasant families of Quechua communities in the high areas of Canchis, Sicuani and Cusco. A revolving fund for native potato seeds and seeders for local production was established, complemented by a local system to provide technical assistance. Technical leaders, or Kamayoq, are chosen by the community to receive training.

Higher levels of potato biodiversity reduced the risks from insect attacks and also climate change. It also provided a greater range of dishes at mealtimes and conferred both status and social recognition. By contrast, development that promotes agricultural modernisation and relies upon high inputs and monoculture approaches has led to the loss of biodiversity. New participatory methods are needed to revaluate appropriate technologies, and to value the culture that has produced such a diversity of potato varieties.

Strengthening community resilience by conserving local seeds

Long periods of drought are becoming more common in much of sub-Saharan Africa, and are predicted to become more widespread as a result of climate change. The Tharaka district lies in dry north-central Kenya. Soils are acidic and of low fertility, and rainfall is low and unreliable. The main crops are sorghum, millet, cowpeas, green grams for food and cotton as a cash crop. Farmers select seeds to plant the following season from varieties that yield best under difficult conditions. Poor farmers do not have the cash to buy new seeds from merchants, and the commercial varieties are often less suitable for drier conditions.

In the past, communities relied on a few farmers who would save enough seeds to supply others when their crops failed due to drought or because they had been forced to eat their own precious seed stock. But recurrent drought undermined these traditional seed-storing and sharing practices. This led Practical Action East Africa to run a programme to improve seed security in Tharaka, from 1994 until 2000. The programme focused on conserving local plant genetic resources through seed bulking (which means producing enough seeds for storage), seed banking and seed shows.

Training on plot management for seed bulking preceded seed-bank training. Each member of a seed-bank group had to deposit two portions of at least one kilogram of each variety of seed that they grew: one portion for their own use and one for the group. At planting season, members withdrew part of their own deposit and the group used its portion to generate income or issue to members wanting to try different varieties. A committee ensured that all seed entering the bank was of top quality: clean, dry, pest- and mould-free. By ensuring access to seeds at the right time, the seed banks have enhanced food security and conserved local plant diversity. Since forming in 1997, one group has expanded its collection from 57 to 140 local crop varieties.

Seed shows enable farmers to sell or exchange surplus seeds, to obtain new seed varieties and to exchange information on the best crops for local conditions. Practical Action first developed seed shows in Zimbabwe and decided to introduce the idea into the Tharaka district, where locals now run them. Each year the number of exhibitors, crops and varieties of seeds displayed increases. An important benefit is the renewed belief in the value of traditional crop varieties, especially by younger farmers.

Another pressure comes from the concentration of ownership in the seed industry into a handful of large corporations. Ten companies now control one-third of the global seed industry, which further threatens agricultural biodiversity. A key aspect of adopting an agro-ecological approach is how different developments can produce synergies, leading to win–win situations such as increased production without additional external resources. Diverse cropping systems yield much more produce per unit of land than the mono-cropping favoured by 'modern' agricultural systems. They are also much more suited to the harsh conditions in which most farmers in sub-Saharan Africa operate.

Senegal: the dangers of large-scale mono-cropping

As long ago as the early 1880s, the French administration, with the help of armed troops, demanded that Senegalese farmers grow peanuts for the French vegetable oil industry. Peanut monoculture expanded rapidly after World Wars I and II and boomed again during the 1950s. Peasants needed cash to pay taxes imposed by the French, and peanuts were the only source of francs. However, the cash crop brought catastrophe, and has served to increase Senegal's vulnerability to climate change. Today, around 40 per cent of Senegal's arable land is used for growing peanuts. Economic dependence on the export crop has led to excessive mono-cropping, soil degradation and forest clear-cutting. Drought cycles of the last two decades have worsened desertification. Vegetation cover has been increasingly degraded, and overgrazing has made the situation worse.

The environmental impact of peanut farming has been comprehensive. Small-scale farmers did not own animals, so manure was unavailable. A fallow period would have allowed nutrients to re-accumulate in the soil, but the people could not afford the time. Instead they grew peanuts until the soil was exhausted, then moved to new land. They chopped down trees, which had held topsoil in place and helped absorb infrequent rains. Before the peanut takeover, the roots and stalks of the millet crop used to be left in place, holding down the topsoil. The peanut, on the other hand, is wrenched from the ground, the soil loosened and clouds of earth swirl away with the dry-season winds.

Small Indian farmers pushed to suicide by government policies

Indian eco-feminist Vandana Shiva has criticised Indian government policies which have marginalised India's small farmers and made them more vulnerable to climate change. 'Policies driven by corporate globalisation are pushing farmers off the land, and peasants out of agriculture', she said in April 2007. In her view, 'this is not a natural evolutionary process; it is a violent and imposed process and the 150,000 farmer suicides are one aspect of this violence.'

Her work with Navdanya – an organic farming organisation she founded in 1991 – has shown how small farms are actually more productive than larger ones and promote biodiversity. Farmers in West Uttar Pradesh, for example, have achieved 62.5 quintal per hectare using a native wheat variety for organic production compared to 50 quintal per hectare for chemically produced wheat. Shiva argues that 'the totally inappropriate model of industrial corporate agriculture has been applied, farmers are in distress, the soil has been destroyed, and the water has been over exploited and polluted.' She feels a change in policy is called for, particularly one that recognises women as the primary food producers and processors.[27]

Sustainable agriculture is a method of farming based on providing for human needs for food, income, shelter and fuelwood. It also builds an understanding of the long-term effect of our activities on the environment. It integrates practices for plant and animal production with a focus on pest predator relationships, moisture and plants, soil health, and the chemical and physical relationship between plants and animals on the farm. Such agroecological approaches consider not just productivity but also system stability, sustainability and issues relating to equity and fairness. The case studies in this chapter show how these approaches are helping those most vulnerable to climate change cope with its impacts. Examples described include diversification of crops (and animals) and seed varieties, agroforestry and tree-planting, using local knowledge and local varieties, organic farming practices, maintaining soil fertility using natural compost and manure, natural pest control, and activities such as terracing and other efforts to conserve soil water levels.

Most sustainable agricultural initiatives seek to reduce soil erosion and to make improvements to the soil's physical structure through its organic matter content and water-holding capacity. Some of the specific techniques for doing this are described in this and the next chapter on water. Water is a clear constraint in many rain-fed systems. When water is better harvested and conserved, it may be the key factor leading to improved agricultural productivity. Provided the soil's nutrient balance is maintained, better water management means better cropping. Techniques that deal with both the water scarcity and water over-abundance typical of climate change include the following.

- *Contour bunding* involves constructing low embankments or 'bunds' of earth or stones along the contour of a field to catch the rain when it falls, so that it has time to soak into the ground rather than run off and be lost. The bunds may be planted with vegetation to help fix them and delay rainwater disappearance. They also help prevent valuable soil being washed away. Bunds may be spaced at intervals across a field or, if the field is small, only along the lowest edge.

- *Gulley plugging* involves the placing of piles of stones across a gulley. This can prevent gulleys caused by heavy tropical rains getting worse and even help 'cure' them as soil builds up behind the 'plug'.
- *Check dams* are small stone or concrete dams, usually constructed across watercourses, designed to delay the flow of rainwater, so it has time to soak into the earth and replenish groundwater supplies whilst keeping adjacent land moist.
- *Tanks.* In India and elsewhere larger dams or bunds were traditionally built to create ponds or tanks to store water. Water seeps from these ponds into crop fields. Sometimes the pond silt is removed and used as fertiliser.
- *Pit planting.* Compost from animal manure and rotting vegetation can be churned into soil, adding nutrients and, equally importantly, helping to retain moisture. As compost is usually scarce, farmers, rather than spreading it across the whole field, may choose pit planting, which involves digging a pit for each plant – usually fruit trees or bushes – and adding the compost to the soil as it is dug in.

Conservation farming increases yields tenfold in Zambia

The Evangelical Fellowship of Zambia (EFZ), a Tearfund partner organisation, is training people to use a technique known as 'conservation farming', which has helped communities in the Monze East area cope with changing rainfall patterns and become more self-sufficient in the face of drought. This is vital in an area that has recorded the lowest river water levels in twelve years and in a country where 17 per cent of the population is HIV-positive (and thus often forced to spend what scant resources they possess on medicines, or are too ill to work) and which has more than 1.5 million orphans.

Conservation farming is a minimum-tillage method that traps moisture, improves soil quality, minimises soil erosion and creates drought-tolerant growing conditions. It lessens the farmers' reliance on rain as crops can use the moisture trapped in the soil. Yields typically increase tenfold when these methods are used.

It is different from traditional farming patterns because it requires sustained periods of moderate farming activity rather than short periods of intense activity. This allows people to continue farming (and so feed their families) when they might otherwise be too frail to cope with the traditional ways of working the land. This is particularly beneficial for women, who are increasingly responsible for agriculture in Zambia.

By encouraging farmers to diversify, EFZ helps to ensure that yields remain high even in times of low rainfall. But in some years, conservation farming of maize alone isn't enough to secure adequate food supplies. When this happens, diversification acts as a vital coping mechanism. For example, cash crops can be grown and then sold to purchase food. Herb cultivation is also being actively encouraged, as herbs can be used to make home remedies to boost the immune system. Yield increases have been so large that farmers are creating community grain stores to provide for the more vulnerable community members.

Organic farming in Leyte

Manong Greg lives on the central Philippine island of Leyte, an area often hit by disasters and exposed to drought. He believes the sun's scorching heat has become more intense in recent years. He has noticed the disappearance of two types of slimy tree frog and asks, 'have they retreated to a place where humidity is more tolerable or are they lost permanently because of the heat?' The intense summer sun also seems to have dried out the medicinal, but rare and endangered, staghorn fern, which grows on branches of the star apple tree. Manong Greg reports that recently seven hens and three roosters died of dungoy or atay, a disease that afflicts domestic fowl during hot months. Fatalities have been increasing in the past few years and spiked during the recent El Niño-induced drought.

Manong Greg has been expanding his farm for the past five years. He knows the climate is changing and he understands that conventional chemical farming techniques could damage his land, health and income stability. He plants disaster-tolerant crops to secure his family's food needs and practises organic rice farming, crop diversification and livestock integration.

Rice hay and husks are gathered and composted in his Vermi worm cast and compost production system. He no longer burns rice hay after the harvest, which contributes to rising greenhouse gas levels. Vermi cast and compost are used as fertiliser along with other natural products like fermented fruit and plant juices and fish amino acids. Oriental herbs are used to combat pest and insect infestations, which threaten crop yields and livestock.

Manong Greg plants pineapples, cassava and squash on the slopes to stop soil erosion and supplement his dry-season income. Gentle slopes are planted with ground-cover crops, tubers and madre de cacao. He also plants some of the 107 organic varieties of rice that he has 'engineered' for the past six years with the help of resource agencies like RDI-Leyte, PhilNet and the Leyte State University in Baybay.

To ensure a steady supply of irrigation water during very dry seasons, Manong Greg diverts water from a nearby stream to his property and has built a pond where he now farms fish and raises ducks. The overflow of pond water irrigates his rice in the fields below, enabling him to maintain three cropping cycles a year despite the erratic climate.

The dry period has become more and more unpredictable. Manong Greg only hopes he has done enough and can continue to find ways to secure his family's daily food supply and income in these challenging times.

Community organisation and empowerment transform lives and the environment in Rajasthan

In recent years, rainfall has been increasingly erratic for people living in the village of Vahigatia in Rajasthan, India. Water levels in wells were sinking by 2 to 3 metres per year, and perennial drinking water sources dried out. As a result, agricultural production was in decline. The farming population had no choice but to leave the village in search of a better life, but at great cost to their children's education, family life and elderly people, who were left behind. Without intervention, Vahigatia would probably have been rapidly engulfed by the great Thar Desert of Rajasthan.

Caritas India is now implementing a project to drought-proof the village through the conservation of soil, water and biomass. People have been trained in organic farming, and efforts have been made to reinstate traditional agricultural practices and increase crop diversity. Farm bunds, dams and contour trenches have conserved monsoon water, decreased water run-off and reduced soil erosion.

Water levels in community wells are now rising due to the recharging of groundwater resources in the project area. The community is enjoying an increase in agricultural productivity and has started to cultivate new crops. In addition, the land area under cultivation has increased due to the project. Areas that once lay fallow are now covered with vegetation. Crop yields have risen by 25 to 30 per cent, and whereas some 40 per cent of villagers used to migrate for work, this number has now decreased. Malnutrition has also fallen due to increased yields and income. Education for children is no longer at risk.

Niger: the story of Hamidou Oussemane

Hamidou is a farmer from the village of Guidan Ali in the district of Birnin Konni in Niger. His extended family comprises forty people.

Climate uncertainty is a way of life for Hamidou. As a young child he remembers the good times when the rains were abundant and more reliable than they are today. But since the drought years of the 1970s and 1980s, the rains have been inconsistent from one year to the next. Adapting to unpredictable and erratic conditions has not been easy, but Hamidou has developed a farming system on which he has raised a family while helping others.

The family's livelihood is based on a mixture of farming, keeping livestock and selling fuelwood. The family farms ten fields covering about 26 hectares, located on different soil types and producing a variety of food crops including millet, sorghum and rice. The women cultivate smaller plots on which they grow sorrel and okra. In a good year, the family produces a surplus, which is stored in the family's granaries and sometimes sold. The family also looks after 61 cattle, 41 of which they own, the others belonging to neighbours and friends. Until 1982, the herd was taken in different seasons either north towards Tahoua, or south to northern Nigeria. But, for a variety of reasons, including conflict and the rising costs of accessing pastures in the dry seasons, Hamidou's sons now look after the herd themselves in the vicinity of the village and use herd manure on the family fields.

Livestock, manure, plentiful household labour, and access to the relatively well-watered clay soils have been the main ingredients behind Hamidou's success as a farmer. Most years he can harvest enough food to feed his whole family and put aside for future years. Since he doesn't need to sell animals or milk to buy grain, the herd can grow relatively fast. Hamidou's system shows the benefits of an integrated crop–livestock farming approach widely promoted by policymakers in the Sahel.

However, such systems are highly vulnerable to climate change and greater rainfall fluctuations. Over the last twenty to thirty years, Hamidou has become more and more sedentary. He no longer takes his animals to more distant pastures and has lost the contacts he used to have with families in other areas of Niger and Nigeria. His farming system is heavily dependent on manure. In the event of a serious drought or a series of below-average years, Hamidou may find it difficult to save his animals as he has no obvious 'refuge area' and local pastures are increasingly scarce due to the pressure of cultivation. Livestock routes are blocked, the institutions managing access to resources are 'corrupted', and there is increasing competition over local resources. The locust plague of 2004 added an extra burden on many farmers in Niger.

The loss of the herd would undermine Hamidou's farming system and livelihood. He now plans to diversify into other areas of economic activity which are less dependent on the rains. Already two of his sons regularly go to Nigeria in the dry season to earn money as labourers. His nephews are planning to set up a small restaurant business in a nearby town. Hamidou is also thinking about buying land in a nearby irrigation scheme. He says he will wait to see what the future brings and whether God will answer his prayers for more rain.

Supporting smallholder agriculture in Ethiopia

Many of the approaches that constitute 'good development' also double as excellent techniques to adapt to the uncertainties of global warming. Smallholder farming in Ethiopia is a case in point. Ethiopia is crippled by unfavourable international trade rules, lack of rural roads and market access, unemployment, debt and environmental degradation. With one doctor per 100,000 people and 15 per cent of the population below the poverty line, when the rains fail in Ethiopia there is nothing to fall back on.

The Ethiopian Orthodox Church, which works with Christian Aid, is addressing these issues through its Rural Integrated Development Programme in Bugna in northern Ethiopia. Project coordinator Deacon Abate Desale observes that 'The land is so degraded in this region that erosion causes floods when the rains come and drought when it does not. Most Ethiopians are dependent on the land for their livelihoods so we must invest in it.' Techniques such as terracing land on hillsides to stop erosion and collect water for irrigation, replanting trees, and protecting areas of land for regeneration are all effective long-term measures to prevent drought and famine.

The Programme shows Ethiopia's potential. In the middle of the dry, unproductive landscape lies an oasis of lush, green vegetation and birdsong. Neighbouring farmers are taught how to grow vegetables and trees using traditional organic methods, enabling them to earn an income and enjoy a more balanced diet. Vegetables such as carrots, lettuces, tomatoes and onions, rarely seen in rural Ethiopia, are intercropped with coffee and fruit trees. Farmers learn about organic pest control, irrigation and water conservation and are provided with seeds and tree seedlings.

Carbate Bazarba is one of 400 farmers benefiting from this project. Like most Ethiopian farmers, Carbate used to only grow cereals. 'The greatest thing I have learnt from the demonstration site is how to plant new crops like fruits and vegetables and how important these things are for our diet. Now my wife and children have a better diet and I earn money from selling vegetables. My only problem now is that my children prefer guava and papaya and won't eat their injera!'

As vital to sustainable agriculture as the techniques and practices listed above are support and organisation:

- Agricultural research at a local level, through formal institutions and local development organisations which work directly with farmers, is essential to develop crop varieties and improve farming practices.
- Demonstration, training and extension services to promote these new crops and techniques to farmers are also important.
- Microcredit – because mainstream banks are usually inaccessible and farmers need access to credit for tools, seeds and transport.
- Combining credit with community grain banks stops poor farmers from having to sell their produce quickly and cheaply, instead enabling them to sell later when prices may be higher. Grain banks can also enhance community food security, and seed banks are a way to save seeds for next year's planting.

Dramatically increasing the support available for small-scale agriculture and an approach to farming based on maximum appropriate diversification is a priority if all the millions of poor people in the world who depend on farming for food and work are going to be able to cope. Highly diverse systems, as opposed to commercial monocultures, have been shown time and again to be more resilient – and more productive. Farming based on expensive and energy-intensive artificial inputs will both be vulnerable to fuel price rises and further add to the problem of climate change.

Vitally, and as demonstrated by many of the case studies in this chapter, small-scale farmers need supporting with a favourable institutional and policy environment and with research that addresses the problems that they, themselves, have identified. New systems that combine new insights and technologies with the wisdom of tradition are needed. Farmers and the NGOs that support them have a wealth of knowledge, skills and experience that can be applied to help them cope with the climate change challenges ahead, but these need placing in context. The case studies also identify a number of challenges relating to the wider political and institutional environment in which farming operates that need tackling if smallholder farmers are to cope. These include corrupt institutions, the blocking of livestock routes, poor government extension services, insufficient government investment in agriculture and appropriate agricultural research, unfavourable trade laws, market concentration and reduced access to land. These broader political issues provide the stage on which climate change will play out, resulting in more and more people going hungry. In the case study above describing how small Indian farmers have been pushed to suicide, Vandana Shiva is particularly critical of Indian government policies in this respect.

Securing livelihoods and boosting production are crucial; doing so requires access to productive land for those who are most vulnerable. Government policies relating to the planting of biofuels on cleared forest land and replacing food crops with biofuels threaten to reduce the amount of land available for agriculture. This provides another example of the importance of the policy environment in which small-scale farmers operate. The dangers of biofuels are discussed in more detail later in the book.

Much more must also be done to tackle the root causes of hunger. That means tackling poverty and the power imbalances that underpin it. The number of people who subsist in extreme poverty (under US$1.25 a day) is just over 1 billion; of whom nearly three-quarters live in South Asia and sub-Saharan Africa.[28]

While remarkable progress against poverty and hunger has been achieved in some regions, progress has been slow in areas where poverty and hunger are severe. Sub-Saharan Africa, for example, is home to some three-quarters of the 162 million ultra-poor people (those who live on less than 50 cents per day).[29] Even allowing for the extraordinary pace of urbanisation in Africa, the majority of the continent's poorest and most undernourished people live in rural areas – especially smallholders, nomadic pastoralists and women. The joint effort to eradicate poverty promised by African and donor governments must therefore deliver rural policies that involve and prioritise these vulnerable groups. Even small improvements in what they produce and earn, in access to health, education and clean water, will have major impacts in reducing hunger, as well as driving equitable growth. The need to give much more support to small-scale farming comes up again and again from the field experience of development groups. Despite this, aid for agricultural production in sub-Saharan Africa dropped by 43 per cent between 1990–92 and 2000–02.[30]

3

Water

The world is already facing a serious water crisis, with roughly
80 per cent of the world's population exposed to high levels of
threat to their water security. Roughly 1.5 billion people already
lack access to clean drinking water and 2.4 billion lack access
to basic sanitation.[1] As with hunger, there are many social and
political reasons for this, but global warming is making the situation far worse. Population growth is already likely to increase the
number of people living in water-stressed situations, and under
some climate change scenarios a further 2 billion people are
expected to be water-stressed by 2055.[23] Scientists estimate that
a future scenario of water availability under climate change and
population growth would see 59 per cent of the global population
facing shortages of water from rivers and irrigation by 2050. This
figure is lower, however, when water evaporating from soils and
transpired by plants is also considered.[4] Earlier estimates by the
Stockholm Environment Institute also put 63 per cent of the
world's population – some 6 billion people – living in countries
with significant water stress by 2025, based upon only a moderate
projection of climate change.[5]

Global warming is exacerbating water stress by changing rainfall patterns, river flows, lake levels and groundwater recharge. In
some places water sources are becoming more depleted, whereas
floods are hitting other areas. Globally, river basins and wetlands – where most of the world's people live – are becoming

damaged and less able to provide the conditions and processes that provide a water supply of adequate quality and quantity to ensure sustainable development and maintain vital ecosystems. Falling water supplies are also making hydropower difficult. In Vietnam, for example, exceptionally dry seasons over the past three years have resulted in low water levels in the reservoirs behind hydropower schemes in the north. This has affected power generation and reduced water supplies for irrigation activities downstream. Climate change could exacerbate this problem with increasing drought conditions in the future. Likewise in Nepal, while rivers can potentially provide 43,000 MW of electricity, changing rainfall patterns and timing of snow melting could reduce this potential.

Falling reservoir and river water levels due to decreases in rainfall reduce water quality because sewage and industrial effluents become more concentrated. This increases waterborne diseases and reduces the quality and quantity of fresh water available for domestic use. Inland fisheries are becoming depleted and degraded, and food security eroded, as good harvests are increasingly difficult to obtain. Both drought and floods, in different ways, favour the spread of waterborne diarrhoeal diseases, as well as diseases such as malaria and dengue.

The effects of changing rainfall patterns are widespread and varied. In Nepal, for example, intense rainfall has made life difficult for people living in traditionally built flat-roofed houses made of mud and stone. Roof leakage and wall erosion are major problems, particularly for low-income families that cannot afford to repair their homes.

Africa, like everywhere else, relies on water for its social, economic and environmental well-being. But given an overwhelming dependence on rain-fed agriculture, the fate of the continent's people is exceptionally sensitive to disruptions in the hydrological cycle. The fact that so many Africans have subsistence livelihoods means that prolonged drought is seriously hazardous for the continent. Southern Africa is one of many water-stressed regions which could see a further decrease in the flow of streams and the availability of groundwater.

In the Nile region, scenarios estimate decreasing river flow of up to 75 per cent by the year 2100. This would severely affect agriculture, as reductions in the annual flow of the Nile above 20 per cent would interrupt normal irrigation. Such a situation could cause conflict because current water allocations – negotiated during periods of higher flow – would become untenable.[6]

The IPCC asserts that 'It seems prudent to expect drought in Africa to continue to be a major climatic hazard', observing that even a small decrease in precipitation combined with higher evapotranspiration could result in 'significantly greater drought risks'.[7] Consequently, the IPCC recommends the improvement of water-use and irrigation systems in Africa, which would, regardless, benefit the region.

Tharaka: the canal that ran dry

Joshua Musyoki-Mutua has every right to be worried about his future. Out of 300 farmers who grew crops around him a decade ago, he is now one of only two who remain – a fact he blames on global warming.

The 36-year-old, who grows chilli, eggplants, green peppers and other crops for the local and export markets, remembers when the land around his plot in Mtitoandei in Tharaka district in central-south Kenya was an oasis of green. That has now changed. The farms were irrigated from a nearby canal, which in 1982 flowed for 7 kilometres. But now the levels of rainfall have dropped and the water only travels half a kilometre. This has forced hundreds of farmers to abandon their farms and livelihoods.

'I would estimate we now get 40 per cent less rain than we used to', reflects Joshua. 'Many farmers have left, mainly because the water no longer runs along the canal like it used to. These people now have nothing. They are destitute. Therefore climate change is increasing poverty.

Joshua says the government and international community could help him and other farmers get back on their feet with irrigation systems and advice on water management. But, he adds, basic work on the current canal could also be a lifeline for fellow farmers. 'In the past there was enough water to compensate for what leaked out of the canal', he explains. 'That is no longer so; now every drop is very important. Making the canal watertight and improving the dam which serves it could dramatically improve the distance the water flows. With water people could work to get themselves on their feet again. Without it, they can do nothing.'

In central Asia, rising populations will place demands on scarce water supplies, directing them away from irrigation farming. This is problematic because most Central Asian countries rely on groundwater to irrigate agriculture. In Iran, for example, agriculture accounts for 94 per cent of water use, and 55 per cent of the water used comes from groundwater sources.[8] Any decreases in rainfall could, therefore, significantly affect both agriculture and the availability of water for human consumption.

Climate change and the water crisis in central Asia

For ordinary people in the former Soviet states of central Asia, access to water is already worsening their many difficulties. In 2000–2001, in response to the worst drought in seventy-four years, Oxfam began working in Tajikistan, the poorest of the five new nations. In the worst affected area, 200 hand pumps were installed to alleviate water shortages for some 9,000 people. Partly on account of increasing aridity, Oxfam is extending its development programme, including introducing farmers to new drought-resistant and less water-thirsty plants.

Because of Tajikistan's mountainous landscape, floods and landslides have also become more frequent and more severe in other areas. In the summer of 2004, serious floods and landslides meant that half the capital, Dushanbe, was without safe water, and the only road between Dushanbe and Khujand, the second city, was seriously damaged with many bridges also swept away. Economic damage was severe. In 1998, a flood swept away a pumping station on the Qizil Soo (Red) river, depriving some 7,000 people in six villages of clean water. Oxfam engineers helped local people renovate the pumping station, and strengthened the riverbanks to guard against another flood.

Global warming is not the only cause of the region's water problems. Many central Asian countries are locked into unsustainable yet expanding water-intensive cotton farming, fed by hopelessly inefficient and wasteful irrigation systems. Now that Soviet subsidies have dried up, there is no money to maintain this dilapidated infrastructure.

Deforestation has added to flooding problems, and Tajikistan's civil war further damaged infrastructure. Now, nearly a quarter of the population use irrigation channels – contaminated by farm chemicals – as their main source of drinking water. Meanwhile, far downstream, the Aral Sea continues to shrink, exposing the fertiliser and pesticide dust washed into it from Soviet cotton fields and creating a toxic wasteland for the people living on its shores.

Melting glaciers are causing grave concern. Much of the water in the Aral Sea Basin comes from glaciers in Tajikistan and neighbouring Kyrgystan, whose glaciers have shrunk by 35 per cent in the last fifty years. Kazakhstan's capital, Almaty, depends on water from the fast-shrinking Tien Shan mountain glaciers. In mountain valleys, melting increases the risk of floods and landslides as glacial lakes burst, and downstream competition for water is increasing.

In mainland Southeast Asia, glaciers and snowfall in the Himalayas play a critical role in the provision of water via snow-fed rivers. As increasing temperatures and other climatic changes cause glaciers to melt and snowfall patterns to change, rivers such as the Mekong will be affected. Flow in the Mekong river may increase in the short term due to accelerated snowmelt, but is projected to decrease in the long term as snow stocks decline. Variation in rainfall and increased sediment yields will also affect river flows. In some areas, wetlands, streams and small rivers that serve as community fishing grounds and important animal habitats may become seasonal with water only when it rains.

In China, rapidly melting glaciers in Tibet could lead to dangerously low water levels in some of its most famous rivers. More than 400 million Chinese people are already living with the problem of desertification, partly brought on by climate change, and China is already facing problems with water shortages, water contamination and unequal water distribution. The area to the north of the Yangtze river, covering about 64 per cent of Chinese land, is home to 46 per cent of the population, 60 per cent of arable land and 44 per cent of GDP. However, the region has only roughly 19 per cent of the nation's water resources. The Yellow River Basin, Huaihe River Basin and Haihe River Basin cover 35 per cent of arable land, contain 35 per cent of the population and provide 32 per cent of total Chinese GDP, but the area has only 7 per cent of China's water resources.

Climate change is intensifying the conflict between water supply and demand in China, especially in the northern regions. Due to temperature increases and changes in rainfall patterns, water resources in northern China have been significantly reduced due to global warming. This is particularly obvious when looking at the reduced discharges of six of China's largest rivers: the Yellow River, the Huaihe River, the Haihe River, the Songhua River, the Yangtze River and the Pearl River. Since the 1980s, the recorded discharge from the Haihe River has reduced by 40 to 70 per cent compared to prior discharge rates, and some studies suggest that global warming could have caused between 35 and 40 per cent of the reductions in run-off that have occurred in the middle reaches of the Yellow River. With increasing evaporation rates and melting glaciers, which traditionally act as a solid backup supply of water, the problems of water availability may intensify. It is estimated, for example, that the annual amount of irrigation water required in the Huang–Huai–Hai Plain is expected to increase by between 66 and 84 per cent if there is a 20 per cent decrease in annual rainfall resulting in major water shortages.[9] The impacts of climate change on large food-producing basins such as this will be felt on food prices around the world.[10] According to the Water Resources 2030 Group, China will face a shortfall in water supply of 26 per cent by 2030.[11]

Bangladesh faces extreme water shortages during the dry months, which is bad news for both ecosystems and agricultural production. On the other hand, floods during the monsoon season inundate more than 20 per cent of the country on average and can flood as much as 70 per cent of the land.[12] Melting snow from the Himalayas provides more than 60 per cent of the water flowing down rivers in the east of Bangladesh. The season in which most snow melts, however, coincides with the summer monsoon season, which intensifies the risk of floods. Accelerated melting of glaciers in the Himalayas will likely increase flooding in Bangladesh, but at the same time the decreasing size of glaciers could lead to more drought in the northern regions of the country as river flows are reduced. Changes in the tide and sea level along with less water flow in rivers has already increased saltwater intrusion in the coastal areas. Saltwater intrusion in freshwater resources is already a major problem for coastal communities.

Unlike many poorer nations, the Bangladesh government is acutely aware of the importance of climate change, and is integrating it into national policies and sectoral plans, particularly in the water sector. Bangladesh also has a wealth of experience in community-based adaptation and disaster-risk-reduction strategies and practices, particularly with regard to floods, cyclones, saltwater intrusion, waterlogging and water scarcity.

All over the world, many different kinds of small-scale community-based activities have developed in response to water shortages and changes in hydrological cycles. Some of these are conceived and developed by the communities themselves, but others receive support from NGOs or government bodies. In India, for example, where rainwater conservation is a priority because the nature of the Indian monsoon is such that most rain falls in a very short time, a wide range of activities are occurring. Farmers are shifting from water-intensive crops to ones that require less water in response to climate change. Several civil society organisations have been working with local communities to develop water-harvesting technologies, as well as to promote local decentralised mechanisms for watershed development. In Rajasthan, for some years now, NGOs like Tarun Bharat Sangh have been involved in channelling water to farmers using locally adapted techniques to help tackle drought in the Alwar district. Such local community initiatives have occurred even without the support of local or national governments, but governments can also play a key role. State policies like mandatory water-harvesting laws in cities such as Chennai are a timely adaptation response in the face of climate variability.

Rainwater harvesting in Gwanda district, Zimbabwe

Practical Action has been working in the communal lands of Zimbabwe, where soils are poor and rainfall is low, for more than twenty years. Work on rainwater harvesting evolved as a good way to increase food production under conditions of falling rainfall and increasing unpredictability.

Mrs Magaye, village coordinator in Humbane village, describes how rainwater harvesting was incorporated into her work: 'The first thing we did was to visit some farmers to learn from them. We went to Zvishavane and Chivi. We liked what we saw, and when we came back we called a ward meeting, so we could share our experience. Traditional leaders in the ward came together.' Following training from Practical Action she describes how farmers began digging contours using an A-frame – an affordable technology. 'We realised if we just dug a contour, the water would overwhelm it, so we dug infiltration pits, to slow it down. Then we ploughed and sowed. Tilling the land was hard, because of a lack of donkeys and ploughs. In the dry season, donkeys don't have enough grass to eat and are weak.'

Before the project there had been no harvest, but following the project quite a few households harvested 500 kilograms of maize. Some 25 per cent of households in 2003 had produced enough food to see them through the year. Many of the other 75 per cent had joined the project later, or only committed part of their land to contour ridging, waiting to see how others fared.

Community water management in Ibans Lagoon, Honduras

Ibans Lagoon is located in the Mosquitia area of north-eastern Honduras. The area is a designated biosphere reserve and has been recognised as a World Heritage Site since 1982 due to its exceptional ecosystem diversity. The reserve is home to three indigenous groups – Miskito, Pech and Tawahka – as well as members of the Garífuna ethnic group and Ladinos from other parts of Honduras. Most people live on the coast or along the major rivers, where they farm, hunt, fish and gather forest products including firewood, timber for building houses and canoes, and medicinal plants.

Coastal erosion is a particularly pressing community concern at Ibans Lagoon. It has been exacerbated by the removal of much of the shore vegetation – including mangroves – for firewood or to create space to build. Older people often tell of when they used to have a house or land in areas now covered by water. Tropical Storm Michelle in 2000 reduced the narrowest point of land between the sea and the lagoon to less than 100 metres. This is worrying because the area is frequented by tropical storms, and sometimes hurricanes. High erosion rates also increase flood risk in the villages.

In 2002, the Tearfund partner and Honduran non-governmental organisation Mosquitia Pawisa Apiska (MOPAWI) began to work with the coastal communities. Reforesting the lagoon shore with mangrove and other species to reduce erosion and improve fish habitats was prioritised, followed by activities to manage waste better, apply the law in relation to resource extraction and house construction on the lagoon shores, and train farmers and foresters in sustainable techniques.

Some of the early areas reforested by individuals or small groups were not respected. As people went down to the lagoon to bathe, play and wash clothes, newly planted trees were trampled on, pulled up and damaged by having clothes hung on them. Many were also eaten by cattle and horses. New plots were therefore fenced to keep out animals. Living fences helped stabilise the soil. These last much longer than normal fences, as the posts do not rot or suffer from termite damage. With some species the new growth can be sold for firewood or as posts. The new, fenced plots have been very successful. Many people helped establish them and everyone in the area knows their purpose.

Whether climate change brings increasing floods and storms or worse drought, it will create havoc for poor farmers,

jeopardising their livelihoods and threatening their food security. It is therefore essential to promote knowledge and methods
which enhance the resilience of small-farmer agriculture and
food production. Many techniques for sustainable agriculture
relate directly to difficult climatic conditions and deal with both
the water scarcity and the overabundance typical of tropical
countries with seasonal, often unreliable, rainfall patterns. These
are detailed in the previous chapter on food and farming.

Storing rainwater in Rajasthan

Helping communities to assess and respond to the risks they face from
extreme events will save many lives. The Discipleship Centre (DC), a
Tearfund partner, is working with five villages near Jodhpur in India
to help communities assess the increasing drought risks and how to
boost their capacity to deal with them. Through this exercise, a Village
Development Committee (VDC) was formed, providing the first opportunity for men and women of different castes to meet together to discuss
how to reduce the impact of future droughts. Already, two ideas have
proved very successful.

The VDC decided to build rainwater cisterns about 3 to 4 metres wide
and 4 metres deep. During the rainy season, channels take rainwater to
the cisterns. Each cistern can store 40,000 litres and is shared by three
families. When full, the cistern can provide year-round drinking water
for the families. It can also store water brought in by tankers in times of
drought.

The VDC also resumed traditional water conservation practices that
had been abandoned or forgotten. They built 2-metre-high rainwater
bunds around fields and dug large ditches in front of the bunds. These
bunds help prevent soil erosion from wind and rain and hold water in the
soil by preventing rainwater from flowing away.

The VDC mobilised the villagers to dig a bund around a field owned
by a village widow. She was unable to survive on what she could grow
and had been forced to find work in a nearby stone quarry. Her children
had to go with her as she had no one to care for them at home. This
meant they dropped out of school and began working in the stone quarry
as well. After the first year, the widow's millet yield doubled and now
other villagers want bunds for their fields.

**Local manufacture and installation of village water pumps
in the Philippines**

Poor access to fresh water in the remote hillsides of the Philippines
means that for many people the journey down steep slopes to collect
water for basic needs can be a difficult one. Furthermore, the absence
of a regular water supply leads to poor hygiene and sanitation, and also
limits agriculture. The Alternative Indigenous Development Foundation
Inc. installs hydraulic ram pumps to provide a good supply of water from
the rivers to the hillside villages. These ram pumps use the power of the
water alone to lift a small fraction of the water up 200 metres vertically,
and sometimes pump it over a kilometre to where it is needed.[13]

Despite the successes of community-based initiatives, many
governments, under pressure from large international lending
institutions, still favour large infrastructure projects such as
dams. Such prestige projects often come with lucrative subcon-
tracting opportunities and financial incentives designed to tip
the scales in their favour. And yet evidence suggests that these
prestige projects are often both dangerous and accompanied by
tremendous social costs. They can also tie governments into
paying back crippling debts for many years.

Indian novelist Arundhati Roy suggested in her 1999 essay
'The Greater Common Good' that at least 30 million Indians
have been displaced to make way for large dams since 1947.
And a report by the International Rivers Network shows that
flood control based on dams and embankments has failed to
stop the rapid rise, severity and number of floods.[14] Dams and
levees can never be fail-proof, and when they do fail they can
cause catastrophic damage. They also create a false sense of
security, encouraging questionable development on vulnerable
floodplains. In 2006, engineers at India's Ukai Dam released
monsoon waters to stop the dam breaching. This action killed 120
people, and many millions of dollars of damage was caused. At
least thirty-nine people walking across the Sind river in Madhya

Pradesh during a religious ceremony in 2006 were washed away by sudden releases from the Manikheda Dam. There have been many other dam-related catastrophes in Asia over the last thirty years in China, Pakistan, India, Afghanistan, Uzbekistan and Kyrgyzstan.[15]

Measures such as restoring wetlands and floodplains, improving warnings and preparedness for evacuation, and reducing development on floodplains can help reduce damage and loss of life. But big infrastructure projects are clearly not a panacea for all development problems, and with climate change many such projects could become even more dangerous. Efforts should rather be made to scale up water conservation activities and river-basin-management strategies.

Coastal areas and sea-level rise

Coastal areas around the world are already experiencing the problems of coastal erosion, flooding and subsidence. Exploitation of coastal resources, development and population pressures add to the pressure. Climate change is expected to intensify these problems.

With sea levels set to rise by up to 70 centimetres in the coming century and continuing to rise for many centuries after,[16] heavily populated areas of low-lying land, such as southern Bangladesh, the Nile Delta, parts of Eastern China, which are home to many of the nation's most prosperous cities and provinces, and many atoll islands of the South Pacific and Indian Oceans face a bleak future. So, too, do the long stretches of low-lying coasts in Western Africa from Senegal to Angola, in South America from Venezuela to Recife in Brazil, and much of the coastlines of Indonesia and Pakistan.

'Overall magnitudes for the developing world are sobering: Within this century, hundreds of millions of people are likely to be displaced by sea-level rise (SLR); accompanying economic and ecological damage will be severe for many. The world has not previously faced a crisis on this scale.'
World Bank, 2007[17]

According to the IPCC, a 1 metre sea-level rise – which could occur by the end of this century without major cuts in greenhouse gases – could flood 15,000 to 20,000 square kilometres of the Mekong River Delta and affect half a million square hectares of the Red River Delta. In this scenario, 2,500 square kilometres of mangrove will be lost, and around 1,000 square kilometres of cultivated farmland and mariculture areas will become salt marshes.[18]

According to the World Bank, Vietnam will suffer most from sea-level rise.[19] Should climate change indeed result in a 1 metre rise in sea-level, the country could incur losses totalling US$17 billion per year and lose more than 12 per cent of its most fertile land.[20] The best agricultural land, together with 50 per cent of the population, is on the low-lying Red River and Mekong River delta regions. Over 17 million people could lose their homes, 14 million of whom live in the Mekong Delta region. Intrusion of saline or brackish water could also affect the irrigation of paddy rice. Mangrove and cajeput forests – important ecosystems in low-lying areas – may die back or be entirely lost.[21] One estimate suggests that with a 90 centimetre rise in sea levels, 33 per cent of reserves and 27 per cent of biodiversity in Vietnam could be lost.[22]

In Thailand, much of the country's most fertile agricultural land is situated in low-lying plains near river deltas. Rising sea levels could cause saltwater intrusion of up to 40 kilometres up the Chao Praya, Tachin and Bangprakong rivers, threatening saltwater-sensitive crops. The Chao Praya river is also the main source of drinking water for Bangkok, with its 10 million or more residents. Bangkok is barely above sea level and already suffering from extensive land subsidence; this combined with only a 32 centimetre projected rise in sea level by 2050 would mean that the expanse of land in Bangkok Metropolitan Area prone to flooding would increase by 26 per cent. This figure rises to 81 per cent of the city with the sea-level rise of 88 centimetres projected by 2100.[23]

Other low-lying nations, such as the Philippines and Indonesia, are also at risk from sea-level rise. Indonesia's environment minister, Rachmat Witoelar, warned in January 2007 that his country – comprising some 17,000 islands where millions depend on fishing and farming – could lose 2,000 small islands by 2030 due to a rise in sea levels as a result of climate change. Thousands of Indonesian farmers in productive coastal areas will have to look for other livelihoods if predictions for sea-level rise come true across the vast archipelago nation.[24]

The Philippines archipelago has the second-largest coral reef cover in the world (26,000 square kilometres) and a coastline which, at 36,289 kilometres, is roughly equivalent to the circumference of the earth. Greenpeace has mapped out areas that are vulnerable to a 1 metre sea-level rise and found that such a rise will affect 64 out of 81 provinces, covering at least 703 out of 1,610 municipalities, and inundating almost 700 million square metres of land. Out of sixteen regions in the Philippines, only one will not be affected by sea-level rise – the Cordillera Autonomous Region. Ironically, this region is at high risk from extreme weather events such as typhoons and increases in rainfall.

In China, the sea level around the coast of the Yangtze River Delta and Pearl River Delta has risen 3.1 millimetres and 1.7 millimetres respectively per year over the past fifty years.[25] Sea-level rise has already combined with storm surges, coastal erosion and saltwater intrusion into fresh water supplies to seriously affect China's coastal economy and the stability of its ecological environment, in some cases bringing huge losses. In 2006, saltwater intrusion and coastal erosion intensified in the Yangtze River Delta region. Frequent saltwater intrusion has already affected Shanghai City's water supply, reducing the quality of groundwater supplies and soils, and having a disastrous impact on local ecosystems. Sea-level rise also influences the reproduction and behaviour of fish living in river estuaries. It is certain to harm the fishing industry, which is already suffering from the harmful effects of overfishing. Coral reefs in Guangxi and Hainan provinces have already shown signs of albinism, perhaps due to increases in sea temperature and other pressures, which could further damage the fishing industry.

The ecology of the Yellow River Delta is particularly vulnerable to climate change. Floods and erosion will damage the tourism industry, water supplies, fish stocks and biodiversity. The United Nations estimates that 40 per cent of delta areas will be inundated if a sea-level rise of about 1 metre combines with a 2–3 metre storm surge. By 2050, the sea level around the Yellow River Delta will likely rise about 0.48 metres and storm surges will be a major challenge. Water supplies, which are already scarce, will be threatened further, and the expected impacts will bring unprecedented challenges to the local ecology and sustainable development of the local economy.[26]

The Chinese government has already taken many important steps to cope with climate change impacts in coastal areas and emphasises the importance of investment in construction to safeguard the coast. However, even if construction proceeds as envisioned by the government, investment will still be far below what the IPCC suggests is reasonable. It is the poor and disadvantaged coastal township communities that will suffer most; the consequence of more intense and more frequent typhoons and storm surges could be disastrous.

'Coastal areas are by far the most populated areas in the world. One has to be very careful about building expensive and sensitive infrastructure along the coasts, such as airports and thermal/nuclear power stations.'
Dr Baba, director of the Indian Institute of Technology, Madras

'We have experienced sea-level changes on certain islands that are unrelated to the tsunami. Coastal sea levels are changing in some places. In Pondicherry, the government started building sea walls because in the last five to six years the sea has started encroaching into the city.'
Evangelical Fellowship of India Commission on Relief, India

In India, sea levels are rising at an average rate of 3.1 millimetres per year. A 1 metre rise would inundate about 1,000 square kilometres of the Ganges Delta. Already, over the past two decades, four islands – Bedford, Lohachara, Kabasgadi and Suparibhanga – have been submerged, leaving 6,000 families homeless. Now, over 7 million people are vulnerable to coastal flooding and rising sea levels.

Development along India's 6,500 kilometre coastline has damaged natural ecosystems, including coral reefs, mangroves, sand dunes and sand bars that have historically provided defence against coastal erosion and acted as a buffer to prevent flooding from wave action or tidal surges. Removal of such defences is common due to fishing practices or construction of embankments and other developments. Such construction can damage natural drainage systems to the extent that, in some areas, the discharge of fresh water is completely cut off. This results in an increase in the salinity of the adjacent area, damaging surrounding ecosystems. The mangrove ecosystems of the Sundarbans are particularly vulnerable to changes in salinity. Some of India's richest biodiversity depends on mangroves, along with many people's livelihoods. Species like horseshoe crabs, which were common in the Sundarbans, have declined drastically due to increased salinity levels.

Bangladesh is one of the world's largest deltas, formed by a dense network of 230 rivers. Most of the country is less than 10 metres above sea level, with about 10 per cent less than 1 metre above the mean sea level. One-third of the country is vulnerable to high tides. Sea-level rise due to global warming during the early part of the twenty-first century is expected to be an average of 2–3 millimetres per year, although this varies by area.[27] Land subsidence can also make the affects of sea-level rise even greater. Combined with coastal erosion, siltation of river estuaries, cyclones, storm surges and drainage problems, this will make life particularly challenging for those who live near the coast. This includes about one-quarter of the population of Bangladesh, who live in coastal areas, in addition to those who depend in some way or other on activities in the coastal region. If the sea level rises by up to 1 metre this century, Bangladesh could lose up to 15 per cent of its land mass[28] and as many as 30 million Bangladeshis could become climate refugees. This would also cost Bangladesh half of its rice land, and some predictions suggest that a 1 metre sea-level rise could lead to a decline in GDP of between 27 and 57 per cent.[29] Much coastal infrastructure, built on the advice of international finance institutions such as the World Bank, has already disadvantaged poor coastal communities, and is likely to reduce their ability to adapt to climate change yet further.

Saltwater intrusion into freshwater supplies in Bangladesh due to sea-level rise will create acute water crises in the future. Saltwater from the Bay of Bengal already penetrates 100 kilometres or more inland up tributary channels during the dry season and this could get worse.[30] Salinity in the freshwater channels and also in the groundwater affects agriculture, forests and biodiversity, as well as human health. Growing populations require more and more water, which will further deplete freshwater supplies.

'Seawater is intruding into estuaries and aquifers, making the estuaries inhospitable breeding grounds for the fish and the aquifer water unfit for human consumption. Besides, salinity intrusion due to sea-level rise and low water flow from upstream during the winter season is causing excessive death of trees in the Sundarban mangrove, including its adjoining areas, and threatens regional/national food security. Recently, the production of our country's famous fish hilsa has declined to a minimum level and some other old varieties are in a state of extinction.'

Koinonia, Bangladesh

The IPCC points out that 'small island states account for less than one per cent of global greenhouse gas emissions, but are among the most vulnerable of all locations to the potential adverse effects of climate change and sea-level rise.'[31] In this respect, small island states are 'canaries in the coalmines' for the rest of the world when it comes to experiencing climate change. Their problems show in microcosm what many other countries face. What is happening today to low-lying communities is a warning to countless other regions around the globe.

Pacific island societies are highly dependent on their natural environment; communities, agricultural land, tourist resorts and associated infrastructure are concentrated in coastal zones and thus particularly vulnerable. Whilst the island nations of the Pacific are in many ways diverse, they share certain characteristics which hamper their ability to cope with the negative effects of climate change:

- small physical size and often a low elevation;
- wide geographic distribution and remoteness;
- proneness to 'natural' disasters;
- rapid urbanisation and dense, growing populations;
- increasing degradation of fragile environments;
- limited natural, human and financial resources;
- loss of traditional coping mechanisms;
- export-dependent, open economies.

Small island states cannot solve many of these problems alone. Political and financial commitment from developed nations is needed. It is long overdue.

Sea-level rise is threatening important mangrove forests in many Pacific island states. Many commercially important fish species breed and raise their young among mangrove roots. Mangroves are also sources of timber and medicines for local communities, and they protect shorelines from storms and tidal surges. The United Nations Environment Programme estimates that some of the region's islands could lose half of their mangroves by 2100.[32]

Water is an extremely limited resource in most Pacific island states and many rely on a single water source. Any changes to the recharging of this source or contamination by saltwater can, therefore, have catastrophic consequences. Changing rainfall patterns can lead to droughts; atoll countries in particular depend on freshwater lenses for drinking and irrigation water. Rising sea levels and leakage from storm surges could contaminate these freshwater supplies.

Many Pacific island nations face the prospect of total inundation, particularly low-lying atoll islands on limestone deposits from coral reefs. Tuvalu and islands in Vanuatu, the Marshall Islands, the Federated States of Micronesia and Papua New Guinea are already affected by rising sea levels. The World Bank predicts that Kiribati could experience flooding of up to 80 per cent of its land mass in some areas due to rising sea waters.[33] In June 2008, Kiribati asked Australia and New Zealand to allow its citizens to move to those countries as permanent refugees. Australian foreign minister Bob Carr announced in 2013 that 'Unless action is taken, Kiribati will be uninhabitable by 2030 as a result of coastal erosion, sea level rise and saltwater intrusion into drinking water.'[34]

With 17,000 kilometres of coastline and 600 islands, many of which are low-lying, sea-level rise is also a key issue for Papua

New Guinea. Some low-lying islands will eventually become completely submerged, as is already happening to Mortlock, Tasmann and the Duke of York Islands. A 1 metre rise could affect up to 50 per cent of the coastline.[35] Natural barriers to storm surges and coastal erosion, such as mangroves and swampy forest ecosystems, will become less effective.

Glacial melt

Glaciers are the freshwater reservoirs at the top of mountain watersheds. They are the origin of many rivers that wind their way through thousands of kilometres of grazing, agricultural and forested land, and are used as a source of irrigation, drinking water, energy and industry. Hundreds of millions of people throughout China, the Indian subcontinent and Latin America, many of whom live far from the glaciers themselves, rely on this water.

The main glaciated areas in the southern South American region are the northern Patagonia ice field with an area of 4,200 square kilometres, the southern Patagonia ice field with 13,000 square kilometres, and Cordillera Darwin with 2,000 square kilometres. Several glaciers in the region are in drastic retreat. The O'Higgins Glacier has shrunk back 15 kilometres over the last century in what is probably the largest retreat in all of South America. A recent thinning of 14 metres a year has been measured at Upsala Glacier, and a record thinning of 28 metres a year has been detected at HPS 12 Glacier in Falcon Fjord.

The incidence and speed of glacial retreat have generally accelerated during the last few decades, with most South American glaciers expected to collapse within our lifetime. This is the case in the Northern Andes, covering Ecuador, Peru and Bolivia, but also further away from the tropics in Chile and Argentina. The Chacaltaya Glacier in Bolivia, which provides water resources to the city of La Paz, is predicted to melt completely before 2015 if the current global warming trend continues.

Peru houses 470,000 hectares of what is known as 'eternal ice'. According to officials at the glaciology unit at the Instituto Nacional de Recursos Naturales, the ice-covered area of the Peruvian Andes reduced by 22 per cent over the 1970–97 period. Mount Huascarán, Peru's most famous mountain, has lost 12.8 square kilometres of ice – around 40 per cent of what was covered thirty years ago.

In Ecuador, glaciers are also shrinking rapidly due to global warming. The ice surface on the volcano Cotopaxi reduced by 31 per cent between 1976 and 1997, and the glacier has shrunk from 21.2 square kilometres to 14.6 square kilometres. In somewhere between seven and seventeen years the country will lose at least four of its eight most important glaciers.

Vanishing glaciers in the Columbian Andes

In glacial terms, sixty years is normally a blink in time. But in the Colombian Andes, the meaning of the term 'glacial' is changing – fast.

In the north-east of Colombia, near the Venezuelan border, El Cocuy National Park covers 306,000 hectares, ranging from 600 to 5,330 metres above sea level and including a mountain range that is home to 30 per cent of Colombia's total glacial ice mass. The glaciers of Cocuy are an integral part of the hydrological cycles of several ecosystems, including lowland and Andean forests and high-altitude savannas known as *páramos*. Up to 80 per cent of the rock substrate in El Cocuy can store and regulate underground water resources, making the area an important provider of environmental services. Together with high-altitude lakes, these systems are vital sources of water and environmental services for the indigenous U'wa and other communities living in and around the Park.

For decades, the ecosystems created and supported by the glaciers on and around El Cocuy have been under assault from below as rural communities marginalised by Colombia's conflict and inequitable socio-economic system have taken agriculture and livestock grazing higher and higher up the mountain. Now, global warming may be an even greater threat.

The area of glacial cover in El Cocuy is now only roughly a quarter of what it was in 1850. This represents a fourteenfold decrease in the volume of glacial ice. The last measure by Park staff (in 2004/05) found an average rate of recession of 15 metres per year. They estimate that at this rate El Cocuy will lose all its glacial cover by 2030.

As the glaciers melt and total volumes of water decrease, the eco-systems and communities that depend on them will experience two waves of change. Currently, higher rates of recession correspond to greater flows of water, which contribute to higher rates of erosion, flooding and mudslides in lowland areas. As the glaciers disappear, however, water flow will tail off dramatically to comprise only rain and snowfall. The giant sponge will dry out and the surrounding communities will have to cope with reduced water flow and greater risks of flooding, mudslides and erosion due to the degradation of the environment.

The Columbian Institute of Hydrology, Meteorology and Environmental Studies, together with the Cocuy National Park team, has established a site for a new climatic station to help monitor glacial recession. Park staff have also begun to discuss the implications of these changes with surrounding communities, but progress is slow. They have launched programmes to improve environmental management of the *páramos*, manage the microbasin, research alpine lakes, reduce human impacts on the *páramos* and increase awareness of the vital importance of the glaciers, the *páramos* and their water resources. There is a critical need to conserve these highlands to guarantee water resources for future generations, but these efforts are already stretching the Park's limited human and financial resources. The speed and scale of the changes under way mean that more effective adaptive responses are imperative.

Only the polar ice caps hold more freshwater than the Himalayan glaciers, yet by 2035 the size of these glaciers could be reduced by as much as 80 per cent.[36] 'Surface temperatures in most parts of India have increased by half a degree Celsius during the second half of the century', says Professor Srinivasan of the Centre for Atmospheric and Oceanic Sciences in Bangalore, adding that 'the surface air temperature in the Himalayas has increased by one degree during the same period. This has led to the rapid melting of the glaciers in the Himalayas.'

Some of India's most important rivers, such as the Ganges, Indus and Brahmaputra, are fed from glaciers in the Himalayas. With the effect that climate change will have on these 'Asian

Water Towers', food security for an estimated 60 million people in the Brahmaputra and Indus Basins alone is at risk.[37] The Ganges is also the source of life for hundreds of millions of people, but 70 per cent of the river's summer flow comes from melting ice and snow.[38] If the Ganges becomes a seasonal river in the near future, as the IPCC suggests, this will affect more than 400 million people who depend on it for drinking water. Farmers will not be able to irrigate their land and hydroelectric power stations will fail. It is no surprise that the IPCC has identified the Ganges as one of the rivers most threatened by climate change.[39]

China has 46,377 glaciers covering an area of 59,425 square kilometres. Because of global warming, some 80 per cent of these glaciers are in retreat; evidence suggests there has been a massive loss in Chinese glaciers in recent years, particularly since the 1990s when the scale of retreat has significantly increased. This is dramatically affecting water resources for both China and its neighbours, because some 60 per cent of glacier run-off flows out of the country.[40] In western China, about 12 per cent of total water discharge is glacial melt run-off, which provides water for 25 per cent of the total Chinese population in the dry season.[41]

Overall, between 5 and 27 per cent of China's glaciated areas are projected to disappear by 2050, and between 10 and 67 per cent by 2100. Water run-off from the glaciers will likely peak between 2030 and 2050, and gradually decline after this, ultimately leading to the long-term exhaustion of glacial water supplies and a consequent reduction in availability of water for both agricultural and human consumption.[42]

Accelerated de-glaciation poses a number of short- and medium-term problems. In the short term, melting could cause reservoirs to overflow, floods and mudslides. In August 2008, when the Kosi river changed course, the Bihar flood in India was probably partly caused by increased river flow from glacial melting. The flood affected 4·4 million people, destroyed 290,000 hectares of land, and cost an estimated US$6·5 billion.[43]

Lakes often form at the front of glaciers, trapped by a natural dam of moraine and ice. But, as temperatures increase accelerating glacial melt and thus increasing water volumes, these dams can break causing so-called glacier lake outburst flood events. These floods can wipe out downstream houses, roads and bridges.

Many glacial lakes in Nepal are now close to bursting. Out of a total of around 2,323, some twenty are potentially dangerous. When outbursts occur the impacts are catastrophic. In August 1985, a glacier lake outburst flood caused a 5-metre-high wave of water and debris to flow down the Bhote Koshi and Dudh Koshi rivers in Nepal for 90 kilometres, leaving a trail of destruction behind it, including a small hydropower project.[44] Likewise in Pakistan, the recent melting of glaciers in the Himalayas and Hindu Kush is causing sudden increases in river volumes, resulting in flash flooding and massive destruction of crops, shelter and lives in areas not historically prone to flooding. The melting of the Tailan Glacier in China also likely explains the increased run-off observed in the Tarim River, which is fed in part by the glacier. This has caused glacial lakes in the region to grow, which has more than doubled the number of glacial lake outbursts in the Tarim Basin in recent years.[45]

The blight of glacial lake outbursts in Shimshal village, Pakistan

Shimshal Village lies at 3,100 metres. The short growing season at this altitude allows cultivation of only one crop per year on surrounding land. Major crops are wheat, barley, potatoes and peas. Shimshal is one of the few communities in Pakistan's northern areas that grows enough agricultural produce to feed itself. It is the sole steward of vast areas of high-altitude pasture, and extensive herding of sheep, goats, cattle and yaks allows Shimshalis to earn much of their income from the sale of livestock and livestock products. But more rainfall in mountain regions could accelerate rates of soil erosion and landslides, and glacial lake outburst floods are a cause of particular concern.

Chughbai, a 65-year-old farmer from Shimshal village, describes how 'In my lifetime I witnessed the disaster of the bursting of the Shimshal lake ... about three times, but one was really destructive as it washed away half of the village... It was summer season when the lake burst, people were busy with their agricultural activities; the high tides of the flood washed away our ripe crops and our fields, houses and gardens. At that time the army was deployed in Shimshal so they assisted the locals in dismantling their houses and shifting their belongings to the safe places. So it was the most destructive disaster I had ever experienced.'[46]

Glacier lake outburst flood in Yigong, Tibet

On 10 June 2000, the moraine lake in Yigong, Tibet, experienced a massive outbreak. Floods stopped the whole of the Sichuan–Tibet Highway from operating, crushing over ten bridges, including Tongmai Bridge and Jiefang Bridge, and flooding over 50 kilometres of roads. In India, which lies downstream from the lake, the effects were even more serious: 30 people died, 100 were missing and 5,000 lost their homes. Some twenty bridges were destroyed. The disaster led to a total loss of about US$23 million.

Glacial retreat near Everest

Sagarmatha National Park is an area of exceptional natural beauty, dominated by Everest (Sagarmatha), the highest peak in the world at 8,848 metres. Several rare species, such as the snow leopard and the lesser panda, are found in the Park. In 1979, the United Nations Educational, Scientific and Cultural Organization (UNESCO) designated the park a 'World Heritage Site', but unprecedented rates of glacial retreat, noted by high mountain communities, are causing concern. Unless urgent action is taken, many Himalayan lakes in and around the Park could burst, threatening the lives of thousands and destroying an irreplaceable environment.

A number of measures can be carried out to prevent outburst floods. These include strengthening lake banks and decreasing lake water volumes to safe levels. Hazard maps and installation of monitoring and warning systems can help, and 'trapping dams' with enough capacity to capture the debris and dissipate impact of the outburst can be built below vulnerable lakes.

Pro Public/Friends of the Earth Nepal, has petitioned UNESCO to place Sagarmatha National Park on the World Heritage Danger List on account of climate change. Putting the Park on the Danger List would oblige UNESCO to assess which glacier lakes are close to bursting and stabilise those most at risk. The petitioners also argue that parties to the World Heritage Convention are legally obliged to transmit World Heritage Sites intact to future generations, and that this requires significant cuts in greenhouse gas emissions (mitigation), as well as action to address the adverse effects of climate change (adaptation). Unfortunately, states that sit on the World Heritage Committee (including the USA), have so far adopted the view that mitigation is only relevant under the United Nations Framework Convention on Climate Change and its Kyoto Protocol, thus trying to avoid these legal obligations.

Whilst water resources may increase in the short term as the ice melts, in the medium term water supplies from glacial melt will be reduced as the glaciers shrink. In South America, glaciers in the tropical Andes could soon disappear, which will change river flows and threaten water supplies for people, industry, agriculture, hydropower and nature in the region. Many large cities in the Andes, for example, depend almost entirely on high-altitude water stocks for their dry-season water supplies. Ecuador's capital Quito receives part of its drinking water from a rapidly retreating glacier on Volcano Antizana, and La Paz in Bolivia also partially depends on glaciers for drinking water. In many dry Andean valleys, agriculture relies on glacier meltwater. For instance, some 40 per cent of the dry-season water in the Rio Santa comes from the Cordillera Blanca in Peru.[47] In areas of China where water availability in the dry season depends on glacial melt, serious water supply problems could occur. Likewise in Pakistan, whilst flash floods cause havoc on occasion, water scarcity is problematic at other times. Many studies in Pakistan and the surrounding region also served by glacial meltwaters have found that the longer-term impact of melting glaciers will be severe water shortages. Disputes over access to water resources are certain to increase as a consequence.

4

Health

As global warming increases, it becomes clearer that it will lead to serious impacts on human health around the world. The range of potential problems sensitive to climate change is enormous:

- Heat stress with associated cardiovascular effects (the direct effect of the thermal environment on health).
- The physical and psychological impact of storms, floods and other extreme events.
- Air pollution (outdoor air quality).
- Vector-borne diseases (such as malaria, dengue, schistosomiasis and tick-borne diseases).
- Water-borne and food-borne diseases (such as diarrhoeal diseases).
- Food security.
- Demographic changes that shift the balance of vulnerable populations demanding different health services.

The effects of climate change will be direct and indirect. Direct effects include heat stress and the impact of extreme weather events, resulting in more frequent humanitarian emergencies, particularly affecting populations in high-risk areas such as coastal zones, river valleys and cities. Even in wealthy France, an estimated 11,435 people above the seasonal average died when a record-breaking heatwave struck in the first two weeks of August 2003. Responding, health minister Jean-François Mattei announced $748 million in extra funding for hospital emergency services, a measure that would either be impossible or stretch to breaking point government budgets in much of Africa.

These direct effects will be especially powerful in the developing world, with its less developed and poorly funded health-care infrastructure. For example, floods in Bangladesh in 2004 caused about 800 deaths, while the cyclone of 1991 killed 138,000 people. While single events such as these cannot be attributed directly to climate change, we know that climate change will increase the likelihood of them happening over time. Deaths caused by extremes of heat and cold will rise in vulnerable groups, particularly those already suffering from heart and breathing problems, the very young, the elderly and the frail. According to the World Health Organization (WHO), the United Nations Environment Programme and the World Meteorological Program, at least 150,000 people die unnecessarily each year and there are 5.5 million 'disability-adjusted life years', (a standard WHO measure to compare disease burdens) as a direct result of global warming.[1]

Indirect effects will happen because of the close relationship between climatic conditions and insects and rodent populations. This will affect the range of vector-borne parasitic diseases like malaria and leishmaniasis. Dengue fever is sensitive to climate, for example, and by 2080 about 6 billion people could be at risk of contracting it as a consequence of climate change, compared with 3.5 billion people if the climate remained unchanged.[2] The World Bank predicts that Kiribati could experience an increase in dengue fever cases of between 20 and 30 per cent.[3] Food-borne diseases are likely to increase as a result of warmer temperatures. Water-borne diseases may also increase because of extra demands on diminished water supplies, which will in turn increase the risk of contaminated supplies reaching the public. This is particularly worrying for countries such as Bangladesh where water-borne diseases are already responsible for 24 per cent of all deaths.

Diarrhoeal diseases, including cholera and typhoid, may increase as a result of more frequent and severe floods and drought.[4] For example, flooding caused by Hurricane Mitch brought a sixfold increase in cholera in Nicaragua.[5] Climate-change-related disasters can also drain public resources for health care.

Warmer and wetter conditions could trigger unprecedented levels of disease outbreaks in both humans and the natural world, and undermine the Millennium Development Goals aiming to reduce child mortality, improve maternal health and combat HIV/AIDS, malaria and other diseases.

'Mosquitoes are spreading into highland areas that were historically free from malaria. There is also an increase in water-borne diseases.'
Tadesse Dadi, Ethiopia

'During floods all the boreholes get damaged by mud. People have to go far away to a river for water – even to drink. People get sick with diarrhoea.'
T.K. Joy, Evangelical Fellowship of India Commission on Relief, India

'Due to lack of pure drinking water there is a rise in water-borne diseases (diarrhoea, dysentery, typhoid and hepatitis A). Due to a shortage of water people are suffering from skin diseases and conjunctivitis. In the summer season due to high temperatures some people are affected with heat stroke and dying. In the winter season due to lower temperatures people suffer.'
Salvation Army, Bangladesh

'Our community is really concerned about the increasing frequency of drought. If drought may happen every year then it will continue to cause infectious diseases in our community and also in our livestock. We depend on our livestock for income generation and to help us with our labour. We village veterinary volunteers have to work hard to encourage villagers to vaccinate animals against common infectious diseases.'
Mr Vanna, 46, voluntary vet with Development Partnership in Action's livelihoods programme, Tareach village, Chumikiri district, Cambodia

---

Malaria, which is already the second leading cause of death in the world for 5- to 14-year-olds, is expected to reach unprecedented levels because of climate change. There are already between 300 and 500 million cases of malaria in the world annually, and it has been estimated that between 260 and 320 million more people are likely to find themselves living in areas with malaria potential by the year 2080.[6]

Malaria is of particular concern in Africa, where it already slows economic growth by up to 1.3 per cent each year.[7] Further changes in temperature and precipitation could trigger malaria epidemics at the current limits of the disease, both in altitude and latitude, where people lack immunity and the impact of the disease is therefore greater. In one highland area of Rwanda malaria incidence increased by 337 per cent in 1987, 80 per cent of which increase could be explained by changes in rainfall and temperature.[8] Previously malaria-free highland areas in Ethiopia, Kenya, Rwanda and Burundi could become vulnerable to the disease by the 2050s, and by the 2080s areas of central Somalia and southern Africa, the Angolan highlands and the East African Highlands with low malaria prevalence at present could become highly suitable.[9] In South Africa, 7.6 million people were exposed to malaria in 2003, and some predict that by 2099 this figure will increase by 247 per cent due to climate change.[10] In addition, flooding – likely to increase as the climate changes – could help mosquitoes breed, thus spreading malaria to otherwise dry areas. The Sahel, which has suffered from drought in the past thirty years and has experienced a reduction in malaria transmission as a result, could be at renewed risk from a malaria epidemic.[11]

Variations in extreme weather typically associated with the El Niño cycle are likely to become more common and more intense. Spending on health care in Bolivia, Chile, Ecuador and Peru fell by 10 per cent, due to the fall in Gross National Product, after the El Niño cycle in 1982–83,[12] and Ecuador, Peru and Bolivia suffered serious malaria epidemics.[13] Following excessive rainfall related to El Niño in 1997, some 10 per cent of all Peruvian health-care facilities were damaged, and droughts in Brazil sparked forest fires, the smoke from which was a major public health problem leading to large numbers of patients with respiratory problems visiting already overstretched health facilities. Cholera had been absent from Latin America for nearly a century when the first cases appeared in Peru following the 1991 El Niño. They were spread out over a 1,000-kilometre-long stretch of coastline as a consequence of an El Niño-related bloom of algae in the rivers and estuaries and on the ocean coastline, combined with poor hygiene and contaminated foods.[14]

The IPCC is unequivocal: 'The impacts of climate change will fall disproportionately upon developing countries and the poor persons within all countries, and thereby exacerbate inequities in health status and access to adequate food, clean water and other resources.'[15]

Poor communities in Africa are likely to be particularly vulnerable. Estimates by Christian Aid suggest that 182 million people in sub-Saharan Africa might die from diseases associated with climate change by the end of the century.[16] Africa's high vulnerability to the impacts of climate change is compounded by widespread poverty. Ongoing drought and floods, and a dependence on natural resources for rural livelihoods, in turn, increase vulnerability. Also, sub-Saharan Africa already supports a heavy disease burden, including HIV/AIDS, malaria, cholera, dengue fever, yellow fever, encephalitis and haemorrhagic fever.

The association between climate change and HIV/AIDS is by no means direct, but it is insidiously real. AIDS lowers productivity as more and more farmers are infected. Survivors have to spend time attending funerals, looking after orphans and managing the estates of the deceased. Absenteeism from school and work is common. At the same time, unreliable rain patterns, which are becoming a permanent feature in some areas, have led to crop failures of such magnitude as to lead to severe malnutrition, which accelerates the negative effects of the disease and poverty. Girls suffer disproportionately, as many are forced into early marriage or prostitution to help their families survive. Many rural folk migrate to towns, where they are more likely to get infected.

Health-related climate change impacts in Chumikiri, Cambodia

Communities in the district of Chumikiri in Cambodia have experienced both floods and droughts in recent years. These have resulted in death and injury to people and livestock, damage to crops, spread of communicable and water-borne diseases, and reduced access to clean water, leading to dehydration and diarrhoea. Longer-term disruption is devastating agriculture and incomes on account of more crop pests and reductions in yields as crops fail. Both disasters and this longer-term disruption have increased migration, which in turn has its own health implications. People who are separated from their families and communities are more likely to contract HIV/AIDS, and people living with HIV/AIDS are more vulnerable to other illnesses, such as malaria, dengue fever, dysentery and cholera, all of which could increase under a changing climate. Families of those living with, or who have lost a parent to, HIV/AIDS are more vulnerable to food security or livelihood-related problems.

Development Partnership in Action (DPA), a partner organisation of CAFOD, has been helping communities cope with these impacts. It has supported community agricultural practices which help people adapt to the changing climate, for example by introducing more resilient strains of rice and encouraging communities to develop disaster preparedness and disaster response plans. DPA has also introduced mobile health clinics and HIV/AIDS prevention and care services in remote communities.

'The changing climatic conditions within our communities are resulting in decreasing rice yields. Villagers, particularly in the dry season, are being forced to migrate outside the village to find jobs, and many have returned having contracted HIV/AIDS. This is a real problem in the communities that we are working in.'

Mam Sambath, Development Partnership in Action, Cambodia

Population movements resulting from drought and environmental degradation can also provoke migration. People forced to leave their home and land may be faced with unsanitary refugee camps with a multitude of associated health problems.

Health is often neglected in the assessment of vulnerability and adaptation to climate change, but understanding of the impacts of climate change on health is steadily improving. Several countries have conducted national assessments to determine their vulnerability to the impacts of climate change and evaluate the capacity of their health infrastructures to adapt.

Rarely considered, however, is the knock-on effect of climate change health impacts on poor and vulnerable communities. How will a greater disease burden affect an already stressed health-care infrastructure? What will be its impact on the provision of education when both economic capacity and the pool of prospective teachers and students are diminished? What effect will it have on the ability of people to work the land, or even rebuild communities after climate-driven disasters? Climate change will not only affect people's health in all the ways described; in doing so it will also hamper people's ability to adapt to a changing, uncertain climate. Given the lack of knowledge about the impacts of climate change on health, it is important to help both map the complex impacts of global warming on health and ensure that the resources are available to tackle them.

5

Energy

Energy cooks the food we eat. It heats our schools, lights our hospitals and powers our industries. It is central to all human economic activity. Access to basic, clean, safe and affordable energy services is essential for sustainable development and poverty eradication. Poverty and energy are inextricably linked. The greatest child killer – acute respiratory infection – will not be tackled without dealing with smoke from cooking fires in the home. Without light in their homes to allow them to read, children will learn less. Water cannot be pumped or treated without energy. Although some 800 million people have been connected to power grids in the last twenty years, nearly 2 billion people still do not have access to electricity, particularly in rural areas.

Providing electricity to the rural poor is a major challenge. Electricity is needed for small industries and enterprises, to run health clinics, and to light schools. The conventional approach to electrification tends to marginalise rural communities that are located far from the grid. Rural population densities are generally low and the cost of energy supplied from new grid connections is high compared with densely populated areas. Electricity companies – public or private – have little incentive to provide services to these areas.

Some 80 per cent of Pacific islanders have no access to electricity. This inhibits opportunities to diversify economic activity, self-sufficiently produce goods (which are otherwise imported great distances) and provide health and education services. Most Pacific island countries do not have their own petroleum resources, and the limited size and remoteness of island markets cannot guarantee the security of fuel supplies. Most electricity is produced by diesel generators; some Pacific countries, such as Niue, have historically spent most of their gross domestic income on diesel imports. Reduced diesel production and increasing and fluctuating prices, which are beyond the control of regional states, could mean Pacific islanders will soon struggle to source diesel, thus further exacerbating their vulnerability to climate change.

Providing the poor with access to safe, affordable energy supplies is central to helping them cope with the impacts of global warming. Those who can secure a good education and access health services and alternative livelihood opportunities will be much better placed to deal with the challenges that lie ahead. But meeting these energy needs without increasing global greenhouse gas emissions, which exacerbate the problem of climate change, and without creating damaging local impacts, for example from pollution or human rights violations, is an enormous challenge.

Looking to the oil, coal and gas industries for solutions is unlikely to reap many rewards. The record of these industries in terms of environmental damage and human rights issues is particularly chequered. British Petroleum (BP), for example, has strong links to the oil extraction industry in Colombia. Oil revenues in Colombia have funded the country's internal conflict,[1] and in July 2006 BP were forced to pay a reported £3 million to Colombian farmers left destitute by the building of a major oil pipeline through their land. Lawyers representing the farmers, Leigh Day & Co., accused BP of failing to compensate farmers for damage reaching back to 1995 and of gaining advantage from terror tactics employed by others to guard the pipeline.

The oil company Chevron is the subject of a campaign over its activities in Ecuador. It is involved in a trial over what has been called locally the 'Rainforest Chernobyl'. Eighty affected communities are seeking legal redress over the alleged dumping of toxic waste. British Gas, meanwhile, has been caught up in controversy over its involvement in plans to expand natural gas extraction in Bolivia. There are fears that existing environmental and social costs will be worsened whilst local people will still fail to accrue benefits. Referring to the new Bolivia–Brazil pipeline, the pressure group Amazon Watch has voiced concerns over 'the divisive tactics being used to undermine established indigenous authorities'.

The vast El Cerrejon Norte coal mine in northern Colombia is one of the world's largest open-pit mines, occupying an original area 31 miles long and 5 miles wide. But El Cerrejon is constantly expanding and eating up villages in its path; it touches on reservation land of the indigenous Wayuu people. The mine is operated by a consortium owned by British-based multinationals Anglo American and BHP Billiton, together with Swiss company Glencore International. In 2001, the Afro-Colombian village of Tabaco was demolished by the mining company, and the nearby village of Tamaquitos is now threatened. The surrounding vegetation is contaminated with coal dust and local children suffer from respiratory problems and malnutrition. The end product, coal, produces even more carbon dioxide when burnt than oil or gas.

Feeling the heat: gas flaring in Nigeria

Nigeria is the world's largest gas flarer. Nigerian flaring has contributed more greenhouse gases than all other sub-Saharan sources combined. In the Niger Delta, gas flares spew emissions equivalent to the UK's annual gas use every three months.[2] Despite international condemnation, the practice of flaring gas in the Delta remains widespread. It has been carried out on a massive scale for nearly fifty years. Flames and fumes are produced twenty-four hours a day, seven days a week, year after year, affecting people's health, polluting the local environment and destroying livelihoods. Nowhere else in the world are communities subjected to emissions on such a large scale.

Particles from the flares fill the air, covering everything with a fine layer of soot. The flares contain toxins such as benzene, and carcinogens such as dioxin. Flaring also emits carbon dioxide. However, venting of the gas without burning releases methane, a greenhouse gas far more potent than carbon dioxide.

Exposed to a cocktail of toxins, local people, who live and work alongside the flares with no protection, complain of respiratory problems such as asthma and bronchitis. Gas flaring at Izombe Flow Station, one of numerous oil installations in the Niger Delta, has led to the complete destruction of crops within 200 metres of the station. Even as far as 1 kilometre from the station, a 10 per cent loss in crop yields has occurred. Acid rain caused by the flaring is also reported to corrode roofs and buildings in the area.

Few Nigerians have benefited from the wealth generated by Nigeria's oil industry. Many of the riverine Delta communities live in poverty, without access to clean water, basic health care, electricity or education. In addition to constant flaring, oil spills are common, frequently contaminating farmland, watercourses and fish supplies.

Gas flaring is also a terrible and expensive waste of resources, costing Nigeria – where nearly 70 per cent of people live on less than a dollar a day and commonly cook on open fires – an estimated $2.5 billion annually in lost potential income. Oil companies ExxonMobil, Shell and Chevron between them flared 23.5 cubic feet of gas in January 2012 alone, and yet there is barely enough energy to power one vacuum cleaner among twenty-five of Nigeria's inhabitants.[3]

The Nigerian government's commitment to end gas flaring is ambiguous. Environmental legislation is lax and there is confusion over the supposed end date.

Livelihoods piped away: the Chad–Cameroon pipeline

The Chad–Cameroon pipeline project, worth $3.7 billion, is the biggest private investment in sub-Saharan Africa today, as well as one of the most controversial. It involved the drilling of 300 oil wells in the Doba region in the south of Chad and the construction of a 1,070-kilometre-long pipeline to transport the oil from Chad through Cameroon to an offshore loading facility on the Atlantic coast. Along the way, the pipeline passes through rainforest, Pygmy territories and major food- and cotton-producing areas.

Project leader ExxonMobil is supported by US-based Chevron and Malaysia's Petronas. The International Finance Corporation and World Bank Group provided over US$330 million for the project, presenting it as an opportunity for Chad to come out of its acute poverty while generating much-needed revenue for Cameroon.

By mid-2002 it was already clear that the project was piping great amounts of misery and devastation into the area. Thousands of people had their lands expropriated, and crops and other plants destroyed, without adequate compensation. The pipeline cuts across sensitive and valuable ecosystems, particularly in Cameroon's coastal rainforest. Project-related upgrading of existing seasonal roads has led to logging and illegal poaching in otherwise inaccessible areas. The pipeline also traverses several major rivers, and construction has already caused oil spills and polluted the water system.

The influx of a migrant workforce, the exponential growth of prostitution, and poor sanitary conditions have led to the spread of communicable diseases, including HIV/AIDS. According to the World Health Organization, 'it appeared that in this project decisions were based largely on cost and profit considerations, giving only passing attention to environmental and social aspects, and little or no decision-making power to the affected populations.'[4]

Transparency International rated Chad the fourth most corrupt country in the world in 2004. The president of Chad used $4.5 million of the signing bonus paid by the oil consortium to buy weapons, rather than investing in public health, education and vital infrastructure as planned. Since the official inauguration of the pipeline in October 2003, the situation in Chad has deteriorated further. The authorities prohibited a peaceful demonstration planned by human rights groups, and the government, in violation of the constitution, closed the country's only independent radio station. 'The World Bank touts the Chad–Cameroon oil pipeline as a model project that will reduce poverty while compensating for environmental impacts. Practice has, however, demonstrated the failure of World Bank rhetoric to match reality', said Samuel Nguiffo of Friends of the Earth Cameroon.

An additional big problem is the continued reliance on fossil fuels for energy. There is some evidence to suggest we are living on the cusp of the so-called 'Hubbert Peak' of oil production. If so, it means that current high oil prices will be just the first tremor of an impending earthquake on the economic Richter scale. The point at which global oil production peaks and begins its decline coincides with endlessly rising demand. The result depends on whether that decline is long and slow – or short and rapid; if the latter, then the chances of global economic chaos are high.

Some mistakenly think that declining oil reserves means that climate change will solve itself: the problematic fossil fuels will simply run out or become too expensive, so that will be the end of the problem. Unfortunately there is more than enough fossil fuel left – especially coal – to trigger catastrophic warming. Critics of the 'Hubbert Peak' theory also point out that new oil reserves are constantly being found, with higher prices fuelling exploration, and new technologies being developed for extracting fossil fuels more efficiently than ever before. This is very bad news for people who want to see greenhouse gas emissions reduced and for those who are particularly vulnerable to climate change.

Much attention is currently focused on the major growing economies of Brazil, China and India, where alternative options to the current reliance on fossil fuels would have a significant impact on future greenhouse gas emissions.

Options for Brazil's energy future

Brazil's energy-related greenhouse gas emissions are, per person, less than half of the world average, due largely to the country's heavy reliance on bioethanol and hydropower, which provide more than 75 per cent of the total power generated. However, Brazil's energy demand is expected to grow, and meeting this demand without increasing global and local impacts is a great challenge. The conventional response focuses on expanding centralised power supply by relying on a massive number of new, large-scale power plants. If Brazil decides to follow this current energy model, used by most industrialised nations, then many of its new power plants are likely to be run on fossil fuels. Under such a 'business as usual' scenario for Brazilian development, electricity-related carbon dioxide emissions will grow by more than 300 per cent between 2004 and 2020.

Friends of the Earth Brazil report that around 84 per cent of installed electricity generation capacity in Brazil comes from large dams, the construction of which has caused the loss of over 34,000 square kilometres of productive lands and forests and forced 1 million people from their homes and land. Despite this, the government has plans for more mega-dams in the Amazon region. Dams proposed for the Madeira and Xingu rivers would drown areas of enormous biodiversity and displace many indigenous peoples.

Claims that dams are the cheapest source of power are misleading. The true costs of dams never appear on the balance sheet. These include biodiversity loss, community resettlement costs, and downstream effects such as disrupted fish migration and resultant livelihood impacts.

Coal is also making a comeback despite irretrievable ecological damage and much damage to the health of mineworkers after decades of mining and burning in southern Brazil. Five of the new proposed coal projects alone, if implemented, will pump 11 million tonnes of carbon dioxide into the atmosphere per year.

Research by the University of Campinas, published by WWF Brazil, outlines alternative future scenarios for the development of the Brazilian power sector by 2020, without increasing global and local, social and environmental impacts.[5] Proposals will also cut the national electricity bill by US$15 billion while creating 8 million new jobs. The research proposes increased efficiency at both the electricity production level and the consumption level, and doubling the use of small- and medium-scale renewable energy (wind, biomass, solar and small hydropower). The overall reliability of the electricity grid would improve due to the move away from centralised systems, which would increase industry efficiency while drastically reducing transmission and distribution losses. Under this alternative future scenario, emissions could be stabilised at roughly the 2004 level, equivalent to avoiding a total of 413 million tonnes of accumulated carbon dioxide emissions over fifteen years.

The way ahead for energy in China

China has now overtaken the United States as the world's largest emitter of greenhouse gases.[6] China has a population that is four times larger than that of the United States; Chinese per capita greenhouse gas emissions are still a fraction of those in industrialised countries. The average American emits 18 tonnes of carbon dioxide per person per year compared to under 6 tonnes per person in China and only 1.38 tonnes in India.[7]

A considerable proportion of the national growth in Chinese emissions is due to the outsourcing of manufacturing industries from industrialised nations and demand from consumers in Europe and America. The launch of China's national climate change strategy is therefore welcome. China hopes to tackle climate change through improvements in energy efficiency, more efficient coal-fired power stations, and renewable energy, such as wind- and hydropower. With continued rapid economic growth, China will inevitably consume more and more energy, resulting in the release of large volumes of greenhouse gases. The main challenges for China in terms of cutting greenhouse gas emissions are its coal-dominated energy mix and lack of advanced clean technology.

India's eleventh five-year plan

India is the world's third-largest greenhouse gas emitter, producing about 5 per cent of global carbon dioxide emissions. Per capita emissions are very small, however. In 2011, they were one-third of the global average of 4.69 tonnes per year (and about twelve times smaller than the per capita emissions of the average American).[8] The main contributor is the energy sector, which the government wants to expand to provide electricity for the half a billion people currently living without it.

India's eleventh five-year plan describes plans to expand its power-generation capacity by using coal-fired power plants to generate 70,000 MW, because coal is supposedly cheap and abundantly available in India. Capital costs for this would come to a conservative US$87.5 billion. It would also be bad news for reducing greenhouse gas emissions from the power sector as the plants would result in 350 million tonnes of carbon dioxide emissions.

Conservative estimates of the environmental cost due to carbon emissions of the proposed 70,000 MW of coal-fired power plant translate to an additional cost of US$4.5 billion. This makes a total of US$92 billion when added to the capital costs. With these additional environment costs, coal seems a costly proposition.

If the government were to consider the environmental costs of coal, then it would see that using a combination of energy efficiency along with renewable energy technologies would be both cheaper in the long run and less carbon-intensive. Energy efficiency measures could generate 30,000 MW more power, with the 40,000 MW balance coming from a combination of wind, solar photovoltaics and biomass for rural electrification. Generating 40,000 MW from renewable energy sources would cost a conservative US$70 billion and the capital cost of energy efficiency measures would be approximately US$7.5 billion. The total cost of meeting the requirement through alternate power sources would thus be only US$77.5 billion.

Coal comprises 53 per cent of India's electric power systems, oil 31
per cent, natural gas 9 per cent, hydroelectric 6 per cent and nuclear 1
per cent. The market in India for renewable energy such as biomass and
solar, wind and geothermal energy, is, however, growing rapidly and its
potential is very high.[9] India is also perhaps the only country to have an
exclusive ministry at the central level to promote renewable energy solutions. Renewable energy could meet roughly 60 per cent of India's total
electricity supply by 2050 in a phased-in manner, but the government
needs to change its spending patterns on energy. In the Union Budget
for 2007–08, for example, the allocation for the Ministry of New and
Renewable Energy is about 25 per cent of the allocations being directed
to the ministries dealing with hydrocarbon energy sources and even less
when compared with the Department of Atomic Energy.

We know that climate change already affects the poorest
people in the poorest countries. We know that bringing the millions of people out of poverty means they need access to energy,
and that this is particularly problematic in rural areas far from
any grids. We also know from Nigeria to the Middle East and
Latin America, that the extractive industries leave a wake of
corruption, pollution, conflict and infringement of the rights of
indigenous people behind them. The solution, surely, is obvious?
A shift to small-scale, decentralised community-based renewable
energy technologies would allow people access to energy in poor
remote areas, help lift them out of poverty, and refrain from
adding to the climate change problem, thus offering a win–win
solution all round. So why isn't this happening?

In India, many homes are opting for energy-saving appli-
ances despite the higher up-front costs. In the village of Binola in
Gurgaon district of Haryana state, a total of ninety-eight households and shops have shifted completely from incandescent bulbs
to power-saving bulbs, reducing the total grid load in the village by
close to 50 per cent. There is, however, a limit to what individuals
or communities, especially those who are most vulnerable, can do
without an enabling policy framework.

The dominance of dirty energy is not a natural state or a rational economic choice. It is largely the consequence of massive, perverse subsidies poured into coal, oil and gas, and the failure to internalise the cost of the environmental damage they cause. Recent estimates from the International Monetary Fund (IMF) put the global scale of subsidies for petroleum products, electricity, natural gas and coal at $480 billion per year on a 'pre-tax' basis. 'Post-tax' – which includes the negative impacts of such energy consumption – this figure rises to US$1.9 trillion. Simply removing these subsidies, the IMF argues, could lead to a 13 per cent decline in carbon dioxide emissions.[10] In contrast to this vast sum, funds for research and development going into renewable energy stood at just US$9 billion globally in 2010,[11] and only 35 per cent of total investment in renewable energy worldwide occurs in developing countries, which is arguably where it is needed most.[12] Highly polluting fuels, like brown coal, are favoured instead because they are plentiful and cheap.

In 2003, fossil fuel projects represented 86 per cent of the World Bank's spending on energy, and renewable energy represented just 14 per cent. This latter proportion has since increased, with roughly a quarter of the World Bank's energy lending going to renewable projects in recent years.[13] However, in the five years prior to 2011 the Bank still increased funding for coal-fired power stations fortyfold, and in 2010 alone it invested US$6.6 billion in fossil-fuel-based projects.[14]

Extracting the World Bank from fossil fuels

International Financial Institutions (IFIs), such as the World Bank, are often criticised for their failure to deliver on poverty alleviation, development and environmental protection. Controversies surrounding IFI involvement in the oil, mining and gas sectors led the then president of the World Bank, James Wolfensohn, to commission an independent review in 2000. Questions were being asked about whether investments in oil, mining and gas met the World Bank's overarching stated objective of poverty alleviation. This resulted in the World Bank Extractive Industries Review (EIR), which was finalised in December 2003 following consultations with multinational corporations, national governments, affected communities and civil society representatives. Its task was to assess World Bank investments in terms of poverty alleviation potential and consistency with sustainable development principles.

The EIR exposed many problems. On average, 80 per cent of the energy produced by World Bank-financed extractive industry projects is exported to rich industrialised countries. The financial revenues obtained by the host country are minimal and project benefits very rarely reach those on the ground. According to Archbishop Desmond Tutu, the consequences of these projects, particularly for indigenous peoples and local communities, are too often 'war, poverty, climate change, greed, corruption, and ongoing violations of human rights'.[15]

The EIR concluded that in the vast majority of cases World Bank extractive industry investments had not alleviated poverty and had failed to promote sustainable development. The review, and a parallel report of the World Bank's own evaluations department, concluded that in countries with weak governance, extractive industry lending fails the Bank's stated mission and is not a suitable use of World Bank funds. The EIR also concluded that free, prior and informed consent of affected communities, respect for human rights, and the protection of internationally established no-go zones in areas of armed conflict and sites of high spiritual or scientific value must be prerequisites.

The EIR recognises climate change as an issue that will affect the world's poor the most. Using public money to subsidise projects managed by multinational fossil fuel energy giants is a fatally flawed strategy for poverty alleviation. The EIR therefore recommended that the World Bank should stop financing oil and coal projects by 2008. IFIs often provide the essential economic guarantee and public legitimacy that allow extractive industry projects to go ahead. So when the World Bank announced in August 2004 that it was not going to implement the EIR in full, it was a huge blow to sustainable development.

National and local governments must also play their part. One municipal council in Saswad, a small town in Maharashtra State near Pune in India, has introduced a building regulation stipulating that all buildings with over 1,000 square feet of floor space must use solar power for lighting. Another example from the same state is that of the Bank of Maharashtra, which has introduced a scheme to finance solar home-lighting systems in rural areas. This may be a response to the crippling power shortages that have plagued the state in the past.

Our current dependence on fossil fuels is absurd because renewable energy is superabundant and it can provide a triple win for human development and an exit strategy from the multiple problems of fossil fuel addiction, only one of which is global warming. In 2011, the International Energy Agency's World Energy Outlook warned that if 'bold policy options are not put in place over the next several years, it will become increasingly difficult and costly to meet the goal ... of limiting a global temperature increase to two degrees Centigrade'. Despite this, global investment in fossil-fuel-based power sources continues to exceed investments in renewable energy, and renewable energy sources (excluding large hydropower projects) account for less than 10 per cent of energy supply globally.[16]

Renewable energy has the potential to meet all human energy needs, and the theoretical potential of the main clean renewable sources is many times greater than current use.[17] Small- and medium-scale applications are particularly well-placed to improve the lives of the 1.3 billion people globally who have no access to electricity, most of whom live in rural areas often remote from ailing national grids. At present, however, families in rural and semi-rural areas are left little choice but to exploit fragile ecosystems to meet their energy needs, ultimately undermining both the fuel source upon which they depend and the rich diversity of plants and animals that live there.

Can't see the trees for the wood: charcoal use in rural Malawi

Along almost any stretch of road in rural Malawi you will find bulging sacks of charcoal and neat stacks of firewood for sale. It is a cottage industry that provides one of the few opportunities for poor households to make a little money, but it is also environmentally unsustainable, and in the long term impoverishes everyone. 'Charcoal production is a very serious issue and is one of the major causes of deforestation in Malawi', the director of the government's forestry department, Kenneth Nyasulu, said in January 2005. 'The damage to trees is causing soil erosion, which in turn causes food insecurity because the fertile soil is lost.' Acknowledging the growing problem of deforestation, the then president Bingu wa Mutharika inaugurated a national tree-planting month in January 2005.

More than 90 per cent of Malawi's 15 million people have no access to electricity. This restricts what they can do at home or work. Alternative sources of income are also needed for rural people. Sustainable forest management will secure livelihoods in the long term. Until a major supply of renewable energy is widely available to poor communities, cleaner fossil fuels such as liquefied petroleum gas offer an affordable alternative fuel for many people in Africa that would remove pressure on the forests and reduce greenhouse gas emissions.

Energy which doesn't cost the earth in Kenya

Demand for indigenous tree species from Kenya's Kakamega Forest for timber, firewood, carving wood, charcoal production and poles is so great that up to 100,000 cubic metres of timber and charcoal may be illegally extracted every year. To preserve the forest, the Kakamega Integrated Conservation Project, in partnership with Practical Action, has introduced firewood-saving stoves, which are acceptable and affordable to local communities. People are made aware of the energy-saving opportunities the stoves offer through discussion, participatory technical training, demonstrations and exchange visits. Local community entrepreneurs have also been trained to commercialise the energy stoves.

The Upesi stove is made of clay and fired in a kiln. The design allows it to burn agricultural residues, such as waste from sugar cane, as well as wood. It can halve the amount of fuelwood needed by a household. Making it provides employment, and it reduces smoke and carbon emissions. Practical Action also introduced a new design of kiln, which substantially reduced the fuel needed to make the stoves.

By the end of the project, communities adjacent to the forest had installed nearly 4,000 energy-saving fuelwood stoves. A production unit for the stoves was in operation, managed by the local community. Ten fuelwood energy-saving stoves had also been installed in schools, institutions, hotels and hospitals around Kakamega Forest.

Better bricks: one solution to environmental problems faced by the poor

In Kenya and Zimbabwe low-cost and low-energy building blocks are being made from stabilised soil. Sun-dried, they can be made close to the building site, so no energy is used in transport. People engaged in production can earn a living and afford to build decent homes and community buildings. The technology is simple. Soil dug on-site, if suitable, is mixed with a small amount of cement. People are trained in soil-testing techniques to determine the best mix. Water is added and the mixture is placed in a block press. The bricks require cement, which often has to be imported, so there is an external energy input cost. However, the bricks offer an alternative to locally made baked-earth bricks, which are fired over two to three days in kilns burning fuelwood; this local industry has contributed to deforestation and is extremely energy-inefficient. The new approach has helped to provide legal affordable housing in low-income neighbourhoods because the stabilised soil blocks compete favourably on cost with commercially made clay bricks. The technology uses little water and produces no waste.

Activities in Uganda take this innovative, home-grown technology one step further. The Appropriate Technology Centre in Mbale, in conjunction with Makere University, Kampala, has been disseminating the use of interlocking stabilised soil blocks across the country and further afield. Bricks produced using ordinary soil with a small portion of cement and water are compressed in a manually operated pressing machine and then dried in the sun before use. The bricks interlock so that structures can be built using only a small amount of cement to hold them firmly and safely together. The pressing machines can make bricks that are straight or curved: straight for construction of houses and other buildings, and curved for the construction of cheap, easy-to-build water storage containers.

More than a third of humanity, 2.6 billion people, burn biomass – wood, crop residues, charcoal and animal dung – for cooking and heating. Just three countries – China, India and Bangladesh – account for more than half of those people without clean cooking facilities,[18] and about 68 per cent of Africans rely on biomass energy for cooking.[19]

Traditional biomass fuels have a complex relationship with climate change. Using solid biomass fuel usually produces higher greenhouse gas emissions per meal than fossil fuels, kerosene and liquid petroleum gas (LPG), even where the biomass fuel is harvested sustainably. This is due to inefficient combustion of the biomass fuel releasing products of incomplete combustion – such as methane – which have a greater greenhouse potential than carbon dioxide. However, biomass energy can be a clean, affordable and environmentally friendly source of energy if used in an efficient and effective manner.

Traditional biomass fuels have significant health drawbacks. Burnt on open fires and rudimentary stoves, the smoke produced from these fuels is the fourth greatest risk factor for death and disease in the world's poorest countries. It is linked to 1.6 million deaths per year.[20] The smoke makes lungs vulnerable to illnesses like pneumonia and chronic obstructive pulmonary disease. In addition, rural women and children spend a significant portion of their time gathering and collecting biomass fuel for cooking and heating their home. What can be done? Billions of people would lead a healthier life if their exposure to high levels of smoke was reduced. Public awareness of the health risks of smoke is a crucial first step. The most effective way to reduce smoke in the home is to switch to a cleaner fuel, such as LPG or kerosene, or to modern biofuels, such as biogas. However, the vast majority of people at risk are too poor to change to a cleaner fuel, or have no access to modern fuels. In these homes, the answer will be to reduce exposure, by using cleaner, more efficient and better-ventilated stoves.

Energy and smoke

Najma Khatun lives in Pazulia village in Gazipur in Bangladesh. Her husband is a farmer; they have two daughters and a son. They have a small poultry farm with 800 birds. Najma used to spend most of her time cooking and managing the poultry waste. She worried that she did not have enough time to care for her children. She was particularly concerned about her youngest child, who is 3, and who was always with her in the kitchen inhaling smoke and dust from their inefficient traditional cooking stove. The stove burned biomass, which produced indoor air pollution and smoke.

Najma was a member of the Bangladesh Association for Social Advancement, which invited her on a two-day training course on biogas plants. Following this, Najma built a 1.2 cubic metre biogas plant inside her poultry farm with technical support from Practical Action. This provided tremendous and quick relief from her problems. She used poultry dung, which was difficult and time-consuming to dispose of, to produce biogas, which she used for cooking and lighting.

Now she has more time to look after her children, who no longer suffer from dust and smoke inhalation. Najma can even do other work while cooking because there is no chance that a fire will start in the house. All this has cost her very little, so she is very happy. Najma's workload has also decreased because she no longer has to collect biomass. This saves her at least one hour each day. Another hour and a half is saved from reduced time spent cooking, because it is quicker and easier when using biogas. Cooking utensils and kitchen cloths do not get as dirty and the kitchen is cleaner, saving Najma a further two and a half hours a day. She also earns 150 taka per month by providing biogas to her neighbour. With the time saved she enjoys caring for her children and plans to expand the poultry farm.

Seeing the cook for the smoke: biomass cooking and health

Practical Action is collaborating with partners in Sudan, Kenya and Nepal to help beat indoor air pollution in ways suited to each community's needs. In each place the choice of technology was influenced by culture, cost, geography, access to fuel and climate.

In the displaced persons' settlement in Kassala, Sudan, the community identified LPG as an appropriate solution once microfinance was made available to cover the initial cost of the stove. The scheme is popular, and already others outside the project are using the 'revolving fund' credit system to buy stoves. Fuel costs are much lower for LPG than for charcoal and wood in Kassala, so repayments can be offset by reduced fuel costs.

In the communities around the town of Kisumu in Kenya, wood fuel is much cheaper than LPG and is often free, so most households have elected to continue using biomass. Smoke hoods and eave spaces combined with fuel-efficient stoves are proving effective in helping reduce indoor air pollution.

In the cold mountain village of Gatlang in Nepal, solutions have been more difficult to identify, as energy is needed to heat the house as well as to cook the food. Gatlang is remote, making LPG or kerosene unavailable. Home insulation has been chosen for retaining room heat whilst reducing the need to burn fuelwood for heating the house. Smoke hoods are currently being developed, along with improvements to the traditional stove to reduce fuel use.

Commercialisation of energy-efficient household stoves in China

The Beijing-based energy company Daxu has developed a stove that can burn crop residues, both loose and compressed, as well as wood. The stove partly gasifies the fuel, and then burns the gas with secondary air. This results in a stove that is 40 per cent more efficient and much lower emissions. Most families in rural China cook and heat their homes using stoves that burn coal or wood. This system can reduce the cost of cooking and heating by 50 per cent. Around 20 million wood and coal stoves are sold each year, so the health and environmental benefits from widespread use of this stove will be significant. Levels of air pollution and smoke in the kitchen are lower, which reduces damage to health from respiratory or eye-related illnesses. Improvements in efficiency and the move towards a renewable biomass fuel also reduce carbon dioxide emissions.

There is a huge market and human demand for sustainable energy, especially in poorer communities. Renewable energy resources and technologies, however, remain largely unexploited due to financial, capacity, market and political barriers.

Africa in particular has enormous potential for renewable energy and energy-efficiency technologies. Energy resources such as biomass, geothermal and hydropower are abundant. On the other hand, the majority of African people have no access to clean modern energy and more than half the population live off the grid. Over three-quarters of sub-Saharan Africans have no access to electricity, compared to fewer than 14 per cent of people living in Latin America and East Asia. Almost half of Africa's countries could profitably produce hydropower, but only a fraction of that potential has been reached to date because of poor infrastructure and the high cost of initial investments. The

African continent accounts for only 1.3 per cent of the world's solar energy facilities, and only four of its fifty-three countries have started exploring underground heat sources.[21]

African people want greater access to energy. The continent has abundant natural resources, but these are often underused, badly exploited or exported to richer countries. Some of Africa's great rivers flow through Mozambique, for example, and in the mountains in the northern and eastern provinces there are many sites suitable for micro-hydropower. Currently large hydropower in Mozambique is transmitted over great distances to South Africa, with little gain to the local people where the power is generated. Africa needs the means to develop local solutions using local resources to meet local needs, and increased access to clean, sustainable energy to support health and education services, households and enterprise.

Unfortunately, the approach adopted by the Commission for Africa favours large power projects. Work is already under way on the development of the Grand Inga hydropower project, supported by the Commission. Such projects absorb billions of dollars of investment and development funds, soaking up all available aid and investment and leaving little to deliver access to energy services for the poorest. They also tend to rely on international technologies, consultants and contractors, meaning that the funds invested will leak out of Africa and very little capacity-building will take place where the projects are built. The Commission's approach to clean energy misses the huge potential for indigenous technology development involving micro-hydro, biogas, small-scale wind power and solar thermal water heaters, for example, to meet local needs now. Without new thinking, a huge opportunity for development could be lost.

There is also a growing interest in renewable energy generation in the Pacific. Currently most Pacific island countries depend on increasingly expensive imported diesel, oil and bottled gas to produce power for electricity, transport and cooking. This trend will only continue unless steps are taken to reverse this development path. Developing renewable technologies, however, must build on past experiences of renewable energy projects that were designed without consulting local communities and without considering the unique cultural and physical context of the Pacific. The development of renewable energy resources is still limited by the availability of appropriate technologies, poor institutional mechanisms and the challenges of developing systems for small remote markets at reasonable prices. Yet technologies such as solar, wind and mini-hydro are clean, affordable, more secure, more reliable, healthier and better suited to the local environment than imported fossil fuels. Solar energy, in particular, has immense potential. In addition, lower fuel bills would allow regional governments and rural communities to spend money elsewhere on water, sanitation and improved living conditions and health services.

---

100 per cent renewable energy for Niue

In 2004, Niue, the smallest nation on earth, had 70 per cent of its infrastructure destroyed by cyclone Heta. Once the immediate needs of the population were met, Greenpeace began helping the government to make Niue the first nation on earth to meet all its energy requirements from renewable sources.

Niue is the largest uplifted coral island in the world. It is an independent country in free association with New Zealand, with a population of 1,700. Niue has one of the highest wind-energy intensities in the South Pacific and ample solar resources, more than sufficient to meet all its energy needs. With electricity prices six times higher than the typical Australian consumer price, renewables should be commercially viable.

The 100 per cent Niue Greenpeace Renewable Energy Project will reduce Niue's dependence on imported fossil fuels, while also creating jobs, because people will be trained to maintain and operate the cleaner technologies. The project will draw new investment into the economy, and help promote local businesses.

Renewable energy technologies offer much more than best practice in the context of sustainable energy. As the Ashden Awards for Sustainable Energy show,[22] projects are saving the sight and lungs of urban street traders and home cooks by using solar lanterns and eco-stoves, utilising solar energy to power communication systems for flying doctors in the rainforest and getting electricity to remote mountain and island communities. Small- and medium-scale renewable energy projects can make use of local manufacturing and technical capabilities, and can be controlled by the communities themselves. Such projects are already delivering human well-being in some of the most difficult human circumstances. They also inoculate against the economic, environmental and political shocks linked to fossil fuels and offer an alternative to the face of the fossil fuel industries, which are tarnished with a reputation for exploitation, pollution and bad development practice.

Solar photovoltaics help small Indian businesses

In South India, solar photovoltaics are enabling small businesses to develop. While viewed as an expensive source of energy compared to grid electricity, for the 57 per cent of the population who do not have access to mains electricity photovoltaic systems are far cheaper than expensive kerosene or dry-cell batteries, and have the added benefit of reducing carbon dioxide emissions. Installing 71,000 systems avoids the emission of around 21,000 tonnes of carbon dioxide per year, including the amount of 'carbon dioxide equivalent' embodied in the manufacture of the system.

SELCO is a private business based in Bangalore, South India, which provides photovoltaic battery charging systems that supply single lamps for street vendors and poor homes. One of the benefits of lighting is extended hours for income generation. The increased income can quickly cover the cost of the system. SELCO's innovation department has also provided other affordable photovoltaic-powered systems: for example, power for sewing machines to increase the productivity of sewing businesses; power for soldering irons for television repair; and small photovoltaic-powered silk looms. As most people who acquire photovoltaic systems require a loan, SELCO further assists its customers through its strong relationship with banks and microfinance organisations. As a winner of the 2005 Ashden Awards, SELCO used some of the prize money as a 'down-payment guarantee' so that banks will provide loans to households who can afford the monthly repayments, but not the down payment.

Boats use solar photovoltaics to service remote Bangladesh

Solar photovoltaics are being used on boats to provide education and information services in the remote region of Chalanbeel in Bangladesh. Here, the charitable organisation Shidhulai Swanivar Sangstha works to improve the quality of life of waterside communities by bringing them services by boat, sometimes on a daily basis. Services include children's education, libraries, training in sustainable agriculture, health advice, mobile phones and Internet access. The boats have been fitted with photovoltaic systems to provide electricity for these services. On some boats the photovoltaic electricity supply is used to charge batteries for the solar home-lighting systems that Shidhulai has supplied to families. Solar lanterns have also been supplied for use in fishing boats.[23]

Renting photovoltaic systems in remote Laos villages

Many poor people in rural areas of Laos rely on firewood and kerosene for lighting. Pollution from both fuels can cause respiratory and eye problems, as well as being unsustainable and releasing carbon dioxide into the atmosphere. Sunlabob Renewable Energies Ltd introduced high-quality photovoltaic systems to rural areas in Laos that do not have access to grid electricity. By renting out portable solar lamps at prices lower than families spend on kerosene for lighting, households can benefit from safe lighting in the evening. Sunlabob also trains technicians in villages to perform day-to-day maintenance.[24]

The solar island

Six kilometres off the mainland in West Bengal, India, lies the sacred Sagar Island. Although home to just under 200,000 people, spread over forty-three villages, each year in January more than 1 million visit on pilgrimage to the Gangasagar Mela festival. But Sagar Island is now becoming the focus for a new kind of pilgrimage, one where people are travelling to see how medium-scale solar power is meeting the needs of thousands who are unable to access energy from the national grid.

Beginning in 1996, the West Bengal Renewable Energy Development Agency now operates nine stand-alone solar photovoltaic power plants that provide grid-quality electricity. The Agency works in cooperation with rural energy development co-operatives formed by the beneficiaries of the power supply, an original feature of the initiative. Over 1,600 families also benefit from solar-powered home lighting systems, and fifty-eight shops and businesses are receiving stable power supplies. Before solar power arrived the island depended on expensive and inadequate diesel generators. More recently a wind/diesel hybrid power plant has been added to the energy mix.

The solar ambitions of Sagar Island are bold. Importantly, the initiative to set up the power plants comes from the local village government Gram Panchayat level. Apart from bringing electricity to homes, the mini-grids aim to power schools and health services. The project also integrates power with water supply systems that bring drinking water to the island's homes. Jobs have been created directly and the local economy has benefited as new lighting and power allow local businesses, markets and homeworkers to work more cleanly, efficiently and safely outside daylight hours.

Gon Chaudhuri, the dynamic director of the Agency, who won the Ashden Award for Sustainable Energy in 2003, emphasises that local people fully understand and promote the radical environmental improvements that solar energy brings: 'Sagar Island has its unique ecosystem. It falls under the Sunderbans delta. Diesel power generation is responsible for environmental degradation not only in Sagar Island but in the entire delta zone. Solar energy is totally eco-friendly. There are no emissions and no sound pollution from solar photovoltaics. Local people are now very conscious about the protection of the environment of "Solar" Island.' Chaudhuri is unlikely to stop until everyone on the island has access to a solar mini-grid.

South India: domestic and municipal waste produces biogas for cooking and electricity generation

Biogas is produced from the decomposition of organic material in anaerobic conditions (without oxygen). The gas can be used directly for cooking, as a safer alternative to LPG (biogas cannot be lit accidentally by a spark). Burning biogas as a fuel also prevents the release of methane from unmanaged decomposition of organic matter, a greenhouse gas that is twenty-three times more damaging than carbon dioxide. Moreover, the effluent from the digester can be sold and used as a fertiliser due to its high nitrogen, phosphorous and potassium content.

Biotech in urban Kerala has developed biogas digesters for managing food waste and other organic wastes in 12,000 households, 220 institutions and nineteen municipal sites. These projects avoid the emission of around 37,000 tonnes of carbon dioxide or its equivalent each year by replacing LPG for cooking and diesel for electricity generation.

Under another scheme in Karnathaka, SKG Sangha supplies biogas plants to households in rural areas of South India. So far, SKG Sangha has installed plants that benefit over 210,000 people. Each plant also saves around four tonnes of carbon dioxide or its equivalent by replacing the unsustainable use of wood. In this region, biogas stoves save women on average two to three hours a day from collecting wood and cooking. The fuel switch from wood to biogas also has many health and welfare benefits as biogas abates respiratory or eye problems associated with wood fires. Additionally, kitchens and cooking equipment are cleaner.

Biogas systems also improve waste management. In rural areas, food waste can be used as food for animals, but in urban environments this is not usually feasible. Urban regions of India, with door-to-door waste-collection services by the local council, often suffer from hygiene problems as animals tear open waste sacks to access food waste. Rural areas with poor waste-disposal schemes can also benefit from improved waste management.

A 6 kilowatt micro-hydro system will drive a mill and provide electric light for a community of twenty families. Once the system is in operation, local people can pay a small charge to use the electricity. This covers maintenance and the eventual cost of replacement. Such micro-hydro systems are designed to operate for a minimum of twenty years if properly cared for. Local people are trained to build and maintain their own systems. Once schemes are set up, they should continue to function indefinitely without external funding. Unlike traditional power stations that use fossil fuels, micro-hydro generators have practically no effect on the environment. And, because they do not depend on dams to store and direct water, they are also better for the environment than large-scale hydroelectric stations. By reducing the need to cut down trees for firewood and by increasing farming efficiency, micro-hydro has a positive effect on the local environment.

Reducing deforestation and providing power in Peru

More than 8 million of Peru's 29 million inhabitants live in rural areas. Some 80 per cent of these people have no access to electricity. Most live in the Andes and the Upper Amazon areas and are very isolated due to the lack of roads and transportation, which makes supplying them with fuel difficult, expensive and unreliable. Micro-hydro is therefore an important energy option for these people.

Practical Action has developed several micro-hydro systems with communities in Peru. These divert stream or river water into a valley, and 'drop' it into a turbine via a penstock (pipeline). Besides providing power for domestic lighting and cooking needs, village hydro schemes can also charge batteries or power income-generating activities, such as grain milling. Only 5 per cent of Peru's potential for hydropower is exploited, so considerable expansion is possible.

Micro-hydro brings power to the Bolivian mountains

Most Bolivian people live in the mountains where steep terrains and scattered populations make grid-based rural electrification impractical. Lack of access to power is driving younger people from country villages to search for work in the towns and cities. But Andres Calizaya and his organisation Prodener have successfully brought small-scale hydro-electricity to communities around Corioco, the main town of the Nor Yungas area. The power runs everything from homes to schools, from health centres to local businesses and restaurants.

Walter Monroi, chairman of the construction committee that built the system for the community of Calle, remarked: 'In the villages on the [main] grid, the electricity is not sufficient and is too expensive; they put on the light just to find a candle. At night the village of Calle is lit up like a Christmas tree, while all the other villages around are dark. I want to help other communities get themselves organised to have a micro-hydro system; it will help them as much as it has helped us.'

Local benefits have been comprehensive. 'The children could not study properly with candles; now with electricity they can study very well', said Don Dionisio, the chairman of the San Juan electricity co-operative, adding, 'We do not just want light; we want to use the electricity to earn income.'

Upgrading water mills in the Himalayas[25]

The Centre for Rural Technology in Nepal runs a programme upgrading traditional water mills (*ghattas*) used to grind flour so that they can operate more efficiently. There are many *ghattas* in the remote villages of the Himalayan Mountains and foothills of Nepal; by upgrading the mills, millers are able to earn more income and work shorter hours. Additionally, the flour from water mills is better than from diesel mills, which have recently come into the region. Although diesel mills are faster, the flour is of lower quality, has a shorter shelf life, is less nutritious and has a lower market value. This is because the higher grinding speeds of the diesel mills heat the flour up more than do the traditional *ghattas*.

While the timber parts of a traditional *ghatta* need to be replaced once every two years, the upgraded and modified water mill only needs replacements every ten years. Such mills can also cope with variable water speeds, so can be used during the dry seasons when water flow is reduced.

Community hydropower in Kenya changes energy policy

Community hydropower schemes in two remote areas of Mount Kenya, Kathama and Thima, between them serve over 200 households and serve to demonstrate the viability of small-scale community-managed hydropower. The projects provide lighting, radio and telecommunications for the households, income generation from chicken farming – electric lighting provides warmth, increasing productivity – and a means to charge batteries. Replacing kerosene wick lamps cuts the need for 18 tonnes of kerosene each year, saving the equivalent emissions of 42 tonnes of carbon.

Practical Action East Africa, in collaboration with Nottingham Trent University and the Kenyan government, installed the schemes in association with local communities. The communities provided building materials, land for the turbine house, labour and financing. They also manage, operate and maintain the projects on their own. They pay monthly charges for power and share their experiences with other communities across the country. The schemes are cost-effective, as households now pay less for better quality lighting, and the project has been financially self-sustaining for several years.

The schemes have demonstrated that despite being small-scale they are operationally and technically viable. Whilst they can contribute to developing national standards and codes of practice for low-cost, off-grid small hydropower schemes, there is a need to build more local manufacturing capacity so that the turbines and their components are readily available.

Roughly 16 per cent of the Kenyan population have access to electricity. By directly involving the Kenyan Ministry of Energy from the start, the project has influenced national policy and contributed to the reform of Kenya's new energy policy and Electric Power Act. Usually, the key constraint to replicating and expanding such projects is a monopoly structure in the power sector, prohibiting independent private power producers. The project has demonstrated the viability of micro-hydropower in reaching communities far from the national grid, and the government has now drafted policies recognising the approach.

The current project has been operating with special permission from the government, but other schemes are expected to follow once the revised policy becomes operational. Community interest is high. Estimates show that Kenya has about 3,000 MW potential power from micro-hydro.

A global framework with major incentives is needed to encourage the shift to renewable energy use and forgo growing dependence on oil and coal. The challenge is how to create access to clean, affordable energy sources, which will allow poorer countries to avoid the 'dirty' energy path that others have gone down, whilst meeting real development needs. These energy options also offer employment and economic development opportunities and help liberate countries from the ball-and-chain of oil-dependency.

For this revolution to happen there has to be a managed withdrawal from fossil fuels towards the uptake of cleaner low-carbon technologies – one that gives developing countries their equitable per-capita shares of the remaining carbon cake that it is still safe to burn. The type of framework that will do this best is a matter of debate. For example, there is the 'Contraction and Convergence' scheme proposed by the Global Commons Institute. It works in stages: agreeing a precautionary concentration target for global greenhouse gas levels; setting an emissions budget to reach it, assuming that everyone in the world has an equal entitlement to emit; and then politically negotiating both the period of time and rate for the target to be met and equal entitlements achieved. In the process of shrinking and sharing greenhouse gas emissions, spare entitlements can be traded to generate income for 'under-emitting' countries.

Another approach is the Climate Action Network (CAN) framework. This promotes a multi-track approach for mitigation and adaptation. Based on the Kyoto framework, it calls for industrialised countries to act first in meeting their obligations to reduce emissions and to help fund development of clean technologies in developing countries as well as the adaptation needs of the more vulnerable countries. It is based on a combination of factors for equity and fairness – including per-capita emissions, ability of a country to pay, and historical responsibility in allocating emissions targets and choosing approaches to mitigation.[26]

Any framework that builds on the current Kyoto Protocol will have to deal with the sense of historical injustice concerning rich countries' ecological debts and current carbon footprints. Without this, the dawn of renewable energy will not arrive. The United States and Australia's per-capita carbon footprint, for example, are both roughly 19 tonnes of carbon dioxide (or equivalent) each year; Qatar's is nearly 60 tonnes. This compares to the comparably insignificant carbon footprints of poor countries such as Ethiopia, whose annual per-capita emissions are a mere 0.08 tonnes, Tanzania at 0.13 tonnes and Mozambique at 0.09 tonnes.[27] Electricity generation from renewable sources and adoption of energy efficiency and conservation measures are indisputably the primary obligation of industrialised countries.

Unfortunately, no framework proposed to date has achieved universal buy-in. Whilst countries party to the United Nations Framework Convention on Climate Change have agreed that a follow-up to the Kyoto Protocol is necessary, the details of this have yet to be negotiated. Current internationally agreed emissions reductions are therefore based on the cumulative sum of voluntary country commitments, which together are unlikely to achieve the emissions reductions needed to keep global warming below 2 degrees Celsius above pre-industrial levels – the level generally held to be that above which 'dangerous' climate change will occur.[28]

Biofuels

As regional instabilities and dwindling oil supplies send fuel prices higher, political leaders and businesses are scrambling to secure energy supplies. Attention is turning to biological sources, such as crops and trees, and climate change is adding extra impetus to this. Plants absorb carbon dioxide through photosynthesis. When burnt they simply emit what they have already absorbed and – in theory – no additional carbon dioxide enters the atmosphere.

Malawi is cultivating jatropha trees for biodiesel, often in areas previously under tobacco cultivation. Many poor people depend on tobacco picking for wage labour; it is too early yet to see whether the new trees will maintain similar employment levels. South Africa has a string of biofuel initiatives, and Nigeria, Africa's largest crude-oil producer, has projects to cultivate cassava and sugar cane for biodiesel. Ghana has a biodiesel refinery for its 20,000 hectares of biodiesel plantations.

India is also exploring biofuels as a component of its energy future and is promoting biofuel crops such as sugar cane, maize, sweet sorghum, karanja and jatropha for transport fuels. A new National Biofuel Development Board has been proposed that would determine the minimum prices for biofuel crops and formulate a national biofuel policy. There are calls for government subsidies and financial support for extraction of oil from seeds and for the blending of auto-fuels. Contract jatropha farming initiatives have started to proliferate in Maharashtra, while state agriculture ministries have encouraged farmers to cultivate jatropha in Chhattisgarh and Gujarat.

In the Philippines, implementation of the Biofuels Act began in 2007. This legislation calls for a mandatory mixing of 1 per cent biodiesel in petrodiesel and 5 per cent bioethanol in gasoline. This has raised fears among some national environmental organisations that the destruction of the country's remaining forests could be accelerated as farmers rush to meet the biofuel demand. It also threatens to increase poverty, as the costs of basic commodities are expected to increase as food and fuel crops compete for land and resources.

For developing countries, shifting towards large-scale export-led biofuel crop production will have big impacts. Some could be positive, such as increased earnings for farmers, farm labourers and exporters. But who benefits depends, like any commodity, on who has power in the markets.

'The great challenge for civil society is how biofuel cultivation can be of benefit to poor upland farming communities, when the reality is that it will surely benefit first the big business companies.'
Nanette Salvador Antequisa, EcoWEB, the Philippines

In practice, the use of biofuels offers negligible or negative carbon savings because the growing and conversion process from crop to fuel is itself energy-intensive and often cancels out the carbon gains of plant growth. Cutting down forests and draining peatlands, both of which hold huge carbon reserves, can mean any carbon benefits resulting from biofuel production on this land are cancelled out.[29]

Global peatlands account for roughly double the amount of carbon stored in all the world's forests while covering only 3 per cent of the land area, and many peatlands are still actively taking up and storing carbon. Research by Wetlands International and the Dutch consultancy Delft Hydraulics reported that deforestation and drainage of peatlands can release phenomenal amounts of carbon dioxide. As the peat dries, rather than storing carbon, it starts to decompose, and emits carbon dioxide at a rate of between 70 and 100 tonnes of carbon dioxide per hectare per year.[30]

A large proportion of Indonesian forests are located on peatlands and about 516 million tonnes of carbon dioxide are emitted each year in Indonesia as a result of peat drainage. A further 1,400 million tonnes of carbon dioxide is released to the atmosphere each year through fires on peatlands. Oil palm plantations on deforested peatlands generally require heavy drainage. It is estimated that at least 50 per cent of future plantations will be developed on peatlands, as much of the more desirable 'drylands' is already occupied. The combination of deforestation and drainage required to meet Indonesia's ambitious biofuel target could result in the emission of an additional 300 million tonnes of carbon dioxide into the atmosphere each year. This implies that for every 1 tonne of palm oil created in Southeast Asia, 33 tonnes of carbon dioxide are emitted – ten times as much as conventional petroleum.[31]

As the competition for land on which to grow food or biofuels grows, inevitably it is the world's poor who will lose out. February 2007 saw riots in Mexico after the price of maize quadrupled, pushed up by the demand for biofuels. Even if high-yield biofuel crops replaced food crops entirely and were grown on all the farmland on earth, they would meet only 20 per cent of current crude-oil energy demands. In 2004, 12 per cent of the United States domestic corn crop, weighing 32 million tonnes, was used to make 3.4 billion gallons of ethanol. This would be enough to feed 100 million people at average world consumption levels, according to the World Watch Institute.[32]

Malnutrition fears in Myanmar

In 2006, the military junta in Myanmar began implementing a plan to replace all of its 40,000 barrels of conventional oil imported each day with biodiesel from home-grown jatropha nut oil. Without any prior announcement, farmers are now being forced to grow this crop. This policy will eventually result in the conversion of between half a million to 7 million acres of land to jatropha plantations.

Currently, Myanmar does not have the technology necessary to efficiently extract and process the jatropha nut oil as a replacement fuel for diesel engines, leaving a product that can be used only in small engines. If this experiment fails, millions of acres of cultivatable land could be lost in a nation where at least 40 per cent of children under 3 suffer from moderate to severe malnutrition.

One argument for the cultivation of jatropha on wastelands in Myanmar is that it will release rural people from their dependence on fuelwood, and therefore prevent deforestation. Yet on Myanmar's south-west coast, jatropha is being grown on the remains of recently cleared rainforest.

Farmers only have the cultivation rights to their land. If they fail to grow crops specified by the state, or the land is deemed useful for other projects, their land will be seized. Already in Chin State the death penalty is in place for anyone who dares to criticise the policy on jatropha.

Biofuels in Brazil

When president, Luiz Inácio Lula da Silva frequently described Brazil's pioneering use of biodiesel – a mixture of conventional diesel and vegetable products – as the country's 'energy revolution'. Flexible-fuel vehicles, with engines that can run on regular fuel or ethanol, made up 22 per cent of car sales in 2004, but by 2009 this figure had shot up to 93 per cent. By February 2008, more than half of all the fuel sold was ethanol as opposed to gasoline. Brazil's share of fossil fuel use in its general energy mix is also low compared to developed countries or to global averages.

But Brazil's growing biofuel industry is not without its problems or its critics. One problem is that land is used to produce fuel instead of food crops. Rising oil prices and demand for oil are radically changing the economics of biofuels. But, in the process, this is sparking the first skirmishes in what may prove a long-term battle for land between food and biofuel producers. 'The line between the food and fuel economies has suddenly blurred as service stations compete with supermarkets for the same commodities', observes Lester Brown, president of the United States-based Earth Policy Institute. In addition, according to government data, Brazil is set to produce most of its biodiesel from soya beans, which have virtually no advantage over conventional fuels in terms of overall greenhouse gas emissions, let alone the millions of hectares of tropical forest that have been cleared for their large-scale plantations. Europe is one of the largest buyers of soya grown on former Brazilian Amazon rainforest.[33]

Pressure to bring more land into production stands to further erode biodiversity by destroying habitats. For example, the widespread mono-cropping of low-cost jatropha in India is being driven by economic incentives due to its assumed 'green' credentials. But research by the Society for Promotion of Wastelands Developments says that the large-scale production of jatropha is significantly affecting surrounding biodiversity. Oil palm plantations used for the production of biodiesel are also a major driver of deforestation and biodiversity loss in tropical Asia, as they require a humid tropical climate to give commercial yields. By 2006, Indonesia had some 6 million hectares of land under oil palm. It had also cleared an additional 18 million hectares for plantations and allotted a further 20 million hectares to oil palm in regional development plans.[34] The Indonesian government actively encourages further expansion by offering incentives and subsidies to attract both domestic and foreign investment in plantations and processing facilities. In 2007 alone, the government signed fifty-eight agreements worth US$12.4 billion in order to produce about 200,000 barrels of oil-equivalent biofuel per day by 2010 and replace 10 per cent of the country's total oil-based fuel needs.[35] The operationalisation of such plans has major implications for Indonesia's forests and those who depend on them. They will accelerate deforestation in a country which globally already has one of the highest rates of deforestation.

Destruction of the Kampar Peninsula, Indonesia

According to Eyes on the Forest, a coalition of three local environmental organisations in Riau, Sumatra, Indonesia, half of the 700,000-hectare Kampar Peninsula natural landscape has been changed to make way for acacia and oil palm plantations. The peninsula is a peat swamp forest, rich in biodiversity with four wildlife reserves and rivers used by local communities for their livelihood. Sumatran tigers, arwana fish, crocodiles and sun bears are among the many species present in the peninsula. A further twenty-one species are on the brink of local extinction due to landscape conversion.

The World Wide Fund for Nature (WWF) and others believe that only biofuels with net environmental benefits, in terms of both reducing greenhouse gas emissions and lowering pollution locally, should be promoted. The organisation is calling for a mandatory eco-certification scheme for all biofuels based on environmental and social criteria, which is also flexible enough to meet local conditions. An urgent assessment is needed of the carbon benefits of different biofuel schemes, the risk of further deforestation, potential socially negative impacts, and whether or not there is an emerging risk of competition between land for fuel and land for food. Rigorous management is needed to ensure that the increase of crops like soya grown for biofuels does not come at an irreversible environmental cost.

6

Disasters

Climate change is not just characterised by an increase in global temperatures. As a result of global warming we are also seeing more extreme weather patterns. It is no coincidence that news of storms, floods, drought and heatwaves now fills our television screens more regularly than ever before. Rain often comes in bigger bursts, leading to floods and landslides; dry spells lead to droughts; heatwaves are increasing, leading to more fires; and storms and hurricanes are becoming more frequent and more violent. Whilst some would describe these as 'natural' disasters, if it is the case that greenhouse gas emissions from human activities are causing them then it is clear that the root causes are far from natural. Whilst it remains difficult to state with certainty that any single event is linked to climate change, the science is clear that the increase in frequency, and in some cases the intensity, of extreme events is directly related to climate change.

A new 'cold war' comes to Bangladesh

According to Jibananda Das, one of Bangladesh's most acclaimed poets, winter in Bangladesh was a time that revealed the 'inner beauty and soul of Bengal'. It was a pleasant season, eagerly awaited and planned for. Nowadays, however, things are different. Winter is severe, with temperatures as low as 5°c recorded in January 2007 – reportedly the lowest in thirty-eight years.

In Gaibandha district in north Bangladesh fields are covered with fog and temperatures are down to single digits at night. The fog is particularly difficult – thick, clinging and cold. Seventy-five-year-old Abdul Husain says life is already harsh and people are ill-equipped to deal with these new low temperatures and with the unusual fogs that damage their crops. Sitting in his front yard, he recalls how winter was once warmer and windier. 'It used to be drier in those days; our skins would chap and feel dry during this month', he recalls. But now things have changed. The water in the river is shallower than it used to be, baigan or bitter gourd can no longer be cultivated, and a lot of health problems develop due to the cold. The damp fog spoils the mangos he grows. Families, especially women and children, are forced to spend hours inside their homes around kerosene lamps or in darkness (as there is no electricity).

The media coverage of the unusual 2007 winter reported that India and Nepal experienced similar cold waves. Over 130 people died and thousands more were affected. Governments, the United Nations and non-governmental agencies like Oxfam and their partners had to launch relief operations. One commentator observed: 'Most of the people have no winter clothes or blankets, and a lot of people died, especially newborn babies. It must be noted that no rich people died. Actually cold waves did not kill; poverty did.'

After over a decade of efforts to achieve the Millennium Development Goals designed to end poverty and save the environment, disasters – driven or exacerbated by global warming – could spell out the end of human development for the poor majority, and perilous political and economic insecurity for the rest of the world. Disasters cost lives, destroy communities, wreak havoc on people's livelihoods and leave a lasting impact not only on physical infrastructure but also on people's well-being.

During the past decade the number of natural disasters has increased sixfold compared to the 1960s, and of the total almost 90 per cent of these are hydrometeorological events such as droughts, storms and floods.[1] Whilst the trend in death rates is downward, the cumulative number of people affected by disasters – a definition that includes being physically injured or made homeless – has grown enormously. According to the annual *World Disasters Reports*, published by the International Federation of Red Cross and Red Crescent Societies, the number of people affected is up from 740 million in the 1970s to over 2.5 billion in the last decade. Virtually all are concentrated in poorer countries. The figure includes a kind of double counting as some people are repeatedly affected, but this merely emphasises how increasingly difficult it is for people and communities to recover.[2] More lives are lost in poor countries than in rich countries. From 1970 to 2008 over 95 per cent of deaths from natural disasters occurred in developing countries.[3] And within poor countries, more poor people than rich people lose their lives. The underlying causes of disaster clearly lie in vulnerability, inequality, discrimination and exploitation.

'Poverty ... plays a big role in keeping people vulnerable to disasters. And in the same fashion, disasters keep the poor in poverty by consistently wiping out the few resources they have.'
World Bank, 2000

While the scale and number of disasters is increasing, so too are the economic costs. Between 1961 and 1970, 1 in 138 persons worldwide were affected by natural disasters, compared to 1 in 28 in the decade 2001–10, and the economic costs associated with natural disasters over the same period increased more than eightfold.[4] The year 2011 was the insurance industry's costliest yet, with Munich Re estimating economic losses from natural disasters to be nearly US$400 billion. The United Nations Environment Programme estimates that the economic costs due to natural disasters are doubling every decade and that if current trends continue disasters could have a global cost of US$150 billion per year by the next decade.[5]

Floods

Massive disruption to the earth's hydrological cycle means that millions will become trapped between the extremes of floods and droughts. How bad the damage from floods will be depends

on a number of issues, such as where people choose to settle and
the quality of flood forecasting, but the IPCC states that global
warming will increase the risk of floods. Floods include those
from rivers overflowing, storm surges, snowmelt and dam break-
ages. People living in low-lying areas of Vietnam, Bangladesh,
India and China are particularly vulnerable to flooding from sea
level rise, for example, and the IPCC predicts that even under the
most conservative scenarios for sea-level rise the annual number
of people flooded in coastal populations in Asia will rise from
13 million to 94 million by the end of the twenty-first century.
Without adaptation, by the 2080s more than 100 million people
could experience coastal flooding each year due to sea-level rise
alone.[6]

Up to 20 per cent of the world's population also live in river
basins that are likely to be affected by an increase in flood risk.[7]
Many human settlements were established on floodplains, which
often provide fertile ground for agriculture, and close to rivers
and the sea for access to water, transport links and marine resources such as fish. But such locations look less appealing now,
with the IPCC predicting a 'widespread increase in the risk of
flooding for many human settlements'.[8]

'Frequency of flooding is increasing due to heavy rainfall or water coming
from surrounding countries and creating waterlogging. Before 1988, we
did not see flood in the Jessore area because Jessore is comparatively
high land. But in 1988, 1998 and 2004, Jessore area flooded... The poor
rush towards safest places during the flood, towards cities in search of
jobs or even for alms. The flood waters damage their crops, houses, local
infrastructures that put them into starvation, isolated, shelterless.'
Salvation Army, Bangladesh

'Periods of heavy rainfall over a very short period of time have been
increasing over the last ten years. This is not usual. The frequency of
cloudbursts is increasing, when there can be 60 millimetres of rain in five
minutes. There have been two of these in the last three years and these

weren't happening thirty years ago (in the northern mountainous areas).
We are seeing many incidences of flash floods even in desert areas where
we experience droughts.'
Evangelical Fellowship of India Commission on Relief, India

In Asia, serious floods have affected Nepal, India, China, Vietnam, Cambodia and Bangladesh in recent years. Record floods in the Mekong Delta in 2000 killed more than 350 people and displaced hundreds of thousands of others. Nearly 500,000 homes were inundated, and in Dong Thap, one of Vietnam's worst-affected provinces, 90 per cent of the land was under water for weeks, and this occurred before farmers could harvest their rice crop. These floods also hit areas upstream in Cambodia, Laos and Thailand, affecting almost a million people. In Cambodia, flooding caused considerable damage in eleven out of Cambodia's twenty-four provinces. River banks in and around the capital were fortified with sandbags, but some outer areas of Phnom Penh were flooded and a state of emergency was declared. Officials said the flooding, which began with unusually widespread and heavy monsoon rains in late July, was the worst to hit Cambodia in seventy years. The rainy season does not usually reach its peak until September. Large areas of farmland were destroyed.

Oxfam Hong Kong and the Red Cross were among the agencies providing flood relief and other assistance in the Mekong River Basin. Temporary latrines were constructed in evacuation areas and strong plastic sheeting provided for emergency shelters. For longer-term rehabilitation, rice and rice seeds for the next crop were provided.

In the summer of 2004, two-thirds of Bangladesh, along with much of Assam and Bihar in India, was under water. Over 50 million people were affected and tens of thousands suffered from diarrhoea and dysentery as sewage mingled with the floodwaters. The main monsoon rice crop was severely damaged and some 20 million people needed food assistance. The floods affected 38 per cent of Bangladesh, destroying more than three-quarters of the nation's crops and leaving 10 million people homeless. Diseases such as dysentery and diarrhoea increased in their wake. Bangladeshis have developed strategies to cope with temporary floods, but with climate change the temporary nature of wet season flooding is fast becoming permanent.

Living with flooding in Bangladesh

At least 174 disasters afflicted Bangladesh between 1974 and 2003. Extreme weather events such as floods, typhoons and river erosion have always been a fact of life and regularly endanger human life and affect livelihoods. Increasingly, however, the impact of these disasters is being exacerbated by climate change. Scientists have warned that a 1 metre rise in sea level would flood about 18 per cent of the land of Bangladesh.[9] Already, typhoons and floods show increased severity and in recent years there have been serious floods in Bangladesh almost annually.

Practical Action has been working with flood-affected communities to increase their resilience to these environmental shocks using a process called Participatory Technology Development. It involves farmers and communities identifying and experimenting with different technological options, followed by self-assessment and reflection.

Technologies developed in communities severely affected by floods cover livestock and crop and fish production. Help with managing livestock feed and disease control during flood periods, and homestead rearing of poultry in pens, has improved the survival of household livestock. Digging pits and enriching the sandy soil with manure for vegetables like chillies and gourds help people grow vegetables at home. Sticks mark pit locations during flooding. Training in how to grow trees and crops during flood periods enables people to be ready for planting out when floodwaters recede. Water-resistant fruit trees are developed by grafting onto different flood-tolerant root stocks.

One technology with great potential is the management of small seasonal ponds for breeding native fish alongside the rearing of stocked carp. Cages for fish breeding are suspended in floodwaters. This practice is benefiting the poorest people. In one year, the production of cultivated species rose by 50 per cent and wild fish production increased threefold as a result of new conservation and stocking initiatives. In one community, 48 people manage a seasonal water body that covers up to 24 hectares during the rainy season. Poor people have limited access to, and control over, natural water basins, but negotiating access to these types of small- or medium-sized bodies of water is easier.

The long-term sustainability of this approach is ensured by training local people who provide technical support and farming inputs to their fellow villagers and are paid by them for their services. So far, over a hundred rural community-based workers are now selling their services to the community.

East Timor is already highly vulnerable to extreme events, such as destructive storms, flooding and landslides, many of which could be caused, in part, by climate change. Following an El Niño year, rainfall can also be higher than average, thus increasing the risk of floods. In the south side of East Timor these often cause landslides, which damage property and rice paddies. Steep topography along with farming practices that remove vegetation from highland slopes and increase soil erosion exacerbate flooding. Forest cover in East Timor already fell by nearly 30 per cent from 1972 to 1999, coinciding roughly with the period of Indonesian occupation.

Monsoon flooding in India

In July 2005, the coastal city of Mumbai was hit by exceptionally heavy rains. Almost a metre of rain fell in one day alone. The metro flooded and as many as 500 people died in the city, many of them from Mumbai's overcrowded slums. In the western suburb of Andheri, a further seventy-two people living in slums at the foot of a hill died in a related landslide. The city was brought to a standstill for several days and communications broke down completely. Outside Mumbai, at least 60,000 villagers had to move into temporary camps because their homes were flooded. The flooding came at the worst possible time, as the planting of the paddy fields had just been completed. The flood water cost an entire harvest for the farmers affected, destroyed farming infrastructure, and left the soil covered in silt washed down from the surrounding mountains.

A year later, the desert area of Barmer in Rajasthan experienced unprecedented floods. Some 577 millimetres of rainfall was recorded in just three days – more than double the average rainfall it receives for an entire year. The floods killed at least 140 people and tens of thousands were displaced from their homes.

Development wasted: the great Mozambican flood disaster

As rescue helicopters flew them to the safety of high ground, survivors of Mozambique's devastating floods of February 2000 looked out over the huge inland sea which covered once-prime farming land. Villages lay covered by silt and vegetation, a train track disappeared either side of an elevated bridge, and cattle waded knee-deep in water or huddled on tiny islands. After landing in Chibuto, a slightly elevated town spared the worst of the floods, the displaced people were taken to camps run by aid agencies. There, a fuel shortage in the town meant that two large water tanks at the main camp sat unfilled and just two toilets served 3,500 people. And longer-term problems loomed large.

A third of the country's crops had been destroyed; in some areas the loss was total. Roads and railway lines were wiped out, entire villages had disappeared, and hundreds of thousands of people were made homeless. But perhaps, more than damage to infrastructure, it was the long-term damage to livelihoods that was most devastating. Estimates put the figure close to 350,000 lost jobs, undermining, through the impact on households, the livelihoods of up to 1.5 million people.[10]

Decades of development work in Mozambique, a country still recovering from years of war, were washed away by these floods. The worst in living memory, they followed unusually heavy rains over southern Africa and tropical storms that accompanied cyclones Connie and Eline. The Mozambique government estimated that £65.5 million would be needed for reconstruction, including for water and sanitation, food aid, medicine and health care, shelter and housing, seeds and tools.

After the great floods, ActionAid–Mozambique conducted interviews with people who used to live in the floodplain of the River Incomati. One respondent recalled, 'I was first alerted to the danger by my son who had heard an urgent warning over the local radio station. But I refused to move, saying "Why should I go? I have been living here since 1937. This is the place where I was born. I'm not leaving!" So when the waters came in the middle of that night I was forced to flee my house and take refuge in a tree, where I was stranded with nothing to eat for four days. There were also many poisonous snakes in the tree, as they had also climbed to escape the water. I saw many dead animals floating past. Eventually I was saved by helicopter and taken to a rescue centre.'

Another respondent observed: 'There was no food; we tried to make platforms in the trees for the children to sit on. Some people died, and some of the children fell into the water, only to be swept away. The adults could not swim after them – they had to sit and watch them float away.'

Tragedy in Belle Anse, Haiti

On 22 May 2004 over a period of thirty-six hours, rainfall caused unprecedented flooding in the communes of Belle Anse, Haiti. Over 1,000 people died and property sustained massive damage.

Deforestation is having a devastating impact on life in Haiti. Parts of some towns are surrounded by mountains where trees have been replaced by small homes and farms, creating particular vulnerability to floods. Over 100,000 inhabitants living in this area are exposed to the consequences of deforestation and climate change. Haiti faces floods caused by regular rainfall and tropical cyclones, with climate change potentially exacerbating these problems. Less than 2 per cent of this mountainous country is now covered by forest, and the interaction between deforestation and climatic factors is proving lethal.

Jean-Baptise Anthony Rabel, a resident of Mapou town, lost his family and livelihood in the 2004 flooding. 'We are facing serious environmental problems in our hometown. A lot of trees are cut down to make charcoal and our government is not upholding its responsibilities', he said. 'We pay the consequences: the place is turning into a desert and there is nothing to keep the water when it rains. Moreover, the climate is warmer than in the past. I am 50 and it was our first flood last year. In my neighbourhood the homes were made with stones linked together with cement and covered with sheet. Before the floods I had my home, my farm and livestock. I used to grow coffee and several other crops in my farm. My wife was also a small merchant. We were able to survive on the money we earned.

'It started raining in the afternoon of Saturday, 22 May 2004. It kept raining until Sunday night. By 8 p.m. the drum in our backyard was full of water. I woke up my wife and my kids and I told them we had to get out. It was the first time this had happened to us. I tried to open two doors but I couldn't. My 9-year-old boy was trying to help me break the third door when my wife cried: "Anthony, we're dead; our home is destroyed." All I knew was that I was floating in the water trying to hold my son in the air.

'A wave came and with the water went my son; all I had left was a shirt in my hands. My arm was broken. I stayed there until the water receded. I had nothing other than the clothes I was wearing that night. I lost everything: my wife and three kids, my home, my livestock and part of my land.'

Droughts

The IPCC states that global warming will increase the risks of drought, particularly in low latitudes and mid-latitude continental interiors.[11] Research by the United Kingdom's Hadley Centre for Climate Prediction and Research looked at the share of the earth's land surface prone to drought and concluded that the proportion subject to extreme drought would increase from 1 per cent to 30 per cent by the end of the twenty-first century due to global warming. The number of extreme drought events per 100 years is predicted to double and the duration of droughts is expected to increase by a factor of six over the same period. Historically a total of 20 per cent of the earth's land surface has been in drought at any one time, be it extreme, severe or moderate. This has now risen to 28 per cent and is predicted to be 35 per cent by 2020 and cover 50 per cent – half the earth's land surface and still rising – by 2090.[12]

Not only will water availability decrease for many people in water-scarce regions, but its quality will deteriorate. Rural areas, where people rely on streams and small rivers, will be particularly hit. And women, the water-carriers, will be far more affected than men.

Africa is already persistently affected by drought, which alongside erratic rainfall has provoked food crises in most countries in Southern Africa and in Ethiopia and Eritrea. The great drought in the mid-1980s triggered the famine in Ethiopia that shocked the world. Local droughts occur every year and continental crises seem to occur once a decade, or, more recently, twice a decade.

'The weather is changing. We used to get heavy rains when the winds came from the west and then came back two to three days later with rain. Now the wind comes from the east, so it brings little or no rain ... these are dry winds. I don't know what is causing this.'

Paul Mayan Mariao, Chief Kaikor, Turkana, Kenya

Access to surface water will be significantly affected across 25 per cent of Africa by the end of this century.[13] About 25 per cent of Africa's 200 million people currently experience high water stress, and this is expected to increase to between 75 and 250 million and 350 and 600 million people by the 2020s and 2050s, respectively.[14] Although the continent uses only a fraction of its renewable freshwater resources, water is becoming one of its most critical natural resource issues. The continent as a whole is warmer by 0.5°c than it was a hundred years ago,[15] which puts extra strain on water resources. By the year 2000, the five warmest years in Africa had all occurred since 1988.[16] Temperature increases will vary between different regions in Africa, and the IPCC expects the continental interior to warm quicker than its coastal areas. Increases in the Sahara and semi-arid parts of southern Africa may be as much as 1.6°c by 2050.[17]

Endless drought in north-west Kenya

In 2005–06 some 25 million people faced a serious food crisis across sub-Saharan Africa, 11 million of them in East Africa. Cows and goats, even camels, died in vast numbers. This was nowhere more apparent than in the Turkana region of north-west Kenya – 2,000 miles of some of the most inhospitable territory known to humankind. In north-west Kenya international aid agencies were supplying 1.7 million people in twenty-one districts with emergency food by late 1999. By the summer of 2004 that had expanded to 2.2 million people.

The Turkana tribe who live there are nomadic pastoralists whose way of life is well suited to the harshness of this land. They are skilful and adept at seizing every opportunity. By being constantly on the move they search out the few watering holes and available pasture on which to graze their cattle, camels, donkeys, sheep or goats during the long dust-dry nine months between one wet season and the next. The Turkana survive a poor rainy season by using up some of their livestock in the expectation that the following year's rains will replenish their stock. But their way of life is under terrible stress. To survive the droughts, people have had to resort to practices that damage their dignity, their long-term livelihoods and their environment, including large-scale charcoal production that intensifies deforestation, fighting over water and pastures, selling livestock and dropping out of school.

Anna Nangolol lives on the banks of what was once a large river (from which she derives her name – *nangolol* means born at a river). 'This drought has been very bad', explained Anna in 2004. 'Past droughts have been short and rains have come. This one seems never to finish and our goats and cattle are not multiplying. Even if the rains do finally come now, it will take a long, long time for us to get back all of our animals.'

Anna Nangolol's impression of the severity of the drought is backed up by scientific data which shows that the Sahel region of Africa saw a dramatic decrease in annual rainfall from the 1970s to the end of the century. Annual rainfall was consistently below the long-term averages. This period of desiccation is consistent with climate change models.[18]

The Turkana have names for the increasingly frequent droughts. 1960 showed sporadic and inconsistent rains and was called *Namotor*, meaning 'bones exposed/emaciated'. 1970 was *Kimududu*, meaning 'the plague that killed humans and livestock'. Nine years later the drought of 1979–80 spread across two years; it was named *Lopiar*, or 'sweeping/cleaning everything away'. The prolonged four-year drought of 1992–95 was called *Longuensil*, meaning 'when the man with no legs from Oxfam came', a reference to an Oxfam member of staff with a disability. *Kichutanak*, meaning 'It has swept everything, even wild animals', began in 1999 and continued until 2004. The 2005–06 drought was called *Atiaktiak ng'awiyei* or 'the one that divided homes' because so many families split up to survive, migrating in all directions to the borders, towns and relief camps. This drought was almost continuous from 1999 when *Kichutanak* began. Hassan Mahmood, one pastoralist, said: 'This drought has no comparison. No other drought has been like this. It's all-encompassing. All regions are affected; there is no place to escape, everywhere is dried out.'

The nomads of Turkana are likely paying with their lives and their way of life for the profligate consumption of fossil fuels by others. Everything must be done to cut emissions and provide sufficient relief aid so that when the rains do eventually come, there will still be a Turkana people to greet them.

New approaches to drought relief in East Africa

Although droughts are becoming more intense and more frequent in north-west Kenya, it is primarily politics that explains the increasing inability of many pastoralists to cope with them. Kenya's arid and semi-arid lands make up more than 80 per cent of the country and are home to over 30 per cent of its population and more than half of its livestock.

Yet nomadic pastoralists are some of the most under-provided-for and politically under-represented people in East Africa. Lacking education and health care for themselves and their children, water provision and veterinary care for their animals, and help marketing skins and animal products means they put increased pressure on the environment and have few opportunities to generate alternative income.

Oxfam and others argue that if the Kenyan government keeps its promises to promote sustainable development in the arid and semi-arid lands, and also creates a national drought contingency fund, pastoralism could be a viable and even profitable way of life, despite climate change.[19]

Aid agencies like Oxfam and Practical Action are also calling for new approaches to emergency relief, including less food aid from abroad. One such approach is a 'meat aid safety net'. In this, people sell their weakest animals – usually goats that would die in the drought – to the agency for a fair fixed price. The animals are slaughtered and the sellers receive both the meat and the hide, which they can sell on. These schemes have been very successful. People receive a good price for what would otherwise be an almost worthless animal, and money they can use to buy food, pay off debts or restock. The money stays in the local economy. Women often use it to buy school uniforms, which means their children can go to school, benefiting from resumed education and school meals. People's main diet is meat, so the system ensures people receive their preferred food, rather than maize and beans, which require lengthy cooking using a lot of fuelwood. Finally, destocking reduces grazing pressure on the dry land.

Other interventions include cash for work, direct cash relief to the most vulnerable, provision of veterinary services and seed distribution. Sesophio, a Maasai pastoralist from Ololosokwan village, Ngorongoro, Tanzania, said: 'It is this development, like cars, that is bringing stress to the land, and plastics are being burnt and are filling the air. We think there is a lot of connection between that and what is happening now with the droughts. If you bring oil and petrol and throw it onto the grass it doesn't grow, so what are all these cars and new innovations doing to a bigger area? Every day diseases are increasing ... diseases we haven't seen before.'

New approaches to tackling drought in Niger

Drought hit Niger hard in 2004–05. This was particularly challenging given that it can take decades for livestock herds to recover from drought in terms of size and health – many pastoralist communities have never fully recovered from the disasters of the early 1970s and mid-1980s.

People's problems in coping with increasing aridity are due as much or more to social and political factors as to the aridity itself. Ongoing poverty, low literacy rates and little access to basic health services combine to weaken people and are reflected in shockingly high child-mortality and malnutrition rates, even in normal times. UNICEF states that one in five children in the Sahel will die before reaching the age of 5.[20] Grain markets are unstable and function badly. During the 2005 famine, grain was often available in markets, but few could afford to buy it.

Another factor is the developed world's failure to deliver aid predict-ably and in accordance with its commitments. The OECD explains how aid to Sahelian countries actually fell by 27 per cent between 1990 and 1997. Per-capita aid to Sahelian countries has also fallen significantly.[21] Annual aid to Niger, one of the world's poorest countries, was US$41 per person in 1982, but a mere US$18 per person in 1999.[22]

Aid agencies working in Niger, like Oxfam, have pioneered new responses to drought. These include calls for less foreign food aid and more direct transfer of cash vouchers to enable people to buy the food that is available at local markets. In the long term, agencies like Tearfund are working with local NGOs like JEMED (Youth with a Mission) to trap rainfall and boost agriculture. Simple structures that capture rainwater – stone lines or earthen half-moon crescents, mini-dams and dykes – can give communities an extra three months' worth of water per year.

Jeff Woodke of JEMED observed: 'The changed rainfall patterns contribute to increased desertification. The decreased production of grass means that it can sustain fewer animals. Drought causes massive loss of livestock. This has a devastating effect on the pastoral people, both Tuareg and Wodaabe, who rely on livestock for their livelihood. It creates chronic food security problems and great social ones as well. At one site called Abrik, a valley that runs east–west serves as a dividing line between the "dead" land to the north, and the "living" land to the south. The northern land is "dead" because of desertification, which has climatic as well as human causes. The valley itself was dying as well. We were able to reverse this process and help the people to adapt to the changing rainfall patterns, for example through building dykes. But then drought struck. For two years the men had to be away from their families, strug-gling to keep their animals alive. Some men did not see their families for six months at a time. However, in spite of all this, the improvements they made in the valley allowed some grass to grow and they could feed a few animals. The women stayed put, and the children stayed in school. The school was one of the most successful in Niger that year.'

What hope for coping strategies? The Tuareg in the Sahel

Since 1990, the local organisation JEMED has been working with the semi-nomadic Tuareg people in Niger to reduce their vulnerability to drought. The Tuareg are well adapted to surviving in the Sahel's dry, marginal land – if pastures fail in one area they move on, taking everything with them. However, the great droughts of 1973 and 1984 decimated herds, and subsequent droughts in 1993–94 and 1997–98 thwarted recovery. Climate change means that already dry areas are likely to get drier. The combination of droughts and the need to graze herds has had a devastating effect on the land, causing famine and poor health.

Women bear the brunt of the famine. While men are forced to leave their communities to search for new pasture for their animals, women are left behind to try and feed their families, foraging for fruit, borrowing from neighbours and trying to find work. When the food runs out the Tuareg are forced to sell their animals – which represent their only wealth and long-term security.

JEMED has been helping Tuareg communities establish 'fixation points'. These do not settle people permanently, but build on a tradition that the Tuareg would spend part of each year camped in a particular place. The fixation point helps the community manage and use surrounding resources better and protect them from encroachment by farmers. Fixation points also help communities develop a social infrastructure and education, training, health and agricultural projects, whilst retaining many of their traditional pastoral ways. Each fixation point has a management committee made up of, and elected by, members of the local community.

The first step is to build wells. In 2002, JEMED helped three communities dig 95-metre-deep wells for all human and animal needs. This directly benefited 390 families, or about 2,000 people, plus another 750 more people who pass through. At each fixation point, cows are loaned to the neediest families to help them re-establish their herds. This results in an increased milk supply, which improves health. The produce from the herds can be sold to provide a small income. JEMED has also helped communities conserve scarce rainwater by building low stone dykes across valley contours. When the rains come, the stones slow the flowing streams, so water sinks deeper into the soil. Behind the dykes, the Tuareg have been able to plant wild wheat. In Intikikitan, an established dyke has increased moisture levels to the extent that plant species not seen for half a century have returned. These measures mean thousands of Tuareg families are more prepared to face and survive drought, and to build up their assets in good years. Their recent experience shows remarkable human endurance and adaptability, but a future of progressive global warming may well push them beyond their abilities to adapt and cope.

Africa is not alone in its susceptibility to drought. Whilst Bangladesh hits the news most often for its dramatic and devastating flooding events, northern districts are facing severe droughts due to higher temperatures, less rainfall and reduced flow of river water, because less rain is falling in the upstream region. These droughts cause livestock and crop losses, malnutrition and disease. Elsewhere, the Tigris and Euphrates rivers in Iraq dropped to about 20 per cent of their average flow in 2001. In southern and western Afghanistan, drought has been more damaging to households than the protracted conflicts there.[23] In March 2007, an eight-month drought in Vose district in southern Tajikistan meant that there was no hydropower and therefore no electricity. Water pumps did not work properly and there was less clean drinking water. This drought was followed by excessive rain causing mudslides that swept away water pipes, including ones constructed by Oxfam engineers. The mudslides effectively finished off the community's water supply system. Now people have to walk over 1 kilometre to get clean water. This has huge health implications, and typhoid and tuberculosis are now rife.

Managing drought in Vietnam

Temperatures in inland Vietnam are rising and the weather is becoming both more extreme and unpredictable. Average temperatures are now 1°C higher than they were around a hundred years ago.

A major study by Kyoto University, Japan, in association with Oxfam in Vietnam, examined links between climate change, communities and government.[24] The study took place in Ninh Thuân province, which experiences regular droughts. The drought in 2004 was the worst on record. Exacerbated by increasing human demands for land, fuel and water causing deforestation and the overexploitation of aquifers, the amount of available water per person declined from some 17,000 cubic metres per year to 4,600 cubic metres in 2005.

Whilst annual rainfall has been steadily increasing, farmers nevertheless experience droughts because the rain now comes in intense, concentrated bursts. Women, in particular, suffer from having to walk far to fetch water in extreme temperatures. Children and old people also suffer more from the intense heat.

Communities are always seeking new ways to adapt. Farmers work together to grow crops and keep herds of goats, and also sheep of the Sultan breed from India, which can tolerate high temperatures. Farmers have switched from growing rice to maize and changed to more drought-resistant varieties. They have devised ways to economise on and reuse water. In particularly difficult times family members will migrate to the cities to find work. Some of these adaptation techniques are productive, but others carry a cost. Migration of young people increases the workload of the older people left behind. Women sometimes go without water in order to give it to their husbands or children.

Rising temperatures need not be a disaster for the people of Ninh Thuân if government and organisations working there take appropriate measures. The most important thing is to involve communities and hear what they want. Such measures could include enhancing weather forecasting; improving water storage and irrigation; enforcing regulations to restrict water usage and allocate it fairly; soil conservation; the provision of micro-credit; along with finance for, and knowledge about, such practices as animal rearing, fodder storage, and the use of improved seeds and new crops. These are all being discussed with the government as a result of the research.

Drought in Chongqing, China

The drought in Chongqing in 2006 was severe, topping all meteorological records kept in China since 1891. Some 3,775,900 hectares of crops were damaged, among which 685,800 hectares provided no harvest at all. The output of spring crops in Chongqing declined by 7,814,100 tons, a decrease of more than 30 per cent compared with regular years. Some 15 million people and 1.3 million cattle experienced temporary shortages in drinking-water supplies. In some areas, people had to carry water from 2.5 kilometres away.

Hurricanes, cyclones and storms

The world watched and the United States woke up to the fear-some potential of global warming when Hurricane Katrina hit New Orleans in August 2005. Yet, both before and after Katrina, there were other major hurricanes that caused widespread dev-astation and yet passed virtually unnoticed by the world's media. The difference? These extreme weather events struck poor coun-tries with their full force, rather than the United States.

One was almost indistinguishable in name. Catarina struck the southern coast of Brazil in March 2004 and left 33,000 people homeless. Only two tropical cyclones had previously been record-ed in the South Atlantic, and Catarina was the first hurricane ever recorded in this region. The speed of Catarina was around 150 kilometres per hour. Twenty-three cities were severely struck and Catarina caused an estimated US$50 million in economic losses. Cities remained without contact with the outside world for a week, some without water and light for three days. Some 80 per cent of schools were damaged, leaving 40,000 students without classes, some for fifteen days.

Previously, in 1998, Hurricane Mitch hit Honduras, causing mudslides and flooding and leading to the loss of almost 10,000 lives. Its impact on agriculture, coral reefs, fisheries and infra-structure was devastating. It destroyed much of the infrastruc-ture of Honduras but also devastated parts of neighbouring Nicaragua, Guatemala, Belize and El Salvador.

Extreme weather in El Salvador and Guatemala

In October 2005, Tropical Storm Stan struck El Salvador, bringing with it a record volume of rainfall. The small streams that cross the city of San Salvador broke their banks, taking with them houses and vehicles. One stream in particular, known as 'El Garrobo', so small that it dries up for several months of the year, carried so much water that it left houses in a number of suburbs totally submerged, some of which were not just flooded but destroyed in the process.

The mountain range La Cordillera El Bálsamo, which crosses a large part of Salvadoran territory, suffered landslides, leaving some communities without communication, electricity or water for five days. At the national level, 100 people lost their lives and tens of thousands were left homeless.

In neighbouring Guatemala a mountainside collapsed, burying a town and killing more than 2,000 people. It was impossible to recover the bodies, and the government declared the zone a national cemetery. Communities struggled to access food and health services. Single mothers were particularly vulnerable and sometimes left their children and their village for a whole day or even a whole week in their desperation to obtain some sort of income in order to get back on their feet. The storm forced the government to recognise the country's environmental vulnerability. The hope now is that they listen to warnings from groups such as Friends of the Earth El Salvador about the increased flooding dangers resulting from deforestation and turning natural watersheds into built-up areas and shopping centres.

Eyewitness accounts from Hurricane Ivan

Hurricane Ivan terrified people across the Caribbean, hitting Jamaica in December 2005. Pauline Adassa Grant, 42, a domestic helper in Mocho, Jamaica, describes what happened:[25]

'Hurricane Ivan was devastating ... I was affected very badly. Everything got damaged, my roof came off, my furniture got damaged, my animals were killed. I didn't really make much preparation for Hurricane Ivan, just a little... Well I tried to nail down the house top, I tried to take care of the animals, but I still got damage... I lost my roof, I lost everything.

'I could have done more, I could have taken the animals to a safer place, and I think I could have put the most important things ... in a safer place. All of my important papers, my birth certificate and whatever, all of those that got damaged ... I think I could have made them more secure... I have to go back and reapply for my birth certificate and that takes me a whole lot of time and a whole lot of money. I think it was late in the hurricane [when I lost my roof] because I didn't leave the house – I stayed until the morning. I tried to put the bed where there was no water; we tried to find a comfortable spot and we stayed until the morning. In the morning, we got up to take the smaller ones [children] to my mother.

Then I returned and started to pack up what I could pack up, and then just picked up everything and left.

'The scariest part of the hurricane was when I was lying down on the bed and when I looked up and saw the sky – that was the scariest part... I felt as if everything was gone, everything was lost, because knowing that the roof is gone, you don't know what next. So I am not comfortable because I don't know what's going to happen next... I think that was a nightmare. It was hard to recover, because I had to spend about a month with my mother, before the things could dry properly. And I had to start all over again.'

In the Philippines, typhoons are growing in intensity year by year and there is evidence that this is as a result of climate change. They are destroying infrastructure, crops and people's lives. Towards the end of 2006, one devastating super-typhoon roared through the central Philippines, leaving around 1,000 people dead, many of them buried under gigantic mudslides. Super-typhoon Bopha struck New Bataan in December 2012, killing over 1,000 people, destroying 216,000 homes and leaving tens of thousands of coconut trees and the region's entire banana crop in ruins – and with it the livelihoods of hundreds of farmers. Bopha was significantly more powerful than Hurricane Sandy, which hit the USA in 2005, but received a fraction of the news coverage.[26] The effects of these weather extremes are exacerbated by the country's denuded hillsides. After sixty years of indiscriminate logging, more than 80 per cent of Philippine forests are gone, most being irreplaceable rainforest. Without trees the thin topsoil washes away, leaving nothing for subsistence farmers or for coastal fishermen, whose catch is displaced by the soil washed into the sea. The Philippines has a low ability to cope with such disasters. Greenpeace mapped out nine tragedies from 1991 to 2006 triggered by extreme weather events. These events have one thing in common – persistent torrential rains, causing landslides and flash floods, killing people and destroying properties and the environment.

'One of the biggest challenges we are facing in our development work is increasing occurrence of natural disaster. What we have achieved over many years is being destroyed by storms and washed away by floods.'
Kim Rattana, Caritas Cambodia

The government of the Philippines recognises the threat posed by climate change, especially along the eastern seaboard. Yet, at the same time as developing disaster-preparedness programmes, the government, pressed by international institutions to pay its debts, is also pursuing so called 'national development' policies that make future disasters more likely. For instance, in the 1990s, the World Bank and the Asian Development Bank successfully pressed the Philippines to liberalise its legal framework and facilitate a massive expansion of mining in the country, financed by foreign direct investment. This was despite strong opposition from the churches, civil society groups, indigenous peoples and even local government. Numerous large-scale mining operations are under development, many of which will practise open-pit mining, which causes extensive deforestation in vulnerable watersheds and will generate millions of tonnes of waste and toxic materials. Mine-tailings ponds in the Philippines are notoriously susceptible to leakage and collapse during storms. Since 1980 at least nineteen major incidents have had huge impacts on the poor, and in some cases have caused serious loss of life. For example, a direct hit to the Australian-owned Lafayette mine on RapuRapu Island by a devastating and unseasonal super-typhoon in November 2006 caused extensive damage. Despite this, major mining companies, including Anglo American and BHP Billiton, are pressing ahead with large-scale mining plans, some on the eastern seaboard.

Vietnam, which has a long coastline facing the South China Sea, is frequently hit by typhoons and tropical storms. At least eighteen people were killed there in November 2005 when typhoon Kai Tak hit. The rains also destroyed thousands of hectares of farmland in ten provinces and disrupted transport, submerging a section of the north–south railway. Kai Tak was the eighth typhoon to hit Vietnam that year.

Tropical storm Bilis hits China

In July 2006, tropical storm Bilis combined with warm moist air flows from south-west China to batter southern China with strong rainfall, causing severe floods, landslides and mud flows. Nearly 32 million people from six different provinces and autonomous regions were affected. Some 843 people died and 3.4 million people were urgently relocated. Over 1,337,000 hectares of crops were damaged, and 263,000 hectares of crops were not harvested at all. Some 391,000 houses collapsed and a further 471,000 were damaged. The direct costs of the disaster reached almost 35 billion yuan.

The frequency of cyclone formation in the Bay of Bengal has declined since 1970 but the intensity of the cyclones formed here and hitting Bangladesh and India is increasing.[27] This is because the temperature of the Indian Ocean is rising, causing higher levels of moisture in the atmosphere, which increases the strength of storms. The people living around the Bay of Bengal are used to cyclones. Bangladesh, for example, has good early-warning systems and cyclone shelters along the coast. These have reduced the loss of life, but houses, infrastructure and livelihoods are still shattered every time a cyclone strikes.

Shelter from the storm: cyclone protection in Bangladesh

In May 1997, a ferocious cyclone hit the Cox's Bazar region in south-east Bangladesh. The cyclone brought winds of 150 miles an hour and lasted for over ten hours, leaving a million and a half homeless, though only 100 dead. It was more ferocious than the one in 1991, when 140,000 were killed, yet the death toll was small by comparison. This was partly because the cyclone struck during daylight and at low tide. However, new cyclone shelters and people trained to alert their community to the impending dangers were also key factors in saving lives.

The Christian Commission for Bangladesh, Gonoshasthaya Kendra, and other NGOs supported by Christian Aid had built a number of cyclone shelters, mostly on stilts. Used as community centres or schools in normal times, when the cyclone struck they provided refuge for the whole community. The low-lying island of Moheshkhali was one of the areas worst hit by the cyclone. Most villagers were left homeless, but on account of the cyclone shelter all survived.

Other programmes to protect against cyclones and flooding include building embankments and raising homesteads and community land. Local organisations are supporting villagers with 'cash-for-work' programmes where earth is moved to build up platforms, to rebuild homes, school playgrounds or other communal areas at a higher level, or so that large groups of people can take refuge.

Coastal fishermen in Bangladesh

Coastal fishermen in Bangladesh are particularly vulnerable to environment-related disasters. Fishermen earn their living from fishing in rivers, estuaries and littoral waters. Of all the open-water fish species, hilsa is the most important, being a major contributor to the livelihoods of coastal fishermen and the nation as a whole. Coastal fishermen contribute 22–25 per cent of the total fish production in the country, but unfortunately they are often the first victims of disasters. During every cyclone or tidal surge, hundreds of fishermen die, and others are driven away to other areas.

On 19 September 2006, a sudden tornado hit the south-western coast of Bangladesh. It caused some 500 fishing boats and trawlers to capsise or go missing. Then on 19 October a violent storm saw some 3,500 fishermen go missing in the rough seas. Several hundred trawlers capsised, but rescuers recovered only 162 bodies. Winds lashed the coastal districts, damaging over a thousand houses.

Coastal communities are poorer than average. They have lower-than-average incomes and calorie intake. In coastal areas, absolute and extreme poverty are higher than in non-coastal areas. Current coping methods include borrowing from local moneylenders, selling labour in advance for fishing or agricultural work, selling fishing gear, sending children to work in urban areas, and selling livestock, land and houses. Climate change will increase this vulnerability and stretch existing coping strategies to the limit.

'I have never seen such high-speed winds ... [the] frequency of depression at the Bay of Bengal is much higher nowadays. We have been experiencing delayed monsoons every year over the last 12–15 years.'

Anil Kr Khara, Bamankhali of Sagar Island, India

Hurricanes, cyclones and storms are on the increase in the Pacific region.[28] In spite of scientific uncertainty on individual cases, there is broad consensus that global warming is likely to increase the intensity of these events. Deaths from weather-related disasters have already increased in the Pacific island region by 21 per cent since the mid-1970s. Cyclone wind speeds could increase by 10–20 per cent over the next few years, and tropical storms are likely to increase in strength and frequency.[29] The World Bank predicts that Fiji could experience a 100 per cent increase in cyclone damage due to climate change in the coming years.[30]

With more disasters related to global warming seeming inevitable, how the international community responds to them will be vital. And following on from immediate response, intelligent recovery from disaster is an important strategy to reduce vulnerability the next time a flood or drought strikes.

'We live in constant fear of the adverse impacts of climate change. For a coral atoll nation, sea-level rise and more severe weather events loom as a growing threat to our entire population. The threat is real and serious, and is of no difference to a slow and insidious form of terrorism against us.'

Saufatu Sopoanga, prime minister of Tuvalu, September 2003

Recovering from disasters

Recovery for whom, or of what, is the question that hangs over any effort towards post-disaster reconstruction. What is the end in mind when an economic reconstruction plan is being designed? Is it targeted towards creating maximum resilience and sustainable livelihoods in the disaster-affected area? Or is its prime aim re-gearing economic infrastructure to meet more abstract economic targets? Being clear about objectives makes it more likely that appropriate strategies will be found.

Post-disaster economic reconstruction will only work if it takes an integrated approach respecting the dynamics of communities' economic, political and cultural lives, and how these interact with the natural environment. It is more important to ask people what they need to recover their daily lives than to rush in foreign contractors to rebuild risks in the familiar shape of major engineering works. Resilient, inclusive and democratic local economies are the best inoculation against the multiple risks wrought by disasters.

Post-disaster economic recovery could include initiatives to:

- *Plan for climate change.* Low-carbon development strategies are needed everywhere to minimise the increasingly hostile greenhouse effect. Risk-reduction strategies must be built into disaster recovery plans. The impacts of globalisation, in terms of trade and financial flows, as well as climate change, are draining the resources needed to deal with disasters in the least developed countries, so these risks must be reduced.
- *Forge sustainable livelihoods* by rebuilding diverse local economies to meet local needs. This is the foundation for human recovery. People's livelihoods are as important as physical defence structures.
- *Diversify local economies* because these are best at maximising employment and respecting economic, social and environmental priorities. They are also more disaster-resilient than agricultural or industrial monocultures. Maximising contributions to the small business sector can help with this. Use grants and micro-credit schemes to increase support to these small businesses and co-operative enterprises.

- *Create employment*, not just wage labour, to maximise long-term secure work, self-help and self-employment. Prioritise secure local employment as an immediate need and ensure that the particular employment needs of women are addressed, such as day care for children.
- *Plug spending leaks* by maximising local procurement to ensure that post-disaster resources recirculate within the local economy, rather than leaking out of it. This will boost short- and longer-term economic recovery. Aid interventions must not undermine incentives for local production or distort markets by undercutting local producers.
- *Improve access to resources for the poorest*, such as micro-credit, land, livestock and farm inputs. This will not necessarily be solved by more foreign direct investment, which – because of higher than usual demands for returns – can drain resources from poor, high-risk economies.
- *Strengthen democracy* to improve recovery planning and efficiency through: stakeholder councils, citizens' juries, and local small business alliances for participatory planning from the pre-disaster phase through to relief and reconstruction.
- *Focus on community disaster resilience* as the primary economic goal of reconstruction rather than export-oriented production. Beware of the economic and environmental vulnerability linked to dependence on a few cash crops. Focusing only on export crops can displace local, community-serving activities.
- *Create new resource-raising mechanisms*: more grant finance, not tied aid, from rich countries; deeper debt relief; and legal compensation for the effects of climate change are needed to compensate low-fossil-fuel-consuming countries for the ecological debt of industrialised nations.
- *Safeguard natural resources that buffer the elements*. Prioritise conservation efforts to protect natural buffers against climate-related disasters – for example, mangroves, forests, coral reefs

and natural river deltas. Minimise the environmental impacts of any post-disaster economic recovery activity that could undermine these natural resources.

Plugging the leaks to ensure that post-disaster resources recirculate within the local economy[31]

'LEAKS' FROM LOCAL ECONOMY	'PLUGS' TO STOP THE LEAKS
Aid staff use foreign-owned hotels and services	Ensure staff localise spending on services
Payments to foreign consultants and contractors	Support local NGOs and businesses
Purchase of foreign reconstruction materials and agricultural/medical inputs	Localise purchase of recovery materials and inputs
Crop and business losses	Introduce disaster insurance against crop and business losses
Profiteering and corruption	Work with governments, NGOs and communities to stop corruption
Market share lost to competitors during economic recovery	Provide small enterprises with flexible credit during recovery period
Long-term development aid redirected to disaster response	Ensure fresh funds for disaster recovery
Long-term commodity price decline	Commodity price support for primary commodity-dependent regions
Higher risk-related returns expected on investment	Ensure 'investment measures' are not undermined
Post-disaster flight of capital	Introduce controls in high-risk areas to prevent destabilising capital flight
Costs of flying aid in rather than procuring locally	Establish targets for local procurement
Local initiative and ownership of recovery undermined by donor-driven aid	Rebuild social economy through community-designed reconstruction

Lifting people out of poverty is the best way to reduce the number of people who have to be lifted out of mud, floodwaters or drought when disasters strike. Investment in local-level economic recovery is better at creating disaster-resilient communities than investment in dams, dykes and concrete.

Much can be learnt from the experience of places highly vulnerable to climate-driven disasters such as low-lying, small island states. Understanding of how to reduce the impact of disasters is particularly advanced in the South Pacific region. Research there identified several factors as enhancing community ability to recover from 'natural' disasters. They include strong, extended family structures, strong local government, and building on traditional approaches to housing and farming. Economic diversity and financial mechanisms to spread losses were also vital (e.g. insurance, disaster funds and community trust funds). A dynamic civil society is important, along with good transport, communications, sanitation, good education and health services, coupled with disaster preparedness and emergency services.[32]

Conversely, the loss of such social and economic fabric hampers post-disaster recovery. A narrow economic base, over-exploitation of natural resources and loss of diversity provide the weakest foundations for recovery.

Renewing rural livelihoods in Mozambique

Despite civil war, major floods and drought, Mozambique has emerged in the twenty-first century as a country of progress and possibilities – a flagship of renewal in Africa. The community of Nwadjahane in Gaza province in southern Mozambique was established in the 1980s following displacement from surrounding areas during the civil war. Over the years, villagers have had to live with political and economic instability, drought, and major flood and storm damage.

Research funded by Oxfam and others on how rural people have adapted to these disturbances revealed that villagers have developed creative and innovative ways of coping and adapting to this uncertainty and change. One fundamental shift is from paying people with cash in exchange for help with tasks on the farm to 'traditional' forms of non-cash bartering, such as exchanging labour. Villagers explain that this is due to the combined drivers of less cash within the local economy, due to fewer crop sales as a result of droughts, floods and storms, and the need for more labour to repair farm infrastructure or replant crops damaged by weather-related disturbances. Social networks have long been important in this area; a positive outcome from this shift is an increased sense of solidarity with neighbours.

The emergency, or 'humanitarian', system must be overhauled, so that it is truly able to deliver prompt, effective assistance on the basis of need. More efficient systems are needed to ensure that this aid is released quickly and that it is well targeted when disasters strike. In particular, it must support people's livelihoods as well as meeting the immediate needs of the hungry. The current stop–start approach must give way to longer-term support to address the underlying causes of food insecurity, including through social protection programmes and through governments, backed by reliable funding. Moreover, the type of aid is still often inappropriate. In 2008 only 33 per cent of global food aid was procured from developing countries.[33] It is not right that the remaining 67 per cent of food aid is still the produce of the developed world: food aid should not be a means of supporting farmers in developed countries. When hunger is caused by lack of access to food as a result of poverty rather than food shortages, the provision of cash can be a more appropriate, faster and less expensive option.

Reducing disaster risks

For over forty years, emergency aid, and food aid in particular, has remained the chief instrument to address food crises. Food aid does save lives, but it does not offer long-term solutions, and at worst it may exacerbate food insecurity. The average number of food emergencies in Africa per year almost tripled from the mid-1980s to 2006, for example,[34] implying that more effort should be spent on preventing disasters in the first place rather than responding to them when they arrive.

Helping vulnerable communities to reduce the risks from climate-related disasters is crucial to positive development, a point acknowledged by poorer countries for many years. Mozambique's Action Plan for the Reduction of Absolute Poverty 2001–2005 stated: 'Natural disasters ... constitute an obstacle to a definitive break with certain degrees and patterns of poverty. Therefore, measures aimed at managing these risks are of the utmost importance.'

In Britain, other European nations and the USA, millions of pounds are invested in reducing the risks associated with floods, earthquakes and droughts. Yet very little of international aid budgets gets spent on helping poor communities to do the same. To illustrate this, six months before the Mozambique flood disaster, the government appealed to the international community for US$2.7 million to prepare for the impending crisis. It received less than half this amount. After the floods came, Mozambique received US$100 million in emergency assistance and a further US$450 million was pledged for rehabilitation.

There is a long history of aid money being used to bandage the wounds rather than prevent the injuries, with the international community concentrating much of its efforts on disaster response. Thousands of lives could be saved each year and economic losses prevented if more emphasis was placed on reducing disaster risks. It can also be highly cost-effective. It has been estimated that for every US$1 spent on preparing for disaster in developing countries, a further US$7 is saved in the cost of recovering from it.[35] For example, in Mozambique a well coordinated community-based early warning system was put in place after the devastating floods in 2000. When another flood occurred a year later, the impact was significantly reduced. As a senior programme officer with UNICEF observed, 'In light of increasingly fragile social, political, economic and natural environments, the longer we delay in addressing risk reduction and preparedness, the greater the impact, scale and cost of emergencies.'

Yet, despite the clear rationale, donor organisations tend to approach disaster risk reduction on an ad hoc basis, normally as a reaction to a major disaster, rather than systematically integrating it into their development planning and programming. This was the conclusion of extensive research on donor policy towards risk reduction conducted by Tearfund in 2003.[36] Much progress needs to be made in donor organisations in terms of understanding, owning and prioritising risk reduction as an integral component of their development work.

Many governments also ignore disaster risk reduction despite the resulting high costs in human and economic terms. People are vulnerable due to the poor design of risk-reduction measures stemming from weak and ineffective state institutions, corruption, lack of transparency and political will, and international structures that create poverty and vulnerability. Their vulnerability is itself a failure of governance. ActionAid has identified eight key policies for governments to promote people-centred disaster risk-reduction:

- *Participation*   In order for development policies to adequately meet the needs of the poor and the excluded, governments need to find ways of ensuring that vulnerable people participate in accountability and decision-making processes.
- *Accountability*   Governments must be held accountable for the promises they make and the policies they either do, or do not, implement.
- *Decentralisation*   Strengthening local government helps to ensure that decision-making is appropriate and enhances government accountability.

- *Freedom of and access to information* People need to have access to adequate information on policies, rights and important government decisions to ensure participation in disaster reduction.
- *Legally enforceable obligations* Government policies and their obligation to protect citizens need to be legally enforceable; without this governments can evade responsibility.
- *Access to justice* Justice for all, based on appropriate legislative frameworks, is essential to protect people, especially the most marginalised and vulnerable.
- *National coordination and cooperation* For disaster reduction to be effective there is a need for national level cooperation between the many different organisations and institutions involved.
- *International cooperation and coordination* Because disasters do not respect international boundaries, agreements ensuring transnational accountability are important to promote safety across borders.

The best approach to reducing disaster risks is a systematic one, which becomes mainstreamed into relief and development planning. This protects programmes from being undermined by future hazards, and ensures that projects do not inadvertently increase vulnerability. As the United Kingdom's Department for International Development observes: effective integration of disaster risk reduction into development 'has the capacity to transform "vicious spirals" of failed development, risk accumulation and disaster losses into "virtuous spirals" of development, risk reduction and effective disaster response.' Gains include a wide range of positive impacts on progress towards the Millennium Development Goals.[37]

Reducing vulnerability to today's climate through disaster risk reduction is also an excellent way to build capacity to cope with the future uncertainties of global warming. Examples of such risk-reduction measures include participatory vulnerability assessments, rainwater harvesting, grain banks, designing and improving evacuation routes and sites, early warning systems for famine and flood, protecting community buildings in flood-prone areas, improved sanitation and access to clean water in poor areas, community disaster preparedness training and better coastal zone management, especially recognising the potential that mangroves and wetlands have to play in reducing flood damage. Such measures are highly effective at saving lives and livelihoods in vulnerable regions around the world. Importantly, many of these risk-reduction measures are low cost and relatively simple to implement.

Preparing for the flood in North India

Since 2002, Tearfund local partner organisation Discipleship Centre (DC) has been working with five villages in Bihar, North India, to reduce their vulnerability to flooding. The villages are poor and geographically isolated. Government aid programmes do not reach them. For three months of every year, they are subject to monsoon floods which destroy lives, livestock, houses and property.

Before DC's programme began, the people had no safe route out of the five villages to escape rising flood waters. With no unity within or between villages, everyone looked after themselves, rescuing possessions, livestock and people in a haphazard, disorganised manner. Boats for rescue purposes had to be hired from local landlords, or banana stems were floated on the water as makeshift rafts. The floodwaters submerged and clogged hand pumps so that the villagers had no safe drinking water. Flood-related diseases were common.

DC mobilised each village to form a Village Development Committee and four teams of volunteers who were trained in flood preparedness. The committees oversee the teams, which are responsible for early warning and evacuation, boat management, resource mobilisation and care of the vulnerable. The teams meet regularly to learn first aid and practise evacuation procedures.

DC mobilised the village communities to build raised embankments to connect the villages to each other and to the main road, providing an escape route during the flood season. Culverts were built to reduce water pressure, and tube wells with raised hand pumps were constructed to guarantee safe drinking water when flood levels rise.

These measures have proved effective in saving lives and property. The monsoon floods in 2003 were severe, but no lives were lost to drowning or flood-related illness, and very few livestock perished. The villagers frequently comment on the difference the measures have made: 'In the past we all used to dread the flooding season ... because we did not know if we would survive. Now we have peace because all the people know they can save themselves.' With a small amount of outside assistance, the villagers are now better able to cope with the floods they have lived with all their lives. As one villager commented, 'we could have done this fifty years ago but no one showed us how.'

The project has had other unexpected benefits. The rescue boats are generating income from being hired out for other purposes, and the raised embankment is providing a valuable connection to the main road for trading. The villagers have learnt the value of community cooperation – they are collecting money for a school – and have developed confidence and leadership skills.

Disaster-resistant housing in Bangladesh and the Philippines

Floods are a normal part of life in much of Bangladesh, and likewise typhoons in the Philippines. Various traditional housing techniques are used to cope with them. Practical Action has worked with communities regularly affected by monsoon floods to develop designs for more disaster-resistant houses. These use available low-cost materials and local skills, and build on local knowledge. The approach could readily be applied in other countries affected by floods and storms, like Mozambique. Success depends on collaboration between local masons and carpenters and outside experts.

Poorer people cannot afford more water-resistant materials like corrugated metal, and thatched roofs, walls of woven grass or palm and bamboo have to suffice. But innovative methods can be applied, building on these traditional approaches. Improved attics were used as living and storage spaces during floods as a result of community contributions on how to improve housing design. Weaving and joining bamboo and timber to form joists, results in a building that can withstand typhoon-force winds due to its very flexibility. Where the floodwater level is not normally too far above the normal water level, houses can be built on raised earthen platforms. Planting water-resistant plants and trees such as bamboo and banana next to homesteads helps to protect the houses from erosion.

Food, household items and crops can be stored on a platform in the main living room. Structures that use woven walls can also be designed to be dismantled in the event of a severe flood forecast, and moved for re-erection on a new site or restoration after floodwaters subside.

Lessons from the 2004 Indian Ocean tsunami

The tsunami of 26 December 2004 was the result of an earthquake, not global warming, but the lessons emerging about managing disasters apply equally to a warming world. Many of the places worst hit in Asia had been developed for fish farming and tourism. In both cases, development required the destruction of natural vegetation and often resulted in the destruction of coral reefs through overfishing or intensive use of motorised boats.

Tropical mangroves are among the world's most important ecosystems, providing a variety of goods and services to coastal communities and protecting inland areas from violent storms and tidal waves. They stabilise sediments, reduce shoreline and riverbank erosion, regulate flooding and recycle nutrients. The government of Kerala state, observing that the tsunami left less destruction in Indian regions protected by mangroves than on barren and exposed beaches, has already started protecting coasts with mangroves. Mangroves also provide key nursery areas for many commercial fish species. Each acre of mangrove forest destroyed results in an estimated 300 kilogram annual loss in marine harvest.

Despite these multiple benefits, in Southeast Asia shrimp farming that displaces the mangroves has been encouraged, aided by World Bank loans. The industry is eating away at more than half of the world's mangroves. What is being projected as an indicator of spectacular economic growth hides the enormous environmental, and ultimately human and economic, costs that countries like Indonesia have suffered.

Myanmar and the Maldives suffered very much less from the impact of the tsunami because the tourism industry had not spread to the coastal mangroves and coral reefs. The large coral reef surrounding the Maldives absorbed much of the tidal fury, thereby restricting human losses to a little over 100 dead. Mangroves also help to protect offshore coral reefs by filtering out the silt flowing seawards from the land.

The epicentre of the tsunami was close to Simeulue Island, in Indonesia. The death toll on this particular island was significantly lower than elsewhere simply because the inhabitants fled to higher ground in time, knowing that a tsunami invariably followed an earthquake. The low death toll and minimal damage to the island was also attributed to the surrounding protective belt of mangroves, which had not yet been destroyed.

The challenge, therefore, is for relief and disaster prevention activities to work with local communities that have perfected time-tested approaches to sustainable management of coastal areas. Fisherfolk often have the expertise to be the primary managers of the health of the coastline and to rehabilitate fisheries. When given the opportunity, they manage the shoreline, mangroves and coastal fishing zones – the source of most of the aquatic diversity and health of the oceans. Working with such fisherfolk, supporting their organisations and using their expertise will help restore their livelihoods, re-equip them for sustainable artisanal fishing, and, in the long term, rehabilitate the coastline and marine fisheries to protect them from future storms and floods likely to occur as a result of climate change.

Disaster preparation in Peruvian schools and communities

Political and economic factors determine that people in poverty also live in areas at high risk of the impacts of climate change. Practical Action works in Latin America to develop training for local communities and organisations where the effect of government centralisation has been to weaken local ability to prepare for, and respond to, disasters. The region is prone to earthquakes, and also to landslides and floods caused by the El Niño phenomenon. Following training, the Ministry of Education built disaster risk reduction into the school curriculum. A regional network has developed a detailed database of local disasters, enabling changing patterns to be tracked.

Project benefits include a transformation in local confidence and the ability to understand the situation. Through drama performances, 17-year-old Lucia felt that she was able to influence her audience. Her relationship with her parents improved because they could see she had learned useful skills and they consequently allowed her more freedom to attend meetings. She spoke about how people now understand that disasters often have human causes and are not merely acts of God. One mayor involved said that before the project, people did not know about the National Civil Defence System, which coordinates disaster preparedness and response. The project also reached out to women and children for the first time. People now understand what to do in an emergency. They know where to go to for safety.

How video helped people in 'the big ditch'

In April 2004 the Argentinean shanty town outside Buenos Aires, El Zanjón (literally 'The Big Ditch') flooded again. Three days later, with mattresses still drying outdoors, two film-makers, Fabio Benavídez and Andrea Santoro, captured local people coming to terms with the twin problems of flooding and climate change. The resulting short film of their meeting shows the community exploring its options for the future. 'You never know when the river will rise', says one individual. 'We wake up with water up to our neck', says another.

Researcher Pablo Suarez from Boston University is unsettled to hear such words from a community flooded on average three times a year. 'Our scientific models have been predicting short-term floods in the Río de la Plata with sufficient lead time and accuracy. We do know when the river will rise', says Suarez. 'The problem is that they, the ones who suffer the floods, do not.' Inequities in access to information remain a fundamental challenge. The most vulnerable people rarely benefit from climate forecasts. Either the information does not reach them or they have insufficient knowledge, resources or power to respond adequately.

During a workshop in El Zanjón, and armed with knowledge that their floods were predictable and likely to become more frequent due to climate change, the community decided to act. They asked for the film to be aired on the local television channel to raise awareness. They organised an advocacy campaign targeting the municipal government. They proposed a simple early warning system using whistles. As a result, a telephone line was provided, and now the port authority calls a local leader when a flood is imminent, triggering evacuation and other disaster-response strategies.

During a similar workshop in the Limpopo river flood plain in Mozambique, the short film from El Zanjón was shown to subsistence farmers (under a tree, using a laptop), revealing the potential of film as a universal language. One of the women farmers remarked, 'I thought that all these recent droughts and floods were sent by God or our ancestors as punishment, and there's nothing one can do to prevent that punishment. But now in the film I see that white women in distant places are suffering just like us. If the climate is changing everywhere, then we should do something about it – we can.'

A simple video from an urban shanty town in Latin America had helped an African rural community to change its understanding of the climate problem, and to seek solutions. Advances in digital technology create new opportunities to use video to help vulnerable communities cope with climate change, particularly in Latin America where common languages allow successful pilot projects for raising awareness to be scaled up.

Disasters, environment and livelihoods in Qingshuiling village

Qingshuiling village in Gansu province, China, is built on arid mountainous land. Severe soil erosion in the area has reduced the fertility of land and has exacerbated the impacts of extreme events like droughts and floods. Village farmland produces poor yields of wheat and corn. The average annual income of villagers is low at around 300 yuan. The villagers cannot afford to buy coal because they are poor, relying instead on gathering wood from the mountain for heating and cooking. Local vegetation is therefore disappearing and the ecosystem is deteriorating. A vicious circle is formed in which poverty leads to ecosystem deterioration, which in turn increases poverty, because with a damaged ecosystem the area and its people are more vulnerable to extreme events like storms and heavy rain.

Oxfam Hong Kong, recognising that disasters, environmental protection and livelihoods are closely linked, conducted an ecological project in Qingshuiling village to explore ways to harmonise the relationship between the three. The project helped solve many problems. Those related to securing farmland fertiliser, livelihoods and equality have been alleviated by raising cattle. Solar cookers have helped solve the problem of finding fuel, and planting clover has helped solve issues relating to water and soil erosion, as well as providing fodder for cattle. The project has also helped villagers build a rain-collection vault for drinking water.

Living with the threat of landslides in the Philippines

The town of Infanta sits at the foot of the Sierra Madre mountain range in the south-eastern part of Luzon Island in the Philippines. It is a major gateway for typhoons entering the Philippines from the Pacific. During the onslaught of four consecutive typhoons in late November 2004, deforestation of the Sierra Madre caused a flow of debris (a deadly mixture of heavy logs, water, soil, rocks and vegetation) that literally buried the towns of Nakar, Infanta and Real in the island's Quezon province.

The landslides occurred largely as a result of excessive rainfall on mountains whose vegetative cover had been severely depleted by logging activities, shifting cultivation and charcoal manufacture. The loose soil structure and steep slopes exacerbated conditions. Growing populations and increasing amounts of land conversion also played a role. Forests continue to be logged despite a government-imposed logging ban, and reforestation efforts just cannot keep up with rampant deforestation rates.

The Sub-Regional Social Action Center of the Catholic Church in Infanta, Quezon province (SAC–Infanta) has started a project to conserve and encourage sustainable use of biodiversity as a means of protecting communities from harsh climatic events. The project promotes diversified sustainable agricultural practices in the lowlands and reforestation and agro-forestry in the uplands. These activities provide the population, particularly the poor, with food, fibre, medicines, building materials, bio-energy and water for households and agriculture. The interventions also secure the mountain slopes, thus reducing the impact of disasters.

SAC–Infanta has also worked to create stronger community coherence. Neighbourhood church-based community groups participate in and strengthen local government disaster-coordinating councils. With help from the state agricultural university, they are experimenting with new soil types to cover land following a landslide. Adapted agricultural technologies are now being practised and new cash crops are providing sustainable sources of income. Integrated farming methods incorporate livestock production and reforestation using income-adding fruit trees and biofuel-producing trees to diversify household livelihoods. SAC–Infanta provides marketing support and access to capital.

There are two responses to danger: fight or flight. With no other place to call home, the communities of Infanta chose to stay put and nurture the goodness that the earth of Infanta has yet to offer.

Community-based flood preparedness in Pakistan

In certain flood- and drought-prone areas of southern Punjab, Pakistan, Oxfam has been running a project on sustainable livelihoods. The project concentrates on the impact that climate-induced changes will have on livelihoods unless effective disaster risk reduction and adaptation measures are taken. Activities to reduce vulnerability to floods and help people to respond actively to flood threats under a community-based flood preparedness programme include:

- Using participatory approaches to mobilise whole communities to form community-based organisations.
- Building community awareness, especially among schoolchildren.
- Networking with government and forming local community forums to raise awareness about disaster risk reduction.
- Small-scale disaster mitigation works, such as building emergency shelters and raising homesteads, and community-based early warning systems, such as forming and training early-warning committees.
- Training in social forestry techniques and soil and water testing.

During the summer of 2006, the early-warning committees in the villages of the Mizafargarh district in south Punjab got timely information about the arrival of floods, giving the communities an opportunity to take proactive action. Community members built a protection bund (embankment) around their villages. The bund was 22 kilometres in length and stretched to five villages. Community members from all five villages built it collectively. The 2006 flood level was higher than the 2005 flood but the timely building of the bund resulted in smaller losses to agricultural land compared to the previous year. In 2005, in the absence of timely access to information through their early-warning committees, people had panicked and run for safer places without protecting their crops and houses. This initiative is a classic example of how community-based early-warning systems can effectively allow communities to take collective action independently of 'outside assistance' to protect their lives and livelihood sources.

Reducing disaster risk in Bangladesh

The Christian Commission for Development in Bangladesh has considerable experience of managing disasters in Bangladesh. It has been working on the island of Moheshkhali to construct several cyclone shelters in response to the inhabitants of Thakurtala village reporting an increase in cyclone occurrence. The Commission has also been working to build community awareness, raise up public places, plant trees and provide relief. It has trained groups of volunteers to help their communities before, during and after disasters. A more recent collaboration between the Commission and the Building Disaster Resilient Communities project – a Christian Aid initiative on climate change adaptation – means the Commission will work with Moheshkhali inhabitants to increase their resilience to growing climate change threats.

Hurricane Wilma struck Cuba in October 2005, leading to the evacuation of 640,000 people, but with little loss of life. When New Orleans was inundated during and after Hurricane Katrina over 1,800 lives were lost. In six major hurricanes that ran over Cuba between 1996 and 2002, only sixteen lives were lost. Wilma took just one of these lives, despite the sea coming 1 kilometre inland and flooding Havana, Cuba's capital city. What is it that a wealthy superpower is doing wrong that a poor country, subject to a long-standing and tight economic embargo from the United States, is doing right? The difference would appear to be efficient organisation and a commitment to social development. Cuba has tangible assets that are like the moving parts of a machine. These include a strong, well-organised civil defence system, an efficient early warning system, well-equipped rescue teams and emergency stockpiles and other resources. But its intangible assets are more important; these are like the oil in the machine that enables it to function properly. They include effective local leadership, community mobilisation, solidarity and a population that is 'disaster aware' and educated in what actions to take, and local participation in evacuation planning. At the heart of the system is a clear political commitment, at every level of government, to safeguard human life. This creates a centralised decision-making process alongside a decentralised implementation process, both being equally necessary for effective emergency preparedness and response.

The Cuban population has developed a culture of safety. Many ordinary people see themselves as actors with important roles to play in disaster preparation and response. 'Any child in school can give you an explanation – how you prepare, what you do. Students, they know what to do, they know the phases [the four emergency phases – information, alert, alarm and recovery], what to do in each phase ... how to gather things in the house and put them away ... shut off the water and electricity. All students, workers and campesinos get this training', explains Mr José Castro, who works for Civil Defence in Cienfuegos. Once a year, at the end of May, the whole country participates in a two-day training exercise in risk reduction for hurricanes. The purpose is to refresh everyone's memory of their role and to familiarise themselves with any changes introduced since the previous year. The first day consists of simulation exercises. The second day is spent in concrete preparatory actions: identifying vulnerable residents, cutting down tree branches which might fall on houses, checking reservoir walls or dams, cleaning wells, identifying places to evacuate animals to and so forth.

Early warnings on the radio

Idalma crossed the bridge at full speed before the hurricane knocked it down. When she arrived at Radio Sandino in Pinar del Río, Cuba, she noticed that the revolving equipment they had to measure wind speeds of up to 50 kilometres per hour was broken by the force of Hurricane Wilma. Remarkably, the hurricane did not lead to any immediate fatalities because warnings were given by radio.

Idalma is one of the journalists who received training from the Proyecto de Ciudadanía Ambiental, which works through community radios in seven Latin American countries. It promotes awareness of global environmental problems and action on climate change, the ozone layer, water and biodiversity. Millions in Mexico, Cuba, Costa Rica, Ecuador, Peru, Chile and Argentina listen to the programmes. Many listeners say they are now aware of how climate change affects everyone. Programmes increase understanding of the environmental connections between production, transport and energy use in the home and at work. But, as well as promoting the reduction of greenhouse gas emissions, the programmes also seek to prepare people for the inevitable impacts that climate change will bring.

The radio project also has a campaign goal to persuade the state to take more responsibility for environmental issues. That means new legislation and education policies, planning in the medium and long term, local and national strategies, as well as financial resources and adequate technologies.

Hazards like hurricanes only turn into disasters – involving the large-scale loss of life and livelihoods – because of inequity, and because the poorest and most vulnerable are left to fend for themselves. In contrast, the Cuban political model is geared towards universal access to services, policies to reduce social and economic disparities, and considerable investment in human development. Is the Cuban model replicable? The Cuban one-party system, and the strong social control that comes with it, are obviously highly unusual and subject to criticism, but some positive elements of the Cuban experience could certainly be introduced elsewhere.

There is a clear political mandate to invest in disaster risk reduction. At the World Summit on Sustainable Development in 2002, all governments agreed to 'Provide financial and technical assistance to strengthen the capacities of African countries, including institutional and human capacity, including at the local level, for effective disaster management, including observation and early warning systems, assessments, prevention, preparedness, response and recovery.'[38] And yet the transformative changes needed regarding the way disasters are managed have not yet materialised. It is not necessary to wait years for more research on climate change before investing in disaster risk reduction. Governments have agreed on the need for action, and tools and methods for protecting communities from disasters are well developed. Now they need to be employed immediately in poor countries and communities on a much greater scale.

Global warming presents a huge challenge to the coherence and coordination of aid, and many donors are focusing strongly on the role of technology. But experience tells us that promoting disaster reduction at the local level by supporting community coping strategies is far more effective and yields immediate benefits that stretch beyond just tackling climate-driven disasters. The integration of disaster risk reduction in relief, reconstruction, development programming and poverty reduction plans should now be a priority. Just as we have argued that 'good development' makes for 'good adaptation' in earlier chapters, it is also clear that 'good adaptation' also makes for 'good development'.

7

The natural environment

Climate change impacts on natural biological systems and bio-diversity are potentially catastrophic. Some ecosystems will be irreversibly damaged or lost entirely. One study of plants and animals in Australia, Brazil, South Africa, Europe and Mexico, covering about 20 per cent of the world's land area, predicts that between 15 and 37 per cent of species in the study's sample regions will be 'committed to extinction' as a result of mid-range climate warming scenarios for 2050.[1] The 2005 Millennium Ecosystem Assessment estimates that 'by the end of the twenty-first century, climate change and its impacts may be the dominant direct driver of biodiversity loss and changes in ecosystem services globally.'[2]

The first known extinction due to climate change – the golden toad of Costa Rica – has already been documented.[3] With the tandem threats of, on the one hand, deforestation due to illegal logging and, on the other, pollution, much of the world's bio-diversity is unlikely to survive.

Food chains are increasingly likely to be disrupted in sudden and unexpected ways. For example, the RSPB reports that climate change has led to the warming of the North Sea by 1°c over the last twenty-five years, which has led to a drop in its levels of plankton – microscopic plants and animals upon which all higher sea life depends, directly or indirectly. Apparently, as a result of this change, populations of small fish known as sand eels – the prey for both larger fish and birds – have collapsed, as have seabird populations off northern Scotland.[4] This type of event is likely to occur more frequently, affecting both people and wildlife.

The Lower Mekong region is known as a 'biological hotspot' on account of its rich biodiversity. And yet of the national parks and wildlife sanctuaries in Thailand thirty-two are also situated in 'climate change hotspots' inasmuch as they will be severely affected by changes in average temperatures and rainfall. A 10 square kilometre area of Thailand's forests could contain up to 750 species of trees and 1,500 species of higher plants; a number greater than the total tree and plant diversity of North America.[5]

Hawksbill turtles declining in the Caribbean

Hawksbill turtles (*Eretmochelys imbricata*) are a 'keystone species' in coral reef and seagrass ecosystems, surviving on a diet of invertebrates and sponges. This means that without them, entire communities and ecosystems could be subject to irreversible changes and maybe even collapse. About 15,000 to 25,000 females nest annually worldwide, 5,000 of them in the Caribbean. Mexico is probably the most important nesting region, with between 1,900 and 4,300 nests per year. The global hawksbill population declined by over 80 per cent during the last century. Like other marine turtles, they are threatened by habitat loss due to coastal development, egg collection, damaging fishing practices, pollution and climate change.[6] Climate change effects include:

- Loss of nesting and feeding habitats due to sea level rise and coastal erosion.
- Extreme events, such as storms, which damage nesting sites, and excessive rainfall, which can flood nests.
- Increased sand temperatures, which can lead to changes in sex ratios (reducing or eliminating male turtle production) or even mortality.
- Increased ocean temperatures, leading to coral bleaching and damage to turtle feeding grounds.
- Changes in ocean currents, which can modify migration pathways and feeding patterns.

Amazonian biodiversity under threat

The Amazon Basin contains a staggering proportion of the world's biodiversity. Thousands of people support themselves by working its land and forests. It provides everything from building supplies to medicine. It contains an unknown number of species of biodiversity, including at least 40,000 plant species, 427 mammals, 1,300 birds, 378 reptiles, over 400 amphibians, 3,000 fish; furthermore, between 96,660 and 100,000 invertebrate species have been identified.[7] The Amazon river is the largest single source of freshwater run-off on earth, representing some 15 to 20 per cent of global river flow. The global climate is therefore sensitive to any changes in the Amazon's hydrological cycle and biodiversity; indeed the rainforest is commonly known as the 'lungs of the world'.

Empirical and modelled data suggest that the Amazon Basin is at particular risk from climate change effects. Projected changes of warmer temperatures and decreased precipitation during already dry months could manifest in longer and, perhaps, more severe droughts and substantial changes in seasonality. This could result is forest dieback with 3–4°c of warming. Coupled with alterations to land use, these changes could have devastating impacts, including increased erosion, degradation of freshwater systems, loss of ecologically and agriculturally valuable soils, loss of biodiversity, decreased agricultural yields, increased insect infestation and the spread of infectious diseases. Once such a 'tipping point' is reached there can be no return.[8]

For those who set little value on the natural world the damage to biological systems and loss of genetic and species diversity might seem of little concern. Does it really matter, after all, if the flowering of certain plants in spring occurs two or three days earlier than in the past? Or if a toad becomes extinct? For the world's poor, however, who depend so heavily on the natural environment for their food and livelihoods, these are disastrous developments. Poor people, especially those living in marginal environments and in areas with low agricultural productivity, are disproportionately reliant on natural resources such as timber, fish, grazing and wild medicines for their subsistence and living. As a result of this dependency, any impact that climate change has on natural systems will threaten the livelihoods, food intake and health of the population.

Fishing livelihoods suffer in Indonesia

Climate change, which has caused high tides and unusual sea temperature patterns in many parts of Indonesia, has negatively affected the income of fishermen in many islands in Maluku province in recent years. Fishermen 'have complained that they can no longer predict the right time and where to catch fish because of the different climate pattern than before', observed Laksmi Prasvita, spokeswoman for Oxfam Great Britain in Indonesia.[9]

In Africa, natural systems form the foundation of the economy of most countries, and most people's livelihoods rely on them. Africa contains about one-fifth of all known species of plants, mammals and birds, as well as one-sixth of amphibians and reptiles. Savannahs, tropical forests, coral reef marine and freshwater habitats, wetlands, and East African mountain ecosystems are all at risk.

In India an estimated 20–30 per cent of plant and animal species are likely to be at increased risk of extinction if the global average temperature rises 1.5 to 2.5°c above pre-industrial levels.[10] Critical ecosystems like deserts, grasslands, coasts and mountains are at particularly high risk. For example, a rapid-warming scenario could have a significant impact on mountain ecosystems which harbour rare and endangered plant species, including medicinal plants that have adapted to colder climates.[11] India's extensive forests, which cover around 20 per cent of its land, provide vital services for biodiversity, the supply of biomass to use as fuel, watershed management and the livelihoods of communities. Around 200,000 villages are located in or near forests. Climate change is likely to cause a shift in forest boundaries and forest dieback, with significant implications for all communities that depend on forest resources and services.[12]

With the extinction of plant species used in traditional medicines, it is expected that the change in climate will affect people's
ability to tackle illness. The World Health Organization estimates
that 80 per cent of the populations of some African and Asian
countries rely on traditional medicine for primary health care. In
many developed countries, too, there is a huge market for herbal
medicine, with annual sales reaching US$5 billion in Western
Europe in 2003–04, and US$14 billion in China in 2005.[13] Some
25 per cent of drugs in modern pharmaceuticals are still derived
from plants – more in fact if synthetic analogues built on proto-
types from plants are taken into account.[14] In Mali, traditional
medicines have declined because many medicinal plants have
been wiped out by constant drought. Tropical rainforests contain
many species that have as yet unknown value in the context of
producing new pharmaceutical products, but increasing aridity
resulting from global warming will damage these forests before
such values can be realised.

Not only do many people depend on biological systems for
their day-to-day existence; they can also be a source of significant income. Many poorer countries depend heavily on foreign
currency from their national parks and reserves. Other consequences are intangible; for example, the national flower of South
Africa, the King Protea, is likely to become extinct in the wild
due to climate change.[15]

Threats to coral reefs, with their high sensitivity to changes
in sea temperature, and their direct link to human livelihoods,
provide one of the clearest examples of how climate change
will affect biodiversity and ecosystems, and hence people's livelihoods. Coral reef bleaching, caused by increases in sea-surface
temperatures, is an important concern for many Pacific Ocean
atoll states. These reefs protect communities from extreme
weather events and coastal erosion. They also protect fish stocks,
enabling them to feed and reproduce. Tuvalu's inner reef areas

and lagoon provide much of its food, for example. While some reefs have been able to keep pace with changing sea levels, the additional stress of coral bleaching may prevent their survival.[16]

Coral reefs cooked by warming climate

Coral reefs are vital to island and coastal communities, which rely on them to support the fishing that provides their livelihoods. They are also complex and have the highest biodiversity of any marine ecosystem. They provide important services and direct economic benefits to the large and growing human populations in low-latitude coastal zones.

The natural habitat of coral reefs near the meeting between land, sea and air can be a stressful environment. Reef organisms have evolved ways to adapt and recover from such stresses. However, recent global increases in reef degradation and dieback suggest that environmental changes are exceeding coral reef coping capacity. This can lead to reefs being displaced by seaweeds and other non-reef systems. Such ecosystem shifts are already well advanced in the Caribbean region, where two of the major reef-building coral species have been devastated by disease. In the Indo-Pacific region, reefs cannot cope with repeated episodes of lethal 'bleaching'.

This crisis is almost certainly the result of pressure from both local human populations and global climatic stresses. The former includes direct destruction, coastal habitat modification, contamination, over-harvesting and increased nutrient and sediment build-ups. The latter includes rising ocean temperatures, contributing to chronic stress and disease epidemics, as well as mass coral-bleaching episodes and lower levels of calcium, which provides the building blocks of coral reefs. Increasing atmospheric carbon dioxide levels can also inhibit calcification. As with many ecosystems, it is difficult to separate the effects of global climate from local, non-climate impacts.

Predicting the future of reefs is difficult because current surface ocean chemistry and temperature conditions have almost certainly never occurred in the evolutionary history of modern coral reef systems. Other uncertainties include the extent to which human activities will continue to alter the environment, what climate change impacts we can expect to see in the future, and what the biological and ecological responses of coral reef communities will be to unprecedented future conditions. It is almost certain, however, that continued climate change in combination with continuing non-climate stresses will cause further coral reef degradation and pose a significant challenge to their global sustainability.[17]

Coping with climate change in the Mesoamerican Reef system

The Mesoamerican Reef system contains the largest barrier reef in the western hemisphere, extending approximately 1,000 kilometres along the Caribbean coasts of Mexico, Belize, Guatemala and Honduras. A wide variety of productive ecosystems are found within the region, and the culturally diverse human population is largely dependent on coastal and marine resources. Overfishing and poorly managed tourism, however, are contributing to a decline in the health and integrity of this fragile ecosystem, along with pollution, largely from farming; coral bleaching, which involves the loss of algae that coexist with the coral and provide it with much of its food, due to warmer water; and a growing variety of coral diseases. Coral reefs have been referred to as the 'canaries of the sea' due to their high sensitivity to rising temperatures and other stresses, such as the 1997 El Niño event.

Reefs in Belize experienced their first widespread coral bleaching event in 1995. This affected over half of the corals and caused an estimated 10 per cent mortality.[18] The 1998 global coral bleaching event triggered the most devastating global loss of coral reefs on record, killing as much as 50 per cent of live coral in Belize.[19] It is not yet known to what extent the reef will recover, or how long this recovery may take – if it occurs at all, given the variety of other coastal development and pollution-related threats to reefs. Thus, climate change and coral bleaching could push many reefs beyond the threshold of recovery.

The predicted rise in coral bleaching due to climate change in the Caribbean poses a major threat to valuable resources. Economic losses from damage to fishing, tourism and livelihoods dependent on the Mesoamerican Reef system could reach US$16.5 million attributable to climate change, and between US$52.5 and US$130.5 million due to the full range of causes of coral reef degradation.

Developing adaptation strategies to improve the resilience of the reefs and livelihoods based on them is crucial to helping the region survive the effects of climate change. Several organisations support the establishment of new marine protected areas, and WWF has initiated a climate-change adaptation strategy for the whole reef system to enhance its long-term viability and the role it plays in livelihoods and in the protection of coastal communities from natural disasters.[20]

Many believe that domino-like environmental effects triggered by existing levels of climate change are already under way. For example, as glaciers and ice shelves shrink, less heat is reflected back from the earth's surface. In some areas, warming leads to the death of forests, releasing more carbon into the atmosphere. Peatlands hold about a third of the carbon contained in soil worldwide and many are important biodiversity reservoirs or stopover points for migratory species; greenhouse gases are released every time they are burnt, drained or converted to cropland. And as global warming is causing the melting of frozen bogs in parts of the world such as Siberia, huge quantities of methane – a much more potent greenhouse gas than carbon dioxide – are being released, thus adding still further to the climate change problem.

Natural biological systems play a key role in helping people cope with climate change impacts. Sustainable management of these systems, and maintenance of genetic, species and ecosystem diversity, will therefore play a key role in helping them cope with future climate change impacts. But many are stretched to breaking point already and will no longer be able to provide these services in the future unless action is taken.

Many people already use natural resources and biodiversity, including genetic diversity, to help them cope with climate change impacts.[21] A larger gene pool will facilitate the emergence of genotypes that are better adapted to shifts in climatic conditions. For instance, alternative crop varieties or wild relatives of food crops that can be used to breed new varieties can often cope better with the changing temperatures, water shortages and pest infestations associated with climate change.[22] The success of agriculture in the Andes, for example, is based on plant genetic variety as well as the people themselves who have mastered appropriate agricultural practices. Some communities cultivate more than 150 distinct potato varieties. Such diversity reduces the impact of the failure of any one, providing a clear example of how conservation of biodiversity and maintenance of ecosystem integrity can help local communities cope with climate change.

Likewise, management of native antelope can offer better returns than cows and goats in dry countries such as Namibia, and could provide opportunities for farmers to adapt to increasingly dry conditions in some parts of Southern Africa in the future.[23]

Well-functioning ecosystems are also more stable and may be better able to adapt to climate change than impoverished systems. It is therefore important to try to limit all other non-climate-related stresses. Wetlands, for example, are important floodwater reservoirs. Vegetation such as hedges protects agricultural land from excessive water or wind erosion in times of heavy rainfall or drought. Vegetation on hillsides reduces erosion and the risk of landslides when rain comes in heavy bursts. Well-vegetated watersheds slow the movement of rainfall to rivers, thus reducing flood risks downstream.

Mangroves, with their impenetrable webbed roots, are well-known coastal buffers, reducing the strength of waves before they reach the shore, and protecting against high tides and cyclone damage. In addition, mangroves sequester carbon and provide a resource base for local livelihoods and income generation. The Sundarbans ('beautiful jungle' in Bengali) is the largest mangrove forest in the world, lying at the mouth of the Ganges river. Mangroves also cover around 26,650 hectares of Cambodia's 435-kilometre-long coastline, where they act as a buffer against storm and tidal surges. They have, however, been cut on a large scale for the production of charcoal, aquaculture and housing. This has increased the vulnerability of the coastal region to climate change impacts and accelerated erosion. Mangroves also protect coastal zones in Vietnam, where their destruction (due to climate change or coastal development) is accelerating coastal erosion. Privatisation of coastal lands has resulted in huge areas of mangroves being cut down for shrimp farming. More frequent and severe typhoons could exacerbate this erosion. Now many international donors and NGOs are helping coastal communities restore mangroves. In Kien Thuy, a 4-metre-high storm surge in 2005 was reduced to a 0.5-metre-high wave by the time it had passed through the restored mangroves.[24]

The real value of mangroves in Fiji

Fiji is already vulnerable to extreme climatic events such as cyclones, floods and droughts. The costs of storm surges account for a noticeable share of annual GDP. Coastal resources are the highest national priority.

Fiji generally receives over US$60 million annually in aid.[25] Between 23 and 36 per cent of this, however, is in sectors potentially affected by climate change. Aside from climate-specific projects, donors and the government have failed to make climate risks a central consideration in their development work.[26]

Coastal mangroves highlight the problem. Mangroves protect against coastal erosion and storm damage, but are themselves vulnerable to sea-level rise and need to migrate shoreward as sea level rises. Pressure from competing land uses, such as agriculture, tourism and housing, militate against mangrove conservation. But mangrove conservation is a 'no regrets' climate change adaptation option given the wide range of other benefits mangroves provide to local communities. These include their role in fisheries, reef protection, coastline stabilisation, timber supply and medicinal uses.

Mangrove cover is being lost in Fiji in part because it is significantly undervalued, which encourages clearing for development. The method typically used by the Department of Lands gives mangroves only a fraction of the value – as low as one-twentieth – assigned to them using other calculation methods that take into account the full range of ser-vices they provide. Another reason for the continued loss of mangroves in Fiji is because traditional clans, or *mataqali*, have communal claims over the physical resources and the environment, including mangroves. The government, however, has limited the amount of compensation paid for the loss of mangroves for reclamation purposes.

Mangrove conservation in Fiji will therefore require greater policy coherence between climate change and development policies – appropri-ate mangrove valuation is one such example. Coastal management plans must also prioritise mangrove conservation, requiring development to be set back from the high-water line to allow mangroves to move inland as the sea rises. To be successful, local communities need to be involved in these processes.[27]

Mangrove restoration and fisheries in Malaysia

The Penang Inshore Fishermen's Welfare Association (PIFWA) in Malaysia has been working for some twenty years to replant mangroves in areas that were cleared for development and aquaculture projects. They began by campaigning to raise public awareness of the importance of wetlands, especially mangroves. Mangrove forests serve as a spawning and breeding ground for marine life, including crabs and prawns, and they reduce coastal erosion. The forests also protect villagers from sea-level rise, strong winds and huge waves, thus safeguarding villagers' lives as well as their livelihoods. The need to restore and protect mangrove forests as well as coastal forests has intensified with the threat of climate change. According to Rousli Ibrahim, 61, an inshore fisherman for thirty-seven years, the mangrove forests in Sungai Acheh have protected villagers each time there is a storm surge or a high tide. The tsunami in 2004 demonstrated the effectiveness of mangrove forests as natural wave-breakers because they protected nearby villages from the worst of the impact.

To date, the fishermen have replanted 100,000 seedlings of Bakau kurap and Bakau minyak in seven places without the help of the authorities. PIFWA, which lends its voice to some 600 fishermen, has encouraged inshore fishermen in neighbouring states to do the same. Additional efforts to lobby the state government to protect the coastal mangrove belt have also been paying off: the Penang government has gazetted 316 hectares of mangrove forests in Balik Pulau and Byram as permanent forest reserves. The state has also drawn up guidelines to deter development, particularly aquaculture projects, which have destroyed vast areas of mangrove forests in the past. It has also identified two other places that will soon be gazetted.

Not only are well-functioning ecosystems more resilient to climate stresses but certain management practices can also promote that resilience. Agroecological practices such as cover cropping to ensure land is never bare, and integrated pest management, can make land more resilient to the erosion and run-off resulting from heavy rainfall. While scientists and policymakers work to find solutions to climate change, local farmers often possess a wealth of experience of how to cope.[28] New measures are therefore needed to ensure that greater respect is paid to the centuries of knowledge accumulated by indigenous people.

Forests

Forests play several major roles in relation to the climate. They are both biodiversity refuges and vital carbon sinks, releasing carbon dioxide into the atmosphere when cut down or burnt. Land use changes, particularly deforestation in tropical regions where forests tend to be very rich in biodiversity, are responsible for roughly 18 per cent of human-driven carbon dioxide emissions worldwide.[29] Deforestation also has devastating effects on both biodiversity and local communities. Forests produce wood fuel, a benign alternative to fossil fuels. Recent analysis suggests that intact forests and those regrowing after disturbance can sequester almost 60 per cent of global emissions from fossil fuel burning and cement production. Unfortunately, the carbon released from simultaneous deforestation reduces this figure to a net sequestration of roughly one-seventh of emissions.[30] This is still significant, however, and clearly, if left alone, forests, soils and forest products can potentially play a key role in slowing global warming in the years to come.

Worldwide, only 21 per cent of original forest cover remains intact, and 47 per cent has been lost entirely.[31] Before deforestation began on a major scale there were 6 million square miles of tropical rainforest on earth. Now only 2.6 million square miles remain.[32] Some areas have suffered more deforestation than others. Forests have virtually disappeared in twenty-five countries; eighteen have lost more than 95 per cent of their forests; and another eleven have lost 90 per cent.[33] In the Asia Pacific region, only 5 per cent of the original tropical and subtropical Indo-Burma and New Caledonia forests remain.[34] The net loss of temperate and tropical forests – which accounts for both deforestation and the offsetting effects of afforestation or natural expansion – is nearly 10 hectares per minute.[35] The World Conservation Union has calculated that about 12.5

per cent of the world's 270,000 species of plants are threatened by forest decline;[36] habitat destruction is also one of the main reasons why threatened mammal species are classified as such in 75 per cent of cases.[37]

Much rainforest is cut down to expand soya plantations. In 2006, Brazil's soy fields totalled an area about the size of Great Britain.[38] Some 97 per cent of the world's soya production is fed to the livestock industry.[39] Just a handful of agricultural commodities giants dominate not just primary agriculture but food manufacturing, transport, processing and retailing. These players extract as much value as they can along the chain, while the costs and risks often fall on those who are weakest – the farmers and labourers at the bottom. Three US-based agricultural commodities giants – Archer Daniels Midland, Bunge and Cargill – are responsible for about 60 per cent of the total financing of soya production in Brazil.[40]

Cutting down rainforests does more than fan the flames of global warming, however. It threatens biodiversity and local livelihoods. Forests contain millions of types of animals and plants, and as much as 90 per cent of the world's land-based species. About 350 million of the world's rural poor and forest-dwelling indigenous peoples also depend on forests for their home, livelihoods and energy supply.

Large-scale industrial investments in timber extraction and plantation forestry do not have a known track record of contributing to sustainable development. More usually, the lands of indigenous peoples are overrun, forests are destroyed and cultural traditions threatened. Although plantations of native trees can be designed to enhance biodiversity by encouraging the protection or restoration of natural forests, to date there is little scientific evidence that large-scale commercial logging can be conducted in primary forest in an environmentally sustainable manner and deliver development benefits to local people.

Deforestation in Brazil

Brazilian forests are the largest on the continent, and critical due to their size and influence on climate, both regionally and globally. A substantial proportion of the world's carbon emissions stems from deforestation, and the Brazilian Amazon is a prime source. Greenpeace says deforestation accounts for about three-quarters of the country's total emissions, which is enough to put the country among the top-ten largest carbon polluters in the world.[41] Despite recent drops, Amazon deforestation still occurs at a rate of 6,450 square kilometres every year – the equivalent of 2,475 football pitches per day.[42] Between August 2003 and August 2004 alone, some 27,200 square kilometres was lost – roughly equivalent to the size of Belgium. About 80 per cent of all logging in the Brazilian Amazon is illegal.[43]

As well as being bad news for the global climate, this logging has also been criticised as being against national interests. Deforestation is said to have made little contribution to raising incomes or increasing development for the local population. And even supporters of the commodity-export-oriented economic model admit that only a small percentage of the forest area so far converted is responsible for producing all the exports of beef and grains from the Amazon region.

In February 2006, an area of the Brazilian Amazon twice the size of Belgium was given greater protection by presidential decree. In a partial victory for many Amazon communities, 1.6 million hectares will be permanently protected. Another 2.8 million hectares will be used for sustainable logging concessions to prevent deforestation and ensure good forest management occurs. Development guidelines will be improved in an additional 2 million hectares of forest. But the protected areas represent less than 2 per cent of the total Brazilian Amazon. Constant threats from logging, soya plantations, biofuel developers and cattle ranchers remain.

Conflict in the Honduran forest

In 2000, Honduras submitted its first report to the United Nations Framework Convention on Climate Change, stressing that its forestry policy should focus on sustainability and abandon the present felling trend and illegal activities. Yet, over a decade on little seems to have changed. In the valley of Río Telica, Olancho, it is politics as usual. The valley, situated to the east of Tegucigalpa, is witness to an unequal battle. On one hand there are farmers who want to protect water sources, and on the other hand there are logging companies that covertly and illegally obtain permits from the State Forest Authority to fell the forest.

According to independent observers, forest sustainability, environmental impacts and local livelihoods have been ignored by officials issuing permits. Timber concessions are taking priority over water conservation and the lives of farming families. Some believe that uncontrolled logging is causing a change in atmospheric temperature and rain patterns and the disappearance of water springs across this and other basins. Farmers believe that the disappearance of twenty-six out of the forty-six sources of water in La Muralla National Park is due to uncontrolled felling.

In 2001, the UN Food and Agriculture Organisation identified the key role that Honduran forests could play in mitigating climate change,[44] and Honduras submitted a proposal to use the Clean Development Mechanism – a device under the Kyoto Protocol that allows projects in developing countries to sell 'certified emissions reductions' to developed countries that emit more than their fair share of carbon – to reinforce forest management programmes and rescue the forests from destruction. These proposals are not without their critics. For example, it is difficult to demonstrate that avoiding deforestation in one place will not lead to deforestation elsewhere. How to measure the amount of carbon sequestered is also controversial. Nevertheless the proposal identified 47,620 square kilometres of forests (42 per cent of Honduras) that could potentially absorb 233 million tonnes of carbon.[45] The sale of this carbon could make the Honduran forests self-sustaining, stop the destruction of the environment and raise the farmers' living standards. But the Honduran government did not take this opportunity, reportedly due to opposition from the logging industry. Large profits with minimal responsibilities rule the day.

Investigations have alleged that government officials acting in the interests of the loggers have created a network of corruption, destroyed the social fabric and promoted displacement of the communities of the Río Telica Valley. With few resources, the Movimiento Ambientalista de Olancho – Environmental Movement of Olancho (MAO) – has campaigned against the destruction. MAO reports that its leaders have been threatened, persecuted and even murdered.[46]

While the United Nations Framework Convention on Climate Change mentions forestry only briefly, the Kyoto Protocol deals with it explicitly. It states that industrialised countries shall undertake policies and measures such as the 'promotion of sustainable forest management practices, afforestation and reforestation' in helping to limit and reduce their greenhouse gas emissions. Under what is known is the 'Clean Development Mechanism' it also makes provision for developed countries with targets for reducing greenhouse gas emissions to buy emission-reduction credits from projects undertaken in poor nations. This provides opportunities to share with poor nations the benefits from projects designed to lower atmospheric greenhouse gas concentrations. The idea was that flows of finance and green technology would enable poorer countries to leapfrog to cleaner and more sustainable development pathways.

Most Clean Development Mechanism projects are located in China, India, Brazil, Mexico and South Africa, however, and have therefore bypassed the world's poorest nations. Many projects also have dubious sustainable development benefits, in part because projects with sustainable development 'frills' can be priced out of the market. Meeting sustainable development objectives can be complex, leading to a 'race to the bottom' of standards as project managers compete to provide the cheapest sources of carbon and reduce barriers to investment.

In the case of Ecuador, 1 tonne of carbon cost US$0.79 cents in 2006, whilst in Holland it was US$8.04. The Dutch company FACE therefore marketed carbon from Ecuador, which was cheaper to buy. But not all the costs were counted: plantation monocultures of exotic plants replaced the fragile ecosystems of the *páramos* in Ecuador. These plantations damaged the hydro-logical cycle and also reduced the amount of land available for the indigenous population.[47]

Whilst forests do store huge amounts of carbon, Friends of the Earth and others have campaigned to oppose the inclusion of such 'carbon sinks' in international agreements on climate change. This is because, although fast-growing trees can seques-ter carbon fast, this provides incentives for large-scale industrial tree plantations, which can generate poverty and inequity and damage food security by replacing traditional land uses, deplete water and soil resources, and slash biological diversity. Planting trees is often a poor alternative to reducing emissions from fossil fuels when it comes to saving the global climate and protecting biodiversity and local livelihoods.

The Plantar Project, Brazil

The Plantar Project, in the state of Minas Gerais, Brazil, is a Clean Development Mechanism project, which aims to use 23,100 hectares of sustainably managed eucalyptus plantations to produce 9.9 million tonnes of charcoal. This charcoal will substitute for the use of coal or coke in the production of pig iron. Replacing fossil fuels with biomass in this way will prevent the emission of 3 million tonnes of carbon. The project also claims local environmental benefits, such as reduced air pollution and erosion, recovery of degraded areas, and provision of shelter to wildlife. The project should provide around 3,000 jobs, and Plantar has said it will promote healthy and socially sound working conditions, and is sponsoring local education and training programmes.

The project has been strongly criticised, however. Greenpeace challenged the permanence and stability of carbon sequestration claims and others have condemned the disastrous local environmental impacts of eucalyptus plantations. The project developers are accused of a wide range of abuses, from expelling local people from their land to burning large amounts of native cerrado forests, fraudulently acquiring community land, poor community consultation, circumvention of Brazilian labour and environmental laws, poor employee care, destroying alternative local industries and incorrect carbon accounting.

In 2007, Sir Richard Branson offered a US$25 million prize 'for an environmentally sustainable and economically viable way to remove greenhouse gases from the atmosphere'.[48] But natural forests had already been invented. Protecting these forests in order to safeguard their immense carbon stocks and benefit local people and biodiversity offers a better way forward than technological solutions. There is some urgency here as forests themselves react sensitively to changing climatic conditions, which has knock-on effects for the industries and communities that rely on them for their livelihoods. There are a number of government and NGO-led initiatives, however, that provide innovative examples of how this can happen.

Forest management in Burkina Faso

Burkina Faso's unplanned use of forests had led to the deterioration of all forest areas around Ouagadougou, prompting a government decision to develop new management techniques. The project aims to develop a national programme for the sustainable and integrated production of wood and non-wood forest products, particularly fuelwood and charcoal. In an area 150 kilometres around Ouagadougou, 80,000 hectares are being managed with the active participation of local people using simple techniques for silviculture. Supported by the United Nations Development Programme and the Food and Agriculture Organization, the government of Burkina Faso has introduced a more rational, planned approach to forest resource use. This has resulted in resource conservation and protection, as well as a 50 per cent increase in income for local people, who are now able to fulfil urban demand for fuelwood and charcoal. Plans are under way for the management of a further 570,000 hectares in Burkina Faso, and other Sahelian countries have expressed interest in adopting similar programmes.

Protecting the Gola Forest in Sierra Leone

The Upper Guinea Forest, which once stretched from Guinea to Ghana, now covers less than one-third of its original area and is highly fragmented. Sierra Leone has only one-seventh of its original Upper Guinea Forest remaining, half of which is made up of the 750-square-kilometre Gola Forest in the south-east of the country.

Following the 1991–2002 civil war in Sierra Leone, there was concern that commercial logging would resume in the Gola Forest, bringing in much-needed but short-term money. Instead, the Royal Society for the Protection of Birds (RSPB) and the Conservation Society of Sierra Leone (CSSL) formed a long-term 'conservation concession' agreement with the Sierra Leone government and seven chiefdoms to ensure the forest is conserved rather than logged.

Under a logging concession, the government and local communities would expect incomes from the concession-holder through fees and royalties. This potential loss of income has to be compensated for by the new conservation agreement. Through this agreement income for the government is therefore fed directly into its Forestry Division to manage and develop the Gola Forest for conservation. Local communities will also receive royalties to put into conservation-friendly community development projects. The agreement also guarantees employment and the engagement of communities in forest management. A trust fund will meet these costs in perpetuity.

Trials and tribulations on the Mosquito Coast, Honduras

The Honduran Mosquitia is often referred to as Central America's 'Little Amazon' due to its extensive moist, tropical broadleaved forests and maze of coastal wetlands. Indigenous inhabitants rapidly repelled incursions by Spanish colonists prior to independence, but now their traditional way of life and the biodiversity on which they depend are increasingly threatened.

Illegal loggers frequent the forest looking for mahogany and royal cedar for the export market. High transport costs dictate that this is the only timber which makes a profit. Landless farmers from other parts of Honduras also come to clear and burn plots to grow their subsistence crops. Wealthier cattle ranchers then buy these plots and convert them into pasture whilst the subsistence farmers move further into the forest.

With a minimal state presence, these new colonists tend to take justice into their own hands, resolving disputes at gunpoint. Transport, schools and health services are poor or absent. Drug trafficking and corrupt officials increase social instability, Mosquitia being one of the preferred smuggling routes between Colombia and the USA.

Community forestry co-operatives, with legally designated forest areas managed by the communities themselves, provide one way to halt encroachment. The most advanced co-operative in Mosquitia is in the small community of Copén in the Sico Paulaya Valley. This co-operative manages an area of 4,149 hectares, producing the only Forest Steward-ship Council (FSC)-certificated sources of mahogany and royal cedar in Honduras.

Co-operative members, however, have a basic primary education at most, and their lack of administration and organisational experience has been problematic. Training and support from NGOs has helped improve administrative practices, and FSC requirements for transparency have helped improve accountability among co-operative leaders.

The economic realities faced in Copén are difficult. The journey from forest to market is a long one, involving mules that carry the timber out of the forest and a tortuous full-day trip in a pickup truck to connect with a paved road. In wetter months these tracks are impassable, so timber is floated 60 miles downstream to the mouth of the River Sico and then taken in small cargo boats 100 miles along the coast to the nearest city. Consultants' fees and FSC audit costs further reduce margins. To date the extra income derived from having a legal product, let alone an FSC-certified product, has been minimal. The co-operative is competing with illegal loggers, who have lower costs, and there is always the temptation to follow the clandestine route. Improved transport links would help, but this could also improve access for illegal loggers and landless farmers, accelerating deforestation.

The experiences in Copén show the importance of long-term investment in training and support if truly sustainable solutions are to be found. With the state virtually absent in these remote areas, locally led initiatives offer one of the few viable solutions for the sustainable management of the area's natural resources.

Community reforestation in Cambodia

Cambodia's rapid deforestation has had devastating consequences for rural people who depend on forests for wild foods and resources. New legislation allowing for formal recognition of communally owned forests means rural villagers can now play an important role protecting the tree cover that is both vital for local economies and could help people cope with climate change impacts.

Cambodia is prone to climate extremes and there is evidence that these extremes are worsening. Summer floods often alternate with periods of drought when the sandy soils dry out. Windstorms and soil erosion are also problematic. Maintaining adequate forest cover helps prevent the worst of these effects, as forests help retain soil moisture, provide shelter from sun and wind, prevent erosion and add vital organic matter to the soil.

The Prey Koki Forest in Svay Rieng province illustrates the difference a community forest can make to the lives of rural people. It was severely degraded during Cambodia's years of conflict, but in 1994 monks from Santi Sena, a local Buddhist organisation, began working with local people to regenerate the forest. A tree nursery was established and seedlings were distributed to over a thousand families in five nearby villages. A variety of species were eventually planted and another NGO, now called Development and Partnership in Action, (DPA) worked with Santi Sena to help local people organise and understand the benefits of community forestry.

Obtaining legal recognition of the Prey Koki community forest was a slow and difficult process, complicated by an attempt by a private company to claim rights to the land. Support from NGOs and the local commune council was essential. Thoeung Setha, a programme officer at DPA, is enthusiastic about the potential the new legislation holds: 'The forestry law seems good. If implemented, it will secure the heritage of this community. During the French era, the forest was policed and intruders ejected. During the conflict it was destroyed. Now it is again a source of fish, wild animals and birds.'

Volunteers now look out for forest fires from a watchtower. The families who tend the forest sell mushrooms and collect leaves for use as cooking fuel. The residents of one nearby village, Ang Khdourch, say the forest has helped to reduce drought and provides a range of local produce.

A large fishpond adjacent to the forest serves as the local fish spawning ground, as it remains full of water until the end of the dry season when other ponds have dried out. During the summer floods its fish are carried to other ponds in the neighbourhood to restock them. The forest helps maintain this water source.

Waving at the expanse of green visible from the forest watchtower, Setha noted: 'This is the young forest which the company wanted to destroy. They thought it would be easy because they had money, but they hadn't reckoned with the local community. They know the value they get from the forest.'

Initiatives that protect forests need to work well at the local and national levels, but they should also qualify for support under international climate change agreements. Paying countries in the tropics not to cut down their trees is one way to do this. This idea has always been one of the most controversial ways to tackle climate change. The use of cost–benefit analysis to commodify and value the natural world has been widely criticised, as has the viability of mechanisms for trading carbon. But some believe it should be encouraged. Every hectare of rainforest contains around 200 tonnes of carbon; developing countries could be granted carbon credits for those rainforests that they save from destruction. These credits could be traded on the international market under the Kyoto Protocol or its successor, giving tropical countries and local landowners an incentive to keep their forests. A hectare of rainforest might cost US$300 to clear for pasture, and then be worth only US$500 to its owner. At current market values for carbon, the same hectare of rainforest, if left intact, could be worth thousands of dollars.[49]

The Coalition for Rainforest Nations, led by Papua New Guinea and Costa Rica, has argued that the issue should be put back on the table at international climate negotiations. Challenges include: measuring the 'baseline' rate of deforestation – the amount of forest a country typically fells each year – in order to calculate the quantity of emissions avoided; demonstrating that slowing deforestation in one place will not simply lead to increases elsewhere, and that reductions in deforestation are permanent; and ensuring that carbon money gets into the hands of the impoverished small-scale farmers and not the landowners who are responsible for much of the deforestation. Monitoring all this is especially challenging in remote regions such as the Amazon, where law enforcement and land tenure are often precarious.

The development of a 'reducing emissions from deforestation and forest degradation' (REDD) mechanism provides one vehicle through which good forest management in developing countries can be made more profitable. The source of REDD funding could come from carbon trading or other mechanisms such as trust funds. Formal mechanisms for REDD under the Kyoto Protocol are still being negotiated, but voluntary REDD projects are starting around the world and show much potential in terms of locking away carbon whilst supporting local community needs.[50]

Because it is much cheaper to reduce 1 tonne of emissions from deforestation than from the energy or transport sector, it is hard to understand the low priority given to tackling deforestation. More stringent measures to protect the world's rainforests from unsustainable logging and environmentally destructive development, including agricultural expansion, are needed. Reducing tropical deforestation is key to reducing overall global greenhouse gas emissions and staying below the 2°C global warming threshold. Countries must adopt clear targets and timetables for reducing deforestation: by expanding local governance and providing economic incentives for sustainable forest management while developing and effectively implementing protected areas. The international community must support poorer countries in this effort with appropriate technology, resources and regulations.

8

Cities

As of 2008, more than half of the world's population live in urban areas. This is projected to increase to 67 per cent of earth's anticipated 9.3 billion inhabitants by 2050. With most population growth expected in towns and cities in poorer countries, global population growth is becoming a largely urban phenomenon concentrated in the developing world.[1]

In Latin America, urban areas already concentrate more than three-quarters of the region's population, around 90 per cent of its economic activities, most of its greenhouse gas emissions, and a very large part of the population most vulnerable to climate change.[2] The region is also unusual in that it has the highest proportion of its population living in 'megacities' – cities with 10 million or more inhabitants – compared to the rest of the world.

Climate change and urbanisation in Brazil

Brazil entered the twenty-first century with over eight out of ten of its 173 million inhabitants living in urban areas, and the number of people living in slums totalling 52 million.[3] In the last few years, the central areas of major cities have grown by 5 per cent while the outskirts where no one wants to live, because they are next to steep hillsides or marshes, have grown by 30 per cent. Land is cheaper here, although transport costs to the city centre may be high.

The urbanisation process, characterised by forest loss and the hardening of ground surfaces (soil compaction), contributes to increases in temperature. Insufficient public transport and growing numbers of private cars are adding to greenhouse gas emissions. Cities like São Paulo,

Rio de Janeiro and Recife are suffering from floods and mudslides. The consequences hit everyone but the worst affected are those who live in poverty, especially women and children. Getting social and environmental movements to work together is difficult, but building bridges between such groups is essential. In one Brazilian debate on a new national law about the occupation of urban land, legalising shanty towns was seen as a crucial conquest for campaigners working for the homeless and slum dwellers. Yet Brazilian ecologists vehemently opposed the law. What is the best solution? Should they be moved to remote areas, increasing the need for transport? Should urban expansion be controlled to preserve the forests? Urgent dialogue is needed to build bridges between the views in the context of climate change and sustainable city management.

The relationship between urban centres and climate change is complex and twofold. On the one hand urban areas, with their energy consumption and burning of fossil fuels, help cause climate change, while on the other hand many city dwellers are particularly vulnerable to its impacts.

Urban areas increasingly contribute to climate change and also concentrate people and enterprises that, in time, must change their ways if greenhouse gas emissions are to be reduced. While it is impossible to calculate the exact proportion of greenhouse gases generated in urban areas, worldwide they are likely to account for most human-driven emissions. This includes both the industry and wealthier social groups with high-consumption lifestyles that are to be found in cities. It also factors in the greenhouse gas emissions from activities that serve urban areas, such as agriculture, forestry, oil and natural gas exploitation, air and road transport, and electricity generation.

Hong Kong's vanishing winter

Hong Kong's winters could vanish within fifty years, with the number of cold days declining virtually to zero, according to the head of the city's weather observatory, Lam Chiu-ying. Speaking in June 2007, he reported that, 'according to our projections, toward the end of this century ... there will be less than one cold day each winter, so winter practically will have disappeared.' Lam attributed the predicted temperature rise of 3–4°c to urbanisation and global warming in equal measure.

According to Lam, cold days are defined as those with temperatures below 12°c at some point during the day. Despite its sweltering summers, Hong Kong enjoys a subtropical climate, with cool winter temperatures. Frost is sometimes found on its highest peak, Tai Mo Shan. Between 1961 and 1990 there were on average twenty-one cold days every winter, but this figure had already halved by 2000.

'Over the past century, temperatures in Hong Kong rose around 1.2 degrees, almost double the global average', observed Lam, who warned that urbanisation would accelerate the loss of the city's winters. 'We would really start losing the very distinct seasonal march throughout the year... We would really look more tropical than we are now.' The number of summer 'hot nights' in Hong Kong, with temperatures above 28°c, has already jumped to thirty a year – an almost fourfold increase from the 1990s, as heat trapped during the day by the concrete city and its teeming skyscrapers is unable to dissipate fully at night.

Climate change will affect people living in urban areas, especially the poorest, who tend to live in illegal squatter settlements or slums. According to the United Nations, nearly 1 billion people alive today are slum dwellers, with that number likely to multiply threefold by 2050.[4] Over 90 per cent of slum dwellers live in developing countries, with 72 per cent of citizens in the cities of sub-Saharan Africa living in slums.[5]

In Dhaka, the capital of Bangladesh, around 40 per cent of the population live in slums and squatter settlements.[6] They earn a living from working in industry (such as garment, textile or leather manufacturing), the transport sector, shopping centres, hotels and restaurants, the construction sector, and as domestic workers. These people are severely affected by floods and water-logging. A field survey conducted during the 1998 flood found that at least one in thirteen people had changed their occupation, while 27.4 per cent were unemployed as a result of the flood. Working hours were also reduced for many people.[7]

Flooding in Dhaka

Dhaka, the capital city of Bangladesh, is one of the world's largest cities, with a population of 13.1 million people living in an area of 1,353 square kilometres. Climate change will affect Dhaka primarily in two ways: through floods and drainage problems and through heat stress. Water-logging and drainage problems due to excessive rainfall and flooding from rivers during the monsoon season are already seriously damaging the city. In recent years, Dhaka has experienced major floods in 1954, 1955, 1970, 1974, 1980, 1987, 1988, 1998, 2004 and 2007. Of these, the 1988, 1998 and 2004 floods were the most damaging.

A massive health crisis occurred during the flood of 2004 as sewage mixed with floodwater swirled through Dhaka. Contaminated water spread all over Dhaka, putting 10 million people at a high risk from water-borne diseases. According to Naseem-Ur Rehman, chief of communications in Bangladesh for the United Nations Children's Fund, the situation for children in urban areas was 'extremely dangerous'. The waterlogged city was filled with filth, and the children playing and walking through this filth were easy prey for infectious diseases. The United Nations said that sludge was issuing from manholes in many parts of Dhaka, and diseases such as acute respiratory infections, diarrhoea, dysentery, jaundice, typhoid and scabies were being reported.

The population of Lagos, Nigeria, is over 20 million, making it one of the world's largest urban areas. One of the first sights that greet the visitor arriving after dark is the fumes and smoke swirling around the headlights of gridlocked traffic on the miles-long Third Mainland Bridge. The acrid smell of exhaust fumes stings the nose and mingles with the overpowering smells from the city's largest slum, consisting of rudimentary shacks built on stilts above the water. Massive influxes of new residents are largely uncontrolled and greatly exceed the capacity of existing infrastructures.

The major danger to people in cities like Lagos will probably be from extreme events, such as increased storm surges, which are related to increasing average sea levels, and temperature extremes. Increasing temperatures will also compound the problems associated with local air pollution and increase the risk of heat-stress-related deaths. Heat stress is much worse in cities compared to rural areas: temperatures are a few degrees higher than in surrounding areas because concrete buildings retain heat, and activities such as vehicle exhaust, industry and the increasing use of air conditioning warm the air. Water supplies – precarious in urban slums at the best of times – may be disrupted. The impacts of climate change on rural areas may further increase the pressures already causing the rural poor to migrate to the cities.

Jakarta's urban poor at risk

The major climate-change-related risks to Indonesia's capital, Jakarta, will come from sea-level rise and flooding, both of which are expected to increase in frequency and severity. Much of the population, an estimated 1.2 million people, is concentrated in the vulnerable coastal slum communities in the north, where population density is 12,635 people per square kilometre – the highest in Indonesia.[8] Over 277,000 people in Jakarta live below the national poverty line, but this figure does not include unregistered citizens in the poor northern communities, who cannot afford basic services like clean water, sanitation and education. Lack of infrastructure in these slum communities leaves residents vulnerable to climate-change-related events, and without the resources to cope.[9]

Sea levels in Jakarta Bay are expected to rise at a rate of 57 millimetres per year, resulting in the predicted submergence of as much as 160 square kilometres of northern Jakarta by 2050.[10] When combined with subsidence due to groundwater extraction and soil compression,[11] poor urban planning and continued upstream deforestation in the watershed, poverty-stricken areas of the city could be left devastated. The impacts of climate change on Jakarta will likely be borne by its poorest and most vulnerable citizens.

Masnellyarty Hilman, a deputy environment minister in charge of drafting a national strategy to deal with climate change, acknowledged that climate change had contributed to the extreme weather conditions in early 2007 which triggered the worst flooding in Jakarta in years. The floods submerged huge areas of the city and its surroundings, killed fifty people and displaced hundreds of thousands more. 'It's a natural phenomenon affected by climate change. It's been made worse by negligent behaviour', Masnellyarty Hilman commented. She added that warmer seas had heated up monsoon winds that carry moisture from the ocean to the land, leading to extra-heavy rain.

Most of Latin America's and the Caribbean's largest cities are coastal and thus vulnerable to sea-level rise. Many are very vulnerable to extreme weather events. Furthermore, a good number of Pacific Coast cities rely on glacial melt for their water supplies during dry summers – a source that will be severely depleted within twenty years at current rates of glacial melt. A high proportion of the region's population live in urban areas. Many are undernourished, have inadequate and unstable income, and lack access to adequate water, sanitation and health care. This makes them particularly vulnerable to climate change.

Well-planned and well-governed urban areas can greatly reduce climate change risks, while unplanned and poorly governed cities can greatly increase them, especially flooding and extreme weather events. Ultimately, the process of tackling climate change for a city such as Lagos or Dhaka cannot be viewed as a separate issue in itself; there are simply too many other priorities. Climate change will need to be framed in the context of achieving sustainable development, which includes poverty reduction and environmental protection. Cities such as Curitiba and Pôrto Alegre in Brazil can teach us much about how to integrate sustainable transport considerations into business development, good water management practices, road infrastructure development, and local community development. Transition to a low-carbon economy is also desirable – developing new industries using renewable energy or developing low-carbon transport systems. There are numerous possibilities for alternative energy technologies, such as solar heating and cooling systems, especially for low-income families and in tropical countries.

Reducing emissions from Mexico City

With a population of over 18 million, Mexico City is one of the largest metropolitan areas in the world. Famous for its air pollution problems, Mexico City also contributes significantly to greenhouse gas emissions, accounting for 20 per cent of the country's total. The city's carbon footprint in 2004 was estimated at 33.5 million tonnes of carbon dioxide (or its equivalent). Due to rapid growth it is difficult for Mexico City to establish an emissions reduction target, so in 2002 it put in place a strategy called Proaire 2002–2010 to tackle air quality and establish climate protection. This involved limiting the growth of emissions, rather than a reduction in absolute terms.[12] In 2008, Mexico City also launched its Climate Action Programme, an inter-agency policy approach to address climate change and reduce the city's greenhouse gas emissions. As of 2012, the costs of the Climate Action Programme alone were estimated at US$4.4 billion.

Results have been impressive. Since 2008 alone, some 745 government housing units have been fitted with solar panels. New regulations ensure that businesses with more than fifty-one people use solar-powered water heating systems. The Ecobici public bicycle system offering the public hired bicycles has 1,200 bicycles and over 35,000 registered users. New buses have replaced older inefficient models and several bus corridors have been introduced. Energy-efficient minibuses have also replaced 325 polluting vehicles, and 1,632 inefficient taxis have been replaced through a programme that provides support to drivers wishing to upgrade. One trolley-bus corridor has been renovated and extended, and another newly constructed. Both now carry a total of 117,000 passengers each day. There are 13,521 hectares of green space in the city and an urban reforestation programme has planted 232,748 trees and other plants to help reduce local flooding and the urban 'heat island' phenomenon.

Between 2008 and June 2011, changes made to the transport sector reduced emissions by 4,551,783 tons of carbon dioxide or its equivalent. Changes to the energy sector reduced emissions by 183,425 tons while changes to the water management sector saved 1,804 tons. Some 127,175 tons of emissions were saved by changes to waste management and 607,846 tons from reforestation.[13]

Planning for climate change in Apia, Samoa

In its National Adaptation Programme of Action, Samoa has identified the 'Zoning and Strategic Management Planning Project' in Apia, its capital, as a key climate change adaptation need.[14] Apia is the centre of all utility services and operations and houses 22 per cent of the population. Its coastal location makes it vulnerable to the storm tides and strong winds that characterise tropical cyclones. Urban growth in Apia and its adjoining areas is predicted to continue to rise, but environmental problems are already apparent. Such problems include waste disposal, overcrowding, flooding caused by building on flood-prone and poorly drained lands, dead animals, mangrove destruction, septic-tank effluent flowing into groundwater and coastal ecosystems, and reduced water quality.

Centralising services in Apia and increasing coastal population levels will place more infrastructure and people in areas vulnerable to sea-level rise and extreme weather events. The project aims to integrate climate change policies and methods into all management plans at national, regional, district and site-specific levels, and mainstream climate change issues into urban planning processes.

9

Women

The impacts of climate change will disproportionately affect people living in poverty in poorer countries, notwithstanding their minimal per-capita contributions to greenhouse gas emissions. It's here where the damage will be greatest and where people have the lowest capacity to cope. According to UN Women, some 70 per cent of people in the developing world living below the poverty threshold are women,[1] yet gender issues receive little attention in the climate change debate. People are vulnerable to the hazards of climate change to a greater or lesser degree depending on factors such as their wealth, education, skills, management capability and access to technology, infrastructure and information. Women's access to these resources is often inferior to that of men, and this increases their vulnerability and limits their ability to cope with the advent of climate shocks and to recover when they have passed. These gender-related inequalities are particularly pervasive in the developing world.

Women and children are fourteen times more likely to die than men during natural disasters. More than 70 per cent of the dead from the Asian tsunami were women; roughly 87 per cent of unmarried women and 100 per cent of married women lost their main source of income when Cyclone Nargis hit the Ayeyarwaddy Delta in Myanmar in 2008.[2] In Bangladesh, social prejudice keeps girls and women from learning to swim and climb trees. Many women cannot leave their homes without accompaniment or consent from their husband or one of their male relatives. Men can more easily warn each other as they meet in public spaces, but they rarely communicate information to the rest of the family. As a result, far more women than men perish in the major floods which characterise life in the coastal areas of Bangladesh.[3] When a cyclone and floods hit Bangladesh in 1991, the death rate for women was almost five times higher than for men.

'Due to the impact of climate change, migration increases. During migration in many cases the children and women are left at home without proper arrangement for food and other survival supports. The children and women left behind are socially and physically insecure. For food and security many of the women choose informal extramarital sexual relations and children embark on hazardous occupations.'

Prodipan, Bangladesh

Research by the London School of Economics found that in a sample of 141 countries over the period 1981–2002, natural disasters (and their subsequent impact) killed on average more women than men, and killed women at an earlier age than men. Boys were more likely to receive preferential treatment in rescue efforts, and women and children suffered more from food shortages and a lack of privacy and safety in the aftermath of disasters.[4] In India, various studies have shown that over the past decade more women than men have suffered from premature deaths on account of heatwaves and cold snaps and other climate-related extreme events. Following extreme events such as storms and floods, the burden of devastation also falls primarily on women, who must keep the family together.

Women who have to find food for their families will find it more difficult if climate change lowers rainfall and increases drought in their home area. Women are usually the main actors when it comes to household food production in developing countries. They achieve this despite unequal access to land and information. If fish populations are affected by levels of salinity in freshwater systems, a primary source of protein relied on by women will be at risk. Changing weather patterns could affect farming activities such as paddy cultivation in Asia, and cash crops such as cotton and tea, the cultivation of which employs many women.

In Africa, for example, women contribute to 70 per cent of food production; they account for nearly half of all farm labour and 80-90 per cent of food processing.[5] Wangari Maathai acknowledged this when she received the Nobel Peace Prize in Oslo on 10 December 2004, describing Africa's women as 'the primary caretakers, holding significant responsibility for tilling the land and feeding their families'. Despite this, women in poorer nations usually have limited access to productive assets, including land, and to other elements necessary for production like credit and education. Indeed, they own only 1 per cent of land in Africa.[6] When a woman does own land, her holdings tend to be smaller and less fertile than those of men. Land reform schemes have often displaced complex systems of land use and tenure in which women had certain rights in common law and local practice, if not in legislation. New land titles are usually registered in the name of a male household head, regardless of women's economic contribution to the household, their customary rights, or the increasing number of female-headed households. Many women find that if their husband dies they are thrown off their land by his relatives.[7] Female farmers worldwide receive only 5 per cent of all agricultural extension services that would help teach them about new crop varieties and technologies. In Egypt only 1 per cent of agricultural extension officers are women.[8] African women also receive less than 10 per cent of all credit going to small farmers and 1 per cent of the total credit to agriculture.[9]

'Climate change induced impacts include livelihood and food insecurity. When livelihood and security is under threat the children and women are the first and worst victims. They have increased working time and less and less food for themselves as the adult males consume most food and also use multiple sources of food (for example eating out in restaurants) where the women and children do not have access due to the lack of control over cash income of the family.'

Prodipan, Bangladesh

'[W]omen and children are vulnerable because they are usually the first to suffer from the impacts of changes in weather conditions such as lack of clean and safe drinking water. Scarcity of food often has a greater effect on nutrition levels of women. Among Filipinos, when there is not enough food for consumption for a certain month, the mother prepares to eat less, giving priority to her husband and her children. Why the husbands? In most cases it has become part of the culture among Filipinos that wives save a meal for their husbands because they are the ones who provide the food, but forgetting that wives also carry the burden of taking care of the children, animal care and other household activities.'

Beth Montazana, the Social Action Centre, the Philippines

Women are also often the main users and carriers of water. They frequently have considerable knowledge about water resources, including their location, quality and reliability, restrictions on collection and acceptable storage methods. In Bangladesh, women and children provide nearly all household water in rural areas, both for domestic use such as drinking, cooking, bathing and washing, and for irrigating gardens and watering livestock. If water resources are nearby and of good quality, this will benefit women's crops and livestock and thus their families' food security. It will also reduce the amount of time and energy women must spend collecting, storing, protecting and distributing water.

The intrusion of saltwater into freshwater resources in the districts of Satkhira, Khulna and Bagerhat in south-western coastal Bangladesh is already having a disproportionate impact

on women, particularly during the dry season. Women are generally responsible for providing their family with salt-free drinking
water. Because nearly all local water sources have high salinity, women must travel long distances by foot every day to find
drinking water, even if they are in poor health. Many women in
south-west Bangladesh must travel at least 5 or 6 kilometres each
day on foot to collect drinking water. This makes finding time
for other household duties difficult, and women are often so tired
they cannot concentrate on other issues. Husbands complain
that their women do not serve food on time; some women are
physically assaulted on account of this. Women suffer more illnesses due to the strain of collecting drinking water. Many are
pregnant or have young babies. They often feel it is unsafe to
leave their children at home while they collect water, so take
them with them, and so their children's health may be affected
too.

The long walk for fresh water in coastal Bangladesh

Aleya is 4 years old and does not know the meaning of the word 'salinity',
but she knows she will have to wake up before dawn and walk 5 kilometres with her mother, braving the morning chill, just to fetch drinking
water. She knows that if they fail, her father will scold her because
the whole family will have to drink salty water from a nearby shrimp-
cultivating gher. Aleya's family and the others of Khaserabad village in
Satkhira's Ashashuni Upazila have no alternative but to walk such distances each day because their local groundwater is now saline. 'We have
to walk this long way as the water of two ponds in our village has turned
to saline and is too muddy to drink', said Aleya's mother Laily Begum.

Women and children are the worst victims of the current salinity
crisis, as they have to fetch drinking water by walking sometimes more
than 10 kilometres along narrow roads. Their ordeal is most acute during
the rainy season, when roads become slippery and difficult to navigate.
'Male members do not go to bring non-saline water. I fetched water,
walking around 2 kilometres, even just before the day I gave birth to this
daughter. Just two days after her birth, I again started fetching water and
now I am suffering on account of the physical troubles', says Laily Begum.

The crisis is even transforming old local customs and creating new cultural barriers. Ashura of Dumuria village in Shyamnagar is 20 years old. She now finds her desire for marriage a distant dream. Her aged parents, fearing that there will be no one to fetch them drinking water, do not want her to marry. People living in areas where the water crisis is more moderate, meanwhile, refuse to arrange marriages for their offspring with people from the worst-hit areas. Salinity has become a social curse, which is likely to get worse with climate change.

Ensuring greater gender equality will benefit society as a whole and help promote sustainable development. However, getting gender issues into debates on climate change and sustainable development is happening piecemeal, extremely slowly, and often as an afterthought. This is in part due to the lack of participation by women in decision-making at all levels. In the Kilombera district in Tanzania, for example, a newly constructed well dried up. Its location had been determined by an all-male local committee, despite the fact that it was the task of local women to dig for water by hand as they know the most likely places to find water. By the same token, at the international climate change negotiations in 2010, women made up only 30 per cent of negotiators and just 10 per cent of heads of delegations.[10] This lack of representation must change, because climate change policies will be unsuccessful if women have no opportunity to influence decision-making, build their capacity, lower their vulnerability and diversify their income sources.

In India, for example, women have played a huge role in improving the public service health sector. A 1992 constitutional amendment mandated the reservation of one-third of panchayat (local government) seats for women. Since then, relative spending on public water and latrines for low-caste communities has increased. particularly when women are in a majority in panchayats.

Education is also key. In most developing countries women are far less likely to receive a formal education than men, and consequently illiteracy rates among women tend to be higher. For example, in Burkina Faso, Niger and Somalia, female literacy rates are very low at 15, 15 and 26 per cent respectively, whereas male literacy rates are roughly double this at 29, 43 and 50 per cent respectively.[11] Illiteracy and poverty often go hand in hand, and day-to-day survival is given higher priority than addressing long-term environmental issues. But environmentally responsible behaviour can be enhanced by formal education which links local issues to the wider world – raising awareness, for example, of the link between burning fossil fuels, climate change and changing weather patterns. In many coastal villages in El Salvador, women have already shifted their livelihoods from selling firewood, in order to preserve the mangrove forests that protect them from an increasing number of floods.

Special attention needs to be paid to the opportunities arising from international climate change negotiations. Many emerging solutions intended to help people cope with climate change involve land use and agriculture in rural areas, a key sector for women.

The dependence of women on biomass energy – for example, burning wood for household cooking – means that they should also be involved in projects promoting renewable energy resources. In El Salvador and Guatemala the primary source of fuel is wood, and it is the job of women and girls to gather it. Many spend as much as three or four hours, three to five times a week, searching for wood. And when they cook food for their households, they are exposed to toxic cooking smoke. Agencies promoting clean, renewable energy, such as solar ovens, have found it vital to target groups of women, who can learn from one another whilst practising the new technologies. Despite this, men often influence the uptake of new energy technologies in this domain too. In one case in Zimbabwe, men are reported to have rejected the use of solar cookers by their wives, since technology and its development are seen traditionally as a male preserve.

Women have a tremendous amount of local knowledge on how to cope with droughts, floods, disease and the other challenges in order to make life in a difficult climate bearable. In Rwanda, women are reported to produce more than 600 varieties of beans, and in Peru, Aguaruna women plant more than 60 varieties of manioc. Such knowledge is a resource well worth documenting, preserving and building on because it contains the details and foundations needed to support new survival strategies in the face of the climatic changes ahead.

Helping women adapt to climate change in Panjhok

Climate change is one of many challenges facing the people of Panjhok village in north-western Tajikistan. This remote community has no road access for up to five months of the year as a result of heavy snow. During winter, their diet depends primarily on grains and potatoes. Winters are cold and heating is inefficient. Fuel – usually a mixture of dung and straw, coal or wood – is scarce, and its collection is labour-intensive. Job opportunities in the village are limited. As a result, many men migrate to Russia for work, and leave the women to care for the family, the garden and the livestock.

CARE, with support from the Canadian International Development Agency (CIDA), worked with a community-based organisation (CBO) in Panjhok village to better understand how climate change will affect the community, and what evidence of climate change is already being observed. When asked about key climate-related concerns, the community members noted that the beginning and end of the winter season were becoming less predictable, and that the snow pack seemed to be increasing. Both of these facts are corroborated by meteorological data from the last few decades. These changes are threatening the livelihoods of a community that already lives in a harsh environment with a short growing season.

The project worked with the CBO to design and implement pilot adaptation strategies in the community. In an effort to target the most vulnerable community members, the CBO prioritised women-headed households. The key issue tackled was the impact of the shifting winter season on food security.

To address the challenge of agricultural productivity in a shortening growing season, the project introduced simple cold frames. These are small greenhouses which are used to start seedlings in the spring and to extend the growing season later in the year. Fifteen women in Panjhok were given cold frames and trained on their use and maintenance. As a result, these families were harvesting greens two months later in the year, and had tomato seedlings ready to plant as soon as the warm weather began in the spring.

The project also addressed the issue of food availability in winter by promoting techniques for food preservation. Female CBO members were trained to preserve tomatoes, onions, peppers and other vegetables commonly grown in kitchen gardens. This increased the variety and nutritional value of the winter diet, providing welcome diversity from the usual bread and potatoes.

Empowering women through carbon sequestration

CARE implemented the Forest Resource Management for Carbon Sequestration project in Indonesia from 2002 to 2005. Project activities were implemented in thirty-six villages in Nunukan district in East Kalimantan. The project aimed to improve household livelihood security and increase carbon sequestration through sustainable natural resource management. Key challenges included illegal logging, forest conversion for agriculture and palm oil production, and the threat of forest fires. Insecure land tenure and unsustainable land-use practices have also contributed to the loss of forest resources, and the low capacity of local government authorities to support sustainable forest management has exacerbated the situation.

Project activities aimed to empower women. Barriers to women's participation in new livelihood activities included early marriage (and consequent low education levels), existing workloads and discriminatory social customs.

A combination of approaches was used to overcome these barriers. Alliances were formed with progressive community groups to address discriminatory social customs. Women were also offered literacy training and men were encouraged to become involved in activities that were traditionally the responsibilities of women, such as childcare and fetching water and fuel.

Community organisations were established to undertake project activities, and women were encouraged to take on leadership roles in them. The organisations worked with communities to map land uses and plan village development. Inventories of forest resources, including carbon stocks, were undertaken, and forest management plans developed and endorsed by local authorities.

Women and water management in the Andes

Ines Rivasplata, a small-scale farmer in Peru's Jequetepeque river valley, prays for water. Like many of Peru's Andean mountain communities, her village has been struck by a four-year drought, with no relief in sight. But Ines has learned to maximise the scarce water that is available after getting help from a natural resource management project run by CEDEPAS, a local non-profit organisation working in the state of Cajamarca and supported by Progressio. The experience proves that water management training and strong local organisations can help combat the negative effects of drought.

CEDEPAS focuses on improving irrigation techniques and the organisation of water management groups, known as irrigation committees. Ines says the training programme has made profound changes in her life. 'Before, women were not allowed to participate in [training programmes]', she explains. 'They were supposed to stay on the farm. But with these workshops, that notion is changing.'

It was realised that traditional systems of water management, which vest control in the hands of men, needed to expand to include women and children. Unfortunately most water-related projects in the region have focused on male household heads – excluding women and children – when, in reality, women and children do most of the daily water resources management.

Ines reported that the presence of one particular development worker helped break the stereotype that water is a man's domain. As a highly qualified female water engineer, she created a space for dialogue between men, women and children on water issues, ensuring that no group was excluded whilst respecting traditional power structures. CEDEPAS also produced a ground-breaking irrigation manual, based on the experiences of a fictional local family, which included the mother, father, grandparents and children.

Standing in the midst of her lush, green mango orchard, Ines said she has learned new techniques that have improved her farm's production. She pointed with pride to circular ditches dug carefully around the base of each tree, joined by a system of inter-connecting irrigation channels. Gone is the exhausting old system of watering by bucket. Now water rushes through the irrigation channels to each tree in the orchard.

We need to improve our understanding of how poverty in general, and women in particular, are affected by climate change.

And we need to ensure that those entrusted with policy development and project work incorporate gender issues. We must continue to listen to the voices of these women and other vulnerable groups over the roar of wealthier countries driving the debate, in order that the consequences of climate change should not lead already marginalised and vulnerable sections of society into further deprivation.

10

Trade

Fossil-fuel-dependent global transport networks have grown in tandem with the trade they help facilitate. Between 1950 and 2008 total world trade grew by a factor of thirty-two; whilst the share of global GDP it represented was only 5.5 per cent in 1950, this figure was 21 per cent in 2007. Clearly, trade in goods and services has grown much faster than GDP.[1] International trade is linked to ever-rising greenhouse gas emissions, and more than a quarter of emissions from some developing countries are linked to products exported to industrialised countries.[2] These emissions, however, are usually marked up under the national carbon scorecard of developing countries they are produced in rather than the developed countries they are consumed in.

The significant dynamic of this process has been the globalisation of production and distribution inside multinational businesses. Globalised production within the subsidiary networks of transnational corporations saw components and parts making up one-third of all trade in manufactured goods by the early 1990s, to a value of US$800 billion. But much international trade lives in a bubble. International aviation and marine fuels are immune from any kind of internationally agreed taxation that would indicate and internalise the real environmental cost of freight and shipping. Greenhouse gas emissions from international freight are also exempt from the emissions reduction targets set for rich countries to meet under the Kyoto Protocol of the UN climate change convention. The transport networks underpinning the movement of goods are hugely subsidised and their contribution to global warming escapes international agreements to control greenhouse gases. As well as the free ride for international marine and aviation 'bunker' fuels, most of the increased demand for freight transport in developing and transition economies is for high-polluting road transport, and this is growing at up to double the rate of GDP.[3]

Whilst benefits to poor countries from trade liberalisation remain the subject of intense academic debate, the social and economic costs of climate change continue to rise inexorably and will have disproportionately negative impacts on developing countries. Economic considerations about which patterns of trade bring real benefits to different trading partners, coupled with the carbon constraints suggested by global warming, point to the need for new models of trade. The specific circumstances for a poverty and climate 'win–win' scenario need to be worked out. Trade will always be an important part of the global economy, and with developing countries accounting for 34 per cent of trade in merchandise – almost double their share in the 1960s – it will be a growing issue for poorer nations.[4] But the picture of who trades what with whom, and how, will have to change if the poorest countries are to benefit and the climate is to be protected.

Mzuzu Coffee Planters Co-operative Union, Malawi

Climate change has wiped out nearly half of the 10 million coffee trees the members of Mzuzu have planted since 2003. At night the temperatures drop lower than they used to, while during the day it is too warm. Trees are not only dying, they are taking much longer to produce their fruit.

To address this challenge, Mzuzu coffee growers receive help from Fairtrade Africa to terrace their fields to retain water, and to plant special grasses which promote soil cultivation and water conservation. They are

also planting shading trees around the coffee bushes to protect them from the sun. In addition the farmers have planted cover crops on bare ground so that when the plants die they turn into biomass and improve the soil quality.
The coffee they produce has been certified 'fair trade' since 2009. Some 3,500 small-scale producer farmers have benefited from this scheme.[5]

There is still enormous pressure on poor countries to liberalise their trade regimes. But for poor countries that depend heavily on selling primary commodities, increased supply and availability to the rest of the world has meant a long-term downward trend in the prices they receive for their goods. Several other factors reinforce this trend, including corporate consolidation of the marketing chains – for example in coffee – and macroeconomic policies pushed by international finance capitalists leading to widespread deflation in rural economies.

There are other problems to do with international trade that receive less attention. In the international trading system, poor countries have to run faster to stay still, whilst at the same time putting greater pressure on their natural resource base and the global ecosystem. A study by the United Nations Environment Programme of the more immediate environmental impacts of trade liberalisation in developing and transitioning economies concluded that there were 'serious negative environmental, and related social, impacts of expanded trade activity'.[6] These included:

- land degradation
- water pollution
- loss of biodiversity
- displacement of local, community-serving economic activity
- loss of common property rights in the shift to export-led activity

- social instability resulting from structural economic changes
- the failure and obstruction of policies designed to mitigate (i) environmental impact, (ii) land-use conflicts, (iii) deforestation and (iv) perverse incentives for resource depletion.

In *Late Victorian Holocausts: El Niño Famines and the Making of the Third World* author Mike Davis looks at the experience of nineteenth-century India, China and Brazil as a parallel for contemporary development dilemmas. According to Davis, the 'forcible incorporation of smallholder production into commodity and financial circuits controlled from overseas' fundamentally undermined food security, and left millions of people exposed to famine during El Niño cycles.[7]

Prior to colonial rule Indian peasants had three practical safeguards against famine resulting from climate instability: domestic grain hoards; (silver) family ornaments; and credit with the village moneylender and grain dealer. Towards the end of the nineteenth century all were lost under the changing balance of power in the rural economy and the trade imperatives of the British Raj. Thirty-one serious famines occurred in the 120 years of British rule of India, compared to only seventeen famines recorded in the previous 2,000 years.

Today, the danger is that the imperatives of trade liberalisation are once again being put before food security and the need to build disaster-resilient economies. The continuing violent incorporation of local economies into world markets looks set to increase the vulnerability of peasants and farm labourers as they become more exposed to disasters – leading yet again to dramatic consequences.

Migration

Hysteria often walks in the footsteps of refugees and immigrants. In Europe, barely a day passes without scare stories of crime, fraud and intolerable burdens placed on public services, with immigrants the implied or overtly stated perpetrators. The well-documented reality that immigrants have always made, and continue to make, a vital contribution to Europe's economy often seems irrelevant.

Yet amidst this irrational fear lies a deeper irony. Refugees could be about to increase dramatically in number over the coming years as a direct result of the way that the rich global elite lead their lives. Global warming, more than war or political upheaval, stands to displace many millions of people. And climate change is being driven by the fossil-fuel-intensive lifestyles that we enjoy so much.

Environmental refugees are already with us. They are people who have been forced to flee their homes and even cross borders primarily in response to environmental factors such as extreme weather events, drought and desertification. There are probably more of them already than their 'political' counterparts. Oxford academic Professor Norman Myers has estimated that there were 25 million environmental refugees in the mid-1990s, compared to around 27 million conventional refugees (people fleeing political, religious or ethnic oppression), but by the time global warming takes hold there could be as many as 200 million environmental refugees.[1] Many millions could be displaced in Bangladesh, the Philippines, Cambodia, Thailand, Egypt, China and Latin America.[2] Reduced river flows in combination with sea-level rise in the Nile Delta will entail massive disruption to one of the most densely populated parts of Africa. Sea-level rise alone could displace between 6 and 7 million people in the Delta.[3]

Migration is the most extreme form of adaptation to climate change and the last option that should be considered. But many will have no other choice. Most refugees will be in developing countries, and many will end up in the slums that surround most developing-country cities. There they face a precarious existence, especially where settlements are established in flood-prone areas such as the drainage valleys of rivers and streams, or on unstable hillsides. The substandard housing found in most slums is vulnerable to flooding, storms, landslides and mudslides, making their new homes far from safe from the impacts of climate change.

Migration is not always to cities. In Latin America, much migration now tends to be towards coastal areas, where it has contributed to the deforestation of mangroves and the destruction of coral reefs, thereby increasing the vulnerability of the coastline to storm surges, tsunamis and sea-level rise. In Mexico, more than 65 per cent of mangroves have already been lost.[4]

Much migration will occur within countries. Devastating episodes of periodic drought in Brazil's north-eastern region, for example, have caused large movements of people for decades. Families who do not own land, but depend on agriculture as a means of subsistence, are the first to lose work when rains cannot support a full crop. Many have no alternative but to migrate in search of income. Last century, internal migration from the north-east of Brazil to south-eastern states was particularly heavy, and, with some climate models predicting huge drops in rainfall and yet further desertification in the north-east, this problem is likely to worsen.

Migration to other countries is also likely to grow. Mexico has experienced a significant drop in production of maize and beans as a result of climate change, which has affected the agricultural poor who depend heavily on the seasons. Unstable production has increased the levels of migration to the United States. Indeed, Mexico is the largest source country for unauthorised immigration into the USA, with an estimated 2 million unauthorised residents in 1990 rising to 4.8 million by January 2000. Mexico's share of the total unauthorised resident population increased from 58 per cent to 69 per cent over the same time period.[5] Most of these immigrants are from the indigenous population, the poorest of the poor in Mexico.[6]

At least five small island states are at risk of ceasing to exist because of flooding or saltwater contamination, which poses several serious unanswered questions. What will happen to the exclusive economic zones of such countries and what status and identity will their populations have? Where whole nations become uninhabitable, should they have new sovereign lands carved out for them in other states? Without proper environmental refugee status, will the world have to create lots of new little Israels for the environmentally displaced? Or would they become the first true world citizens? If there is no state left, how can the state protect its citizens?

The Carteret Islands (Papua New Guinea) and Tuvalu are likely to be the first Pacific islands to be evacuated due to climate change, but Kiribati, the Marshall Islands and many other parts of the Pacific may also have to face this catastrophe. Internal relocation due to shoreline erosion and rising sea levels has already occurred in Vanuatu, Kiribati and Tuvalu.

Sea-level rise in the range expected by the IPCC would also devastate the Maldives, most of which is just 1.5 metres above water. In 2008, the then president of the Maldives, Mohamed Nasheed, began planning for this when he announced proposals to divert a portion of the country's tourism revenue into buying a new homeland in Sri Lanka, India or Australia for his 300,000 islanders. 'We do not want to leave the Maldives, but we also do not want to be climate refugees living in tents for decades', he said.[7] Without international legal protection, however, their people could become potentially resented minorities in Sri Lanka, itself threatened, or India, with enormous problems of its own.

Forced migration from Tuvalu

Tuvalu is one of the places most vulnerable on earth to the impacts of global warming. Most of Tuvalu is just 2 metres above sea level, with its highest point a mere 4.6 metres above sea level. Sea-level rise could spell complete disaster to the 11,000 Tuvaluans currently residing on nine low-lying coral atolls. Its entire population could have to relocate to other countries over the next few decades.

Currently, Tuvaluans live by fishing, receiving financial support from relatives working overseas and accessing an international trust fund set up in 1987. But the rising sea levels are taking their toll on infrastructure and on those who have not left the islands already.

Assistant secretary for foreign affairs in Tuvalu, Paani Laupepa, made it clear that they 'feel threatened, [their] whole culture would have to be transplanted'. Tuvalu has twice approached the Australian government for assistance by accepting climate change refugees. So far it has refused. However, an ad hoc agreement has been reached with New Zealand to allow phased relocation.

Like many peoples across the world facing the devastating impacts of climate change, Tuvaluans stress that becoming 'climate refugees' is not their primary goal.[8] 'Taking us as environmental refugees is not what Tuvalu is after in the long run. We want the islands of Tuvalu and our nation to remain permanently and not be submerged as a result of greed and uncontrolled consumption of industrialised countries. We want our children to grow up the way we grew up in our own islands and in our own culture' said Tuvaluan governor general Sir Tomasi Puapua in September 2002.

The Carterets, Papua New Guinea

Citizens of the Carteret Islands are also being moved because of sea-level rise. The Carterets are six small islands that surround an atoll about 25 kilometres wide. The islands are approximately 1 metre above high tide and made of sand. The communities occupying them are losing access to fresh water, with consequent health effects, and the advancing saltwater is destroying crops.

According to Bernard Tunim, chief of Piul Island and community spokesperson, 'we are frustrated, and we are angry at the same time. We are victims of something that we are not responsible for. We believe that these islands are ours, and that our future generations should not go away from these islands. I think it's about time these industrialised countries realised that these island countries in the Pacific are taking the toll. We are bearing the brunt of all these gas emissions.'

It is a sad irony that the people of the Carterets, with a carbon footprint one of the lowest in the world, are among the first to have to abandon their islands because of rising seas attributable to emissions from nations elsewhere.

Climate refugees in Tegua, Vanuatu

A small community living in the Pacific island chain of Vanuatu has become one of the first to be formally moved as a result of climate change. The community has been relocated higher into the interior of Tegua Island after coastal homes were repeatedly swamped by storm surges and waves. The relocation occurred under a project called 'Capacity Building for the Development of Adaptation in Pacific Island Countries', a project of the Secretariat of the Pacific Regional Environment Programme (SPREP).

In recent years, more and more flooding has triggered an escalating variety of problems including malaria and skin diseases among children. A 1-metre-high coral reef – previously a line of defence against high tides and waves – is increasingly being swamped. According to Taito Nakalevu, climate change adaptation officer with SPREP, 'people are being forced to build sea walls and other defences, not just to defend their homes but to defend agricultural land'. Under the project, water tanks able to collect rainwater have been supplied and installed in the interior, enabling the community to move.

The effects of the scale of population movement expected will be highly destabilising to the global community unless carefully managed. Without action, the countries least responsible for creating the problem – poor developing nations, which are already the largest recipients of refugee flows – stand to carry the largest share of additional costs associated with environmental refugees. As a consequence of global warming, Bangladesh, one of the poorest countries in the world, expects to have between 15 and 20 million such environmental refugees in the coming years.[9]

The United Nation's Guiding Principles on Internal Displacement are widely used in reference to internally displaced persons, although they do not confer any legal status. They consolidate existing principles on human rights and international humanitarian and refugee law and then apply them to the needs of people forced to leave their homes but remaining within their countries of origin – including as a result of natural or human-made disasters such as climate change. In certain circumstances, however, suggesting that the solution must lie purely at the national level is absurd, since the national level may be under water.

Creating new legal obligations for states to accept environmental refugees would be one way to ensure that industrialised countries accept the unintended consequences of their fossil-fuel-intensive lifestyle choices. Just as the 1951 Geneva Refugee Convention provides protection for people fleeing persecution, a new international treaty could address the current gap in the international legal system by conferring special status and rights on environmental refugees forced to flee their country of origin either because it no longer exists or because it cannot meet their needs due to the scale of climate change impacts.

Alternatively, a reinterpretation of existing international law could provide better protection for environmental refugees. People can already claim refugee status where persecutory action by states leads to the oppression of individuals, and 'environmental persecution' has been used to provide protection for the victims of deliberately flooded valleys, or for those who have lost their livelihoods through deforestation. Policies that either fail to abate, or worsen, global warming could fall into the category of 'environmental persecution' and may offer opportunities for protecting environmental refugees as a result of climate change in the future.

Numerous poor countries already cannot afford to meet the basic needs of their people. Without status, environmental refugees could be condemned by a global problem to a national economic and geographical lottery, and to the patchwork availability of resources and seemingly ad hoc application of immigration policies. There is wide acceptance that current national policies would not be remotely capable of handling the scale of the problem. Environmental refugees need recognising, and the problem needs managing before it manages us.[10]

12

Conflict

As the effects of climate change bite, limited resources such as water and land will become scarcer, leading to conflict. Whilst some feel the evidence for a causal link between climate change and violent conflict is weak,[1] it is hard to disagree with the statement that

> climate change increasingly undermines human security in the present day, and will increasingly do so in the future, by reducing access to, and the quality of, natural resources that are important to sustain livelihoods. Climate change is also likely to undermine the capacity of states to provide the opportunities and services that help people to sustain their livelihoods... in certain circumstances these direct and indirect impacts of climate change on human security may in turn increase the risk of violent conflict.[2]

A less reticent United Nations Environment Programme report, however, attributes the conflict in Darfur, Sudan, which broke out in 2003 and left between 200,000 and 500,000 dead, to climate change and environmental degradation.[3] Whilst the report acknowledges the immediate cause of the conflict to be a regional rebellion, it suggests the true genesis of the conflict pre-dates 2003 and is to be found in failing rains and creeping desertification. Rainfall reductions of up to 30 per cent over forty years and the advance of the Sahara by well over a mile every year exacerbated tensions between farmers and herders over disappearing pasture and evaporating waterholes. Achim Steiner, the United Nations Environment Programme's executive director, stated that 'It doesn't take a genius to work out that as the desert moves southwards there is a physical limit to what [ecological] systems can sustain, and so you get one group displacing another.' The report goes on to threaten an era of wars triggered by climate change across Africa unless more is done to contain the damage.

Poor and hungry people are vastly more likely to fall into violent conflict than rich and well-fed populations. And as the climate gets tougher, people will migrate more. Nomads from the drylands of northern Darfur went into the more-humid farm regions of southern Darfur in the 1980s in search of water for their livestock. Similarly, migrants from other parts of the African Sahel, such as Burkina Faso, moved south towards the coastal regions, into the Ivory Coast and other coastal countries. In both cases, the migrations triggered conflicts.[4]

Conflict over water in Isiolo

In Kenya's Isiolo district, Sambarwawa is a place where groups of pastoralists congregate in times of drought. Each group is allocated a space on the dry riverbed to dig a shallow well for water. They are allowed to bring their animals to drink here once every four days. 'It's a sort of cafeteria system to ensure everybody has a chance to get water for their animals', says local leader Wako Liba. But the system has been under extraordinary strain because of almost a decade of drought. By December 2005, some 10,000 herders with 200,000 animals had descended on tiny Sambarwawa, many trekking 400 kilometres from the epicentre of the drought in the Turkana and Wajir. Although the village had not seen rain for a year, they knew they could still find water under the riverbed. But then the shallow wells began to dry up.

'As the water level dropped, I foresaw conflict', says Liba. 'Some herders started encroaching on boreholes owned by different communities. As one group pushed to water its livestock, another moved to restrict access to the few boreholes that had enough water.' As the drought intensified, the pressure finally led to killings.

'Gunshots reverberated the whole night', Liba recalls. 'By the time I came down, seven people had died. There were dozens of injuries. Animal carcasses littered almost a kilometre stretch of the valley.' David

Kheyle, 37, was queuing for water when fighting broke out. 'There was grumbling that evening. A good number of boreholes didn't have water so the queues were relentless', he says. 'People were becoming impatient. Suddenly there was a scramble at the northern end of the valley... it was a free-for-all. But it later took on an ethnic dimension when people aligned with their kind to defend themselves.'

Edwin Rutto of the Africa Peace Forum, says that there is an 'established correlation between drought and violent conflict'. With recurring droughts associated with climate change, poor pastoralists are stuck in an ever-tightening poverty-trap. 'After people go through a period of relative recovery, then another drought hits. People are living in a state of perpetual suffering', says Rutto.

Global warming could tip the former Soviet states of central Asia into conflict with each other over access to water. Many experts have pointed out how the regional water-sharing systems, once closely woven together by Soviet design and management, have unravelled. Access to water must now be managed by five fractious and poverty-stricken new countries (and also Afghanistan) that have shown relatively little willingness to cooperate, each wanting more water for national development. Oxfam has encouraged local civil society in Tajikistan to begin debates on how to manage water resources fairly and efficiently and to move away from cotton-dependency, which uses so much water. At the same time, dialogue will need to encompass Tajikistan's neighbours so that water becomes a source of peace not conflict in the region.

Researchers at the Institute of Development Studies argue that it is difficult to identify climate change as the 'smoking gun' that causes violent conflict, because conflict always has a multitude of political, economic and environmental causes.[5] Others agree that the effect of climate change on armed conflict depends on a number of political and social variables, and that these can better predict where conflict is likely to occur than knowing where climate change impacts will strike.[6] Helping people adapt to climate change can, however, be a way to build peace, and, likewise, building peace can be a way to help people cope with the challenges of global warming. Some pastoralists in the Horn of Africa, for example, are coping better with more frequent, severe and longer droughts due to new agreements with farmers who sell them hay and permit their livestock to graze on crop residues left on drought-stricken fields. Many development agencies now find themselves involved in peace-building activities as part of their work, helping those in some of the world's most inhospitable environments cope with climate-related challenges.

Climate change conflicts in north-west Kenya

The Turkana – nomadic pastoralists who graze huge herds of cattle and other animals on the dry savannah of north-west Kenya – are used to dealing with drought and food shortages. But, in line with climate change predictions for sub-Saharan Africa, droughts are now more frequent and more prolonged. Opportunities to recover from a poor rainy season before the next is upon them are now infrequent. Also, rain is less predictable now. The Turkana used to know, from natural signs, when rains would come and where they would fall. Now rain, when it comes, may be sudden, violent and unpredictable.

There have always been tensions between the Turkana and other pastoralist groups for access to water and pasture. But these have increased as water sources have dried up and pastures have been lost. Because the water table is not being recharged, the wetland areas that the Turkana could traditionally fall back on in times of drought have dwindled. Even the huge Lake Turkana has receded.

Territorial disputes have become more common as the lake recedes. Many such disputes are settled peacefully, but each time one party or the other is perceived to have broken an agreement, the willingness to trust the next time, and to respect borders, is eroded.

Cattle raiding is also linked to drought. Raiding has always been used as a strategy to restock herds during or after a drought, and more droughts and more cattle deaths are leading to more raids. A particularly big raid in 2004 saw a coalition of the Toposa from Sudan and the Dodoth from Uganda take away large numbers of Turkana cattle. And raids lead, in turn, to new cycles of retaliation.

Traditional forms of raiding are also being replaced by more predatory approaches where well-armed gangs and rebel groups seize Turkana cattle to sell for profit. These raids, unlike those undertaken in order to restock cattle, can be large scale and extremely violent. They obey none of the traditional rules that tended to limit violence. Guns and bullets are cheap and plentiful, spilling over from the long-running conflicts in neighbouring southern Sudan and northern Uganda, and the increase in violence and killings is marked.

As a result of droughts and growing insecurity, the Turkana have moved from a state in which they are able to cope most of the time to one in which destitution and vulnerability to famine are a constant danger. International aid agencies like Oxfam have been providing relief food. Oxfam's approach is not just to give out food, however, but to link human and animal health, relief and development, and to help Turkana institutions that are trying to tackle the problems of cross-border raiding using conflict reduction and peace-building techniques.

Peace-building between tribes in northern Kenya

Recurring drought in arid and semi-arid lands of northern Kenya has long been a major natural hazard, causing mass livelihood losses, hunger, conflict and internal displacements. Rainfall in such areas is always unreliable and erratic, and mostly seasonal sandy streams are only active for short periods during any rainfall event. Climate change is reducing rainfall amounts and changing rainfall patterns. Coupled with other pressures on rangeland natural resources, pastoral farmers are increasingly in conflict with each other over access to scarce water.

During the dry periods they get water for themselves and their livestock by scooping into the sand beds of the dry streams. Water in such sites is usually clean enough to drink but quickly runs out. Sand dams can enhance this traditional practice by putting extra water into the sand beds. Sand dams are made by building a concrete wall across the channel at specific sites to trap and hold back the sand during flooding, thus creating an additional bank of sub-surface water.

With careful siting, sand dams can store over 6,000 cubic metres of water. They have been used successfully in Kenya in Kitui, Machakos and Samburu districts. Other dry countries such as Ethiopia and Namibia have also used them. Compared to other water-harvesting techniques, benefits include provision of clean water for households and control of erosion. Sand dam sites witness plant growth which attracts animals and helps restore ecosystems threatened by drought. Building sand dams can be costly in terms of getting people involved, and it is labour-intensive, but it is culturally acceptable and can alleviate water shortages and benefit livelihoods.

Constructing sand dams gave Practical Action the opportunity to help build peace between tribes in conflict over scarce resources in northern Kenya. Teams of Samburu and Turkana men and women worked together to build the dams. Practical Action insisted that equal numbers of each tribal group and of men and women should work together. This helped informal interaction and renewed recognition of common problems between the tribes.

Improved water availability has reduced the deaths of both people and livestock. Water troughs have been constructed, allowing more animals to drink and reducing congestion and conflicts between water users. Coupled with better management, these improvements to existing water resources have opened up underused rangelands and increased livestock productivity, despite poor rainfall.

13

What next?

Members of the Up in Smoke coalition are in agreement that there are three overarching challenges for tackling climate change:

1. How to stop and reverse further global warming.
2. How to live with the degree of global warming that cannot be stopped.
3. How to design a new model for human progress and development that is climate-proof, climate-friendly and gives everyone a fair share of the natural resources on which we all depend.

Stopping and reversing further global warming is largely the responsibility of industrialised nations. Much of the historical responsibility for climate change lies with these countries and their use of fossil fuels over the last 150 years. They must therefore take the first steps to reduce greenhouse gas emissions. Such countries need to go far beyond their targets for reducing emissions set under the Kyoto Protocol. Instead they need to cut emissions to a level commensurate with halting global warming and so that temperature rise is kept well below 2°c above pre-industrial levels – a goal of the European Union since 1996.

Scientists say that the threat of major and irreversible climate change, with potentially enormously damaging impacts, becomes far greater as temperatures increase, and that we have less than ten years before global emissions must start to decline. Instead they are rising remorselessly. This means there is not a moment to lose. Wealthy countries need to make plans to implement cuts is emissions of greenhouse gases of between 60 and 80 per cent by 2050. The negotiations under way in the United Nations Framework Convention on Climate Change (UNFCCC) and the Kyoto Protocol must deliver a fair, effective and equitable agreement that deepens current greenhouse gas reduction targets in the industrialised countries and allows greater contributions from some of the larger developing countries.

Why focus on limiting warming to 2 degrees?

Although a temperature rise of 1.5°c above pre-industrial levels will be disastrous for many, such as those in small island nations, scientific consensus seems to be converging on the fact that 2°c marks a line which once crossed will mean damage will become progressively less manageable, perhaps uncontrollable. 'Once temperature increase rises above 2°c up to 4 billion people could be experiencing growing water shortages. Agriculture will cease to be viable in parts of the world and millions will be at risk of hunger. The rise in temperature could see 40–60 million more people exposed to malaria in Africa. The threshold for the melting of the Greenland ice-sheet is likely to have been passed and sea-level rise will accelerate. Above 2°c lies the greater danger of 'tipping points' for soil carbon release and the collapse of the Amazon rainforest.'[1]

Taking account of the internationally agreed principle that wealthy countries must act first and fastest to cut emissions, poorer developing countries must also play their part. Countries such as Brazil should work to reduce, and eventually halt, deforestation, because deforestation is estimated to contribute to 18 per cent of global greenhouse gas emissions. Wealthier developing countries like China, India and South Africa must also work to develop in such a way that prioritises both energy efficiency and the use of renewable energy, and developed countries, as well as international donors and financial institutions, need to help these and other poorer nations to leapfrog 'dirty development' and the exploitation of fossil fuels to meet growing national energy needs. In Africa, Asia and Latin America alike, this exploitation does little for the development or security of its people. The potential for sustainable and renewable energy on these continents is enormous.

Taking responsibility for reducing greenhouse gas emissions is not just something for wealthy countries to act on. It is high consumers throughout the world who add most to the levels of greenhouse gases in the atmosphere. A wealthy businessman in India can have just as big a carbon footprint as a wealthy businessman in America.

In some instances, individuals and companies are taking responsibility for their actions; in others, nation-states are leading the way. NGOs like those in the Up in Smoke coalition have played a key role in influencing public opinion and government action alike, and several faith-based groups are also leading the way in encouraging people, as well as governments, to change their behaviour.

The churches and climate change

Churches have been taking a lead role in encouraging their members to take action on climate change. And church leaders are increasingly speaking out against climate change, which many see as a human rights issue, because of the disproportionate affect that it will have on the world's poor.

Carlos Tamez, a Presbyterian pastor in Mexico who leads Latin American work stemming from the World Council of Churches (WCC) Climate Change initiative, has outlined his region's vulnerability to increasingly severe and frequent hurricanes, drought and desertification, hunger and forced migration. The Catholic Archbishop of Bulawayo in Zimbabwe, Pius Ncube, has noted the affects of climate change in Matabeleland over the past few years. 'There has been a big climate change within living memory', he reports, 'and the rainy season, which used to run from

October to April, now starts around mid-November and ends in February.' The Argentine ecumenical patriarch Elias Crisostomo Abramides has also described the effects of climate change in Argentina. 'We are dealing not only with a technological issue', he said, 'but with a spiritual crisis that has taken us to the present situation.' In the UK, in 2004, the then Archbishop of Canterbury, Dr Rowan Williams, endorsed remarks made by Sir David King, the government's chief scientist, describing climate change as 'a weapon of mass destruction'.

In Zambia, the Catholic bishops issued a letter in 2004 deploring that 'We have not taken the best care for this environment on which we depend for our survival.' In South Africa, the Church has begun raising awareness on the issue of energy, particularly encouraging the development of renewable energy. Local ecumenical groups in South Africa, such as the Diakonia Council of Churches in Durban, are incorporating climate change into their Bible study materials.

In December 2004, Reverend Ishmael Noko, from Zimbabwe and head of the Lutheran World Federation, spoke of the tsunami disaster that month: 'It is a reminder that we would do well to heed, at a time when even the relatively inadequate efforts by the international community to address climate change continue to be subverted and undermined by some of those most responsible.' His concerns were shared by Reverend Dr Sam Kobia, a Kenyan Methodist and the head of WCC, who called on powerful nations that had not signed the Kyoto Protocol on greenhouse gas emissions to do so.

Speaking at an event in 2005, Andres Tamayo, a Catholic priest from Honduras and director of the Environmental Movement of Olancho, spoke of the impact of deforestation and global warming on his region. 'Our forests could play a part in climate change mitigation' he asserted, 'but, sadly, 64 per cent of them have been cleared in the last 30 years.' He has organised two Marches for Life where thousands of Hondurans walked to the capital city, demanding a logging ban. Elsewhere the Catholic Bishops of Northern Mexico have criticised lumber companies for having 'no vision of the future' and 'placing economic incentives before all else'.

When the Pacific Churches' Consultation on Climate Change met on Kiribati in 2004, they produced the Otin Taai declaration. Acknowledging the impacts of human-induced climate change, signatories promised to engage Christian churches internationally in education and action on climate change. Specialised church-related ministries for emergency response, development and advocacy were called on to integrate climate change and adaptation projects into their work. Churches were also asked to encourage companies that produce or consume large amounts of fossil fuels to move towards cleaner, renewable energy sources.

Over the past few years, the WCC Climate Change Programme has challenged inaction by the United States Government over the issue. In the United States itself, the Catholic Bishops' Conference issued a statement in 2001, *Global Climate Change: A Plea for Dialogue, Prudence, and the Common Good*, in which they stated that the level of scientific consensus on global warming obligated taking action to avert potential dangers. 'Since our country's involvement is key to any resolution of these concerns,' it said, 'we call on our people and government to recognise the seriousness of the global warming threat and to develop effective policies that will diminish the possible consequences of global climate change.' The Bush administration was urged to undertake initiatives for energy conservation and the development of renewable energy. American citizens were asked to reflect on their lifestyles as 'voracious consumers' and consider living more simply.

The question of how best to live with the degree of global warming that cannot be stopped is in part addressed by all the stories and subsequent recommendations made in this book. But it is important to remember that industrialised nations have a moral and ethical obligation to help vulnerable nations and people deal with current and expected climate change impacts given that the poor did little to create the problem in the first place. Signatory countries to the United Nations Framework Convention on Climate Change acknowledged this responsibility by signing up to the fact that all of them, and especially the developed countries, had an obligation to assist the poorest and most vulnerable countries, namely the Least Developed Countries and the Small Island Developing States, to adapt to the impacts of climate change.[2]

Helping poor countries cope with climate change will cost money. It is important that any funding provided for adaptation is additional to existing funds and not just redirected from other important development budgets or reclassified, thereby meeting targets on paper alone. This funding should not be seen as 'aid' or given in the spirit of philanthropy. Rather, it should be seen as the responsibility of the rich countries that created the problem and that thus have an obligation to help.

The World Bank has estimated that the overall annual costs for developing countries to adapt to projected climate change are likely to be US$70–$100 billion each year from 2010 to 2050.[3] Such sums may seem large, but they need to be put in perspective. For instance, following the lethal European heatwave in the summer of 2003, when an estimated 11,435 people died in France, US$748 million in extra funding was announced for hospital emergency services in that country alone.[4] Or consider the fact that global subsidies to fossil fuel industries totalled US$557 billion in 2008 (an increase from US$215 billion in 2007).[5] Of a different magnitude altogether, the total amount of US federal government money injected into the financial markets in order to save private banks had reached US$8.5 trillion (or US$8,150,000 million) by the end of 2008.[6] As Chilean economist Professor Manfred Max-Neef asks, 'US$8,150,000 million, instead of saving private banks, could generate 270 years of a world without hunger. Would not a world without misery be a better world for everyone, even for the banks?'

Given that people are particularly vulnerable to climate change if they are poor, it seems obvious that any steps taken to reduce poverty will help people cope better with climate change. The cancellation of outstanding, unpayable international debt, and trade justice that promotes a fair and sustainable trade system, rather than trade liberalisation as an end in itself, would help tackle deepening poverty and thus vulnerability to climate change.

The importance of promoting more sustainable lifestyles and energy efficiency, particularly among high-consumption nations such as the United States, has been stressed. But all policies and programmes relating to health, infrastructure, education and the economy in every nation should also be tested to see whether they are both 'climate proof' and 'climate friendly'. This means asking whether they will be able to stand the test of time in a climate-change-constrained world – for example, there is no point reinforcing sea walls in Cotonou, Benin, if ultimately sea-level rise means people have to move inland. And it means asking if policies will leave people in developing countries more vulnerable to the effects of global warming – for example, looking at whether governments should be supporting investment in renewable energies or traditional fossil-fuel based energy systems.

A lack of public understanding regarding climate change means that effort is needed globally to raise awareness about the problem. Many countries are developing national climate change strategies and action plans that can help address this problem. For example, China launched its national climate change programme in June 2007. This includes strategies to reduce greenhouse gas emissions, alternative ways to fuel its huge and growing need for energy, as well as ways to cope with the worst effects of climate change ahead. Civil society organisations in China are also increasingly active in work to combat climate change. More knowledge is needed, however, on what makes one community or country more or less vulnerable than another, and what approaches and tools can be used to increase resilience at regional, national and local levels.

Whilst awareness about climate change issues is growing, developing-country governments still tend to prioritise other pressing concerns, such as education, health, housing and providing enough food for their people. Until people realise that global warming is intimately linked with all these concerns and will considerably exacerbate the challenges under them in the future if not tackled now, this is unlikely to change.

The need for awareness-raising in Tajikistan

Climate change is affecting communities in Tajikistan. People in Khatlon and Pamir, when interviewed in 2007 under a Christian Aid-funded research programme, felt strongly that the climate had changed for the worse over the previous five years. Farmers like Burkhoni Saidbek from Sughd province are already adapting their farming techniques to the new conditions. But the research also revealed that three-quarters of those interviewed said they had insufficient information on climate change and possible adaptation measures. This may be because the Tajik government and media do not prioritise the issue, and because of the relatively small number of environmental non-government organisations operating in the country (just twenty compared to 200 in neighbouring Kyrgyzstan). It is no surprise, therefore, that so few of the people questioned could correctly identify increases in greenhouse gas emissions as the principal cause of global warming.

A range of adaptive measures are available for these communities, including improved systems for measuring and forecasting hydrological changes, increased crop rotation, sustainable pasture management, crop insurance schemes, efficiency measures for irrigation, riverbank strengthening and the development of disease-resistant varieties of wheat and cotton. However, minimal government funding prevents the rolling out of these measures. Although the Tajik government developed a National Action Plan on climate change in 2003, funds have not been made available to oblast or district authorities to carry out adaptive measures, in spite of the importance of agriculture for the national economy.

Raising youth awareness in Fiji

The University of the South Pacific's Institute of Applied Science and the Pacific Centre for Sustainable Development are organising workshops for Fiji's youth, training them on the use of songs and traditional dances to raise awareness about climate change, biodiversity, sustainable development and the need to understand how these issues are connected. Drama consultant Sukulu Rupeni described how youth capacity-building workshops had been conducted in three village communities – Naboutini in Cakaudrove, Muaivuso in Rewa, and Univanua in Tailevu. The workshops involved about sixty-five young people from fifteen villages who were given role-play exercises after each topic had been taught. The exercises reinforced the messages.

Youths learnt how climate change affects coastal areas, the agriculture, water and health sectors, and marine and terrestrial biodiversity in small island countries. They learnt how climate change will devastate coral reefs and how changing rain patterns threaten land-based biodiversity. Participants also gained an understanding of the impacts of climate change on food sources, traditions, culture and livelihoods. Tourism is a major source of income for Fiji, with the nation's marine biodiversity attracting many visitors. The workshops also raised awareness about the significance of village marine-protected areas as food sources.

The two-year project will include Vanuatu, the Solomons and Tuvalu, where lessons learnt in Fiji will be replicated. The next step is for community drama troupes to work with their provincial council offices to coordinate village community theatre performances. Community theatre groups will also help other NGOs and government departments working to raise awareness of similar issues in other provinces.

Recently donor governments have emphasised the role of 'new technology' in tackling climate change, in particular in the context of energy efficiency, renewable energy, sustainable transport or improved weather forecasting. Development groups, however, believe adaptation must be more than this: it has to be about strengthening communities from the bottom up, building on their own coping strategies to live with climate change and helping them to participate in the development of climate change policies. Identifying what communities are already doing to adapt is an important step towards discovering what people's priorities are and sharing their experiences, obstacles and positive initiatives with other communities and development policymakers. Giving a voice to people in this way can help to grow confidence, as can valuing their knowledge and placing it alongside science-based knowledge.

One thing is certain: a one-size-fits-all development approach will not work. Effective responses to climate change will differ everywhere depending on local circumstances. The greatest challenge is to build climate resilience and resistance, and to secure livelihoods at local level.

New models for human progress

This book has so far focused on defining the grave challenges presented by global climate change, described some of the ways in which poor people are dealing with these challenges, and emphasised the urgent need for new development models. Tackling climate change in a way that helps the people who are most affected by it clearly needs a new model for human development that reaches far deeper than merely offsetting the carbon emissions resulting from a family holiday in Majorca.

'It is clear that current mitigation and adaptation responses are inadequate and that the model of development currently being pursued globally will only exacerbate the worsening impacts of climate change. The Fourth Assessment Report of the Intergovernmental Panel on Climate Change states: "There is high agreement and much evidence that with current climate change mitigation policies and related sustainable development practices, global GHG emissions will continue to grow over the next few decades." This growth in emissions will exacerbate problems in vulnerable developing states and could easily lead to economic and social turmoil, in turn posing an even greater threat to the environment, human life and global security. Therefore, the current pattern of development pursued worldwide will continue to endanger the well-being not only of citizens in developing countries but also of those in the developed world.'

R.K. Pachauri, chairman of the IPCC; director-general of The Energy and Resources Institute; and founding director of the Yale Climate and Energy Institute

'Climate change, important as it is, is nevertheless a symptom of a deeper malady, namely our fixation on unlimited growth of the economy as the solution to nearly all problems. Apply an anodyne to climate and, if growth continues, something else will soon burst through limits of past adaptation and finitude, thereby becoming the new crisis on which to focus our worries.'

Professor Herman E. Daly, ecological economist at the School of Public Policy, University of Maryland, and author of *Steady-State Economics*[7] and *Beyond Growth*.[8]

'The current model from the industrialised countries which develops through the use of fossil fuels as the driving source of energy cannot be sustained. We must find a balance to improving our quality of life while not undermining the environment, and therefore the capacity of our species and other forms of life to continue. This can be controlled by investing in renewable sources of energy low in carbon – solar, wind, hydropower; sources of energy that will help us to develop without sacrificing the environment. We all need to recognise that wherever we are, even if we feel that we are very far from the forest that is being logged in the Amazon, the Congo or Southeast Asia, environmentally we are not far; we are indeed a global village. What is happening in faraway places that undermines environment, the damage that is being done, will affect us all.'

Professor Wangari Maathai, Nobel Peace Prize winner

This final section explores what new policies we should focus on developing, what fresh ways we could be thinking about development and sustainability, what fundamental principles of our economic system need changing, and what steps we need to take to achieve an alternative model of growth and development. Many of these alternatives are currently within our reach. Learning from and applying some of these approaches may yet help us achieve a development model that is sound and sustainable, and hence move us towards a better future.

But before we go about suggesting alternative models for human development, it is worth stopping for a while to ask what 'development' is and what we actually mean by it. Most definitions of development have common characteristics. Typically, they say something about: improving human well-being and realising our potential in safe and clean environments; creating fair and just forms of governance; providing economic and political freedoms for all; and, allowing us to lead dignified and fulfilled lives.

These ambitions are almost universally supported, at least in word. But their achievement is set heavily in the context of conventional global economic growth. And such growth is hard-wired at the planetary level to the increased use of already-overused resources. Questioning the benefits of growth tends to cause a reflex action among most policymakers and economists. It is, for many, still heresy.

Yet an active debate about the merits or otherwise of growth has raged at the margins for more than four decades. In 2007, Adair Turner, current member of the UK's Financial Policy Committee and former chairman of the Financial Services Authority, the Confederation of British Industry and the UK government's Committee on Climate Change, commented: 'We should ... dethrone the idea that maximising the growth in measured prosperity, GDP per capita, should be an explicit objective of economic and social policy.'⁹

Nevertheless even now, according to received wisdom, you can't have development without all that global economic growth entails in terms of its human and environmental costs. The logic runs in circular fashion, rather like accepting that you must work hard, in often poor conditions, worsened sometimes by the economic activity itself, to earn the money, to buy the medicine, to cure yourself of the illness from which you are suffering, because of your overwork in poor conditions. Regardless of the logic, the strategy in practice, along with the typical sets of policies that come attached to it, has proved increasingly inefficient and ineffective in recent decades.

The conviction that development is dependent on global economic growth is a major driver of the destruction of the natural environment. It is as if we hope that by turning natural capital into financial capital we can somehow disengage ourselves from our dependence on the natural environment and the ecological limits of our world. In climate change we find evidence that this approach is misguided, myopic and unsustainable. In terms of natural resources – clean air, minerals, forests, clean water and fertile soils – there are simply not enough to support ever-growing levels of consumption. Humans already use more natural resources and produce more waste than global ecosystems can replace and absorb. The last year that humanity's levels of resource use fell within the means of our life-supporting natural assets was 1987.[10] But why has it taken mainstream economists so long to recognise the links between environment and economics, and why do so many still fail to make this link? What kind of development is it that potentially bankrupts its own life-support system? And what kind of meaningful development is possible if the life-support system is chronically compromised?

Research in 2006 revealed that for everyone to live at the European average level of consumption at the time, more than double the biocapacity available – the equivalent of 2.1 planet Earths – would be needed to sustain this. And if everyone consumed at the US rate, nearly five planet Earths would be required.[11]

Growth as a means of ending poverty has been failing on its own terms too, with a shrinking share of benefits reaching those who need them most. Thus we end up with the paradox that the already-rich now have to consume ever more, to deliver a shrinking share of benefits to the poorest. In the 1990s, to achieve a single dollar of poverty reduction, for those living on less than US$1 per day, it took US$166 of extra global production and consumption, generating enormous environmental impacts which counter-productively hurt the poorest most. Thus global economic growth is an extremely inefficient way of achieving poverty reduction.[12]

At the level of most governments, in rich and poor countries alike, there appears to be no consideration of a fundamental alternative to this view of development. Faced with critical flaws in the basic model, the official response seems to be to soldier on and hope for the best. For some reason, changing course for a different sea or safe harbour is not considered an option. We must steam ahead, holed below the water line, through iceberg-ridden waters, simply because that is the course originally set – a course that no one feels able to correct.

Climate change is a serious threat to human development. But it also holds opportunity. Rethinking how to share a finite planet, and meeting our collective needs whilst living within environmental limits, could not only rescue civilisation (yes, the stakes are that high) but be a way to tackle deeply entrenched problems of social injustice, and greatly improve overall human well-being.

Not everyone subscribes to the traditional narrow view of development. Critical voices are increasingly being raised. Some key ones are in this book. Four world-leading thinkers from poor countries – all development practitioners whose experiences cover Asia, Africa and Latin America, as well as the corridors and meeting rooms of the international financial institutions – were asked about what they felt any new models for human development in a climate-change-constrained world should include in order to make people's lives happier and healthier. They are: Professor Jayati Ghosh from India, Nobel Prize winner Professor Wangari Maathai from Kenya, and the development economists Professor Manfred Max-Neef from Chile and David Woodward based in Cambodia. None of the alternatives they propose are underpinned by global economic growth – indeed they are based on broader interpretations of development that do not require global growth in order to succeed.

Jayati Ghosh makes the case for pursuing new, less materialistic and aspirational role models for human development in the light of climate change and resource scarcity. Without this, poorer countries are being set up to fail. She explains that the way wealthy nations like the United States have developed has left them vulnerable, and is not the path for others to follow.

Jayati Ghosh: Rethinking material realities

'Relatively small minorities of elite and middle class groups have dominated the process of economic growth across the world, especially in the past two decades. The large and growing inequalities within countries have meant that production has been disproportionately geared towards meeting the changing lifestyle requirements of the rich everywhere, rather than ensuring basic needs for all.

This means that coping with climate change also necessarily requires a reduction of income and wealth inequalities within countries. This is not going to be easy. It will require the global elite, spread across both developed and developing worlds, to curb extravagant lifestyles. It will require wage shares of national income to rise from their current very low proportions, with corresponding declines in the shares of profits and interest. It will require governments everywhere to be more responsive to the needs of the bulk of their citizenry rather than bow to the interests of a privileged minority.

But it will also mean that, even among the less wealthy, the presumptions and aspirations of what constitutes a civilised life will have to be modified. The model popularised by "the American Dream" is perhaps the most dangerous in this context, with its emphasis on suburban residential communities far from places of work, markets and entertainment and linked only through private motorised transport.

Indeed, the automobile industry provides a telling example. In the United States, the original home of the automobile, the role of big car companies in influencing policy has been problematic. It was associated not only with the systematic destruction of the public transport network in large parts of the USA, but with associated patterns of residence and occupation that required people to be constantly dependent upon automated mobility for work, entertainment, domestic provisioning and even social interaction. This led to the emergence of huge personal dependence upon private transport in all aspects of life.

This model is now being exported to countries in the developing world, as the personally owned automobile moves from being considered a luxury to be aspired for, to being seen as a necessity for 'normal' life. Along with this, as elites and middle class groups with "voice" opt for the personal vehicle as the preferred transport option, public transport is underfunded; it becomes even more inadequate and increasingly unattractive as a viable alternative. This has already led to massive problems of urban congestion in the metropolitan areas of many developing countries, and is further encroaching upon life even in semi-urban areas.

Capitalist markets created this want and then proceeded to over-supply it: we now have substantial overcapacity in automobile production globally. And the automobile companies have as a result been among the first to be badly affected by the global economic slowdown. Yet in this period of crisis, much of the efforts of governments across the world, beginning with the USA, are directed towards saving these automobile companies, by providing financial lifelines, offering tax sops and generally trying to create more of the same problems that were already proving to be unmanageable. The immediate fears about job losses if some of these companies do shut down have completely overshadowed any questions on the longer-run appropriateness of such production.

The issue involves moving beyond such palliatives as 'green cars' that reduce carbon emissions, although that is obviously desirable. It requires a shift in the way we organise our societies, our locations, our lives. To start with, a much greater emphasis on creating communities that do not require major and continuous movement of individuals on a daily basis – by bringing together home, work and leisure locations as far as possible – is important. Second, a major impetus must be given to affordable, efficient and fast public transport networks. Third, there must be incentives to reduce unnecessary mobility, for example by using the possibilities created by newer information and communication technology...

The current multilateral negotiations on climate change have thus far been hugely disappointing, especially to people in the developing world, because they have barely addressed the crucial issue of technology transfer. It is no surprise that new and green technologies are dominantly being developed in the North by large corporates: after all they have the resources and now even the fiscal incentives to do so. But the increasingly octopus-like grip of intellectual property rights denies producers in developing countries access to these technologies except under very onerous and typically monopolistic conditions. For any meaningful action on mitigating and adapting to climate change, much more democratic access to new technologies is absolutely essential. And with it, finance to enable producers in the developing world to adopt such technologies is also required.

It is more than obvious now that unfettered markets are simply unequal to these complex and enormous tasks. Not only are they obsessed with short-run profitability, but the incentives thrown up by current relative prices all operate to direct production and consumption in precisely the opposite, unsustainable, direction. So government intervention – within countries and spanning across countries in multilateral efforts – is absolutely essential. Fortunately for those who have been pointing to the need for government action for some time, the state is back in fashion in economic terms. The de facto nationalisation of banking in many important capitalist economies, the need for large firms to keep turning to governments for large bailouts and other props, the recognition that free cross-border trade often operates to worsen environmental damage – all these make the case for public policy much more persuasive.

So we are clearly entering a global phase of much intervention in the economy, and we can certainly use this opportunity to create the changes in patterns of accumulation, production and consumption that will be more sustainable in future as well. But that means we must be continuously conscious of the need to ensure that such governments themselves are democratic, transparent and accountable in their functioning.'

Professor Jayati Ghosh is Professor of Economics at Jawaharlal Nehru University, New Delhi, and the executive secretary of International Development Economics Associates (IDEAS)

Wangari Maathai argues for a revolution in democratic participation and inclusion in the way that important economic development decisions are made. Both to adapt to climate change and to leapfrog dirty development, significant new financial resources will be needed, along with appropriate technology transfer. Equity and the maintenance of the environment, as the basis for people's livelihoods, must take centre stage in policy decisions. She stresses that 'For humankind to manage and share resources in a just and equitable way, governance systems must be more responsive and inclusive. People have to feel that they belong, and the voice of the minority must be listened to, even if the majority has its way. We need systems of governance that respect human rights and the rule of law and that deliberately promote equity.'

Wangari Maathai: What does Africa need against climate change?

'A post-carbon society and addressing climate change mean much more than constraining carbon usage. While Africa is rich in resources, her people are poor; to counter this poverty, Africa needs to develop. For development in Africa to be successful, we need to ensure the right conditions in society that facilitate respect, equity and sustainability.

In trying to explain my work and philosophy, I often look to the traditional African stool to articulate the relationship between peace, good governance and sustainable development. Just as the African stool is made out of a single block of wood, so each leg, or pillar, is reinforced by the others and formed from the same grain. The issues must be addressed together and simultaneously.

The traditional stool comprises a seat and three legs. The first leg represents democratic space, where rights – whether human, women's, children's or environmental – are respected. The second leg symbolises the sustainable and accountable management of natural resources both for those living today and those in the future, in a manner that is just and fair, including for people on the margins of society. The third leg stands for what I term "cultures of peace". These take the form of fairness, respect, compassion, forgiveness, recompense and justice. The three legs of the stool support the seat, which in this conception represents the milieu in which development can take place. Citizens, feeling secure that the three legs are in place – that their country has strong democratic principles, equitable distribution of resources, and strong cultures of peace – can be educated, productive and creative. In this situation, the spirit of the citizenry not only welcomes development, but drives itself, because individually and collectively the people feel they have the opportunity to contribute. A secure seat also provides the environment in which governments can receive money from multilateral agencies, lending institutions or private donors, and use it accountably and responsibly – free of corruption – for the benefit not of the few, but of the many.

Having a stable stool means ensuring that a holistic approach to development is adopted, placing a priority on democratic governance and respect for human and other rights; equitable, sustainable and accountable use of all resources; and affairs of state that are managed in an accountable and responsible way. When all these are in place, the stool is secure, the state has stability, and development can take place.'

Professor Wangari Maathai is a Nobel Peace Prize winner, founder of the Greenbelt Movement and author of *The Challenge for Africa*[13]

Manfred Max-Neef dismisses the notion that there are no alternative directions that the global economy can take. He believes that globalisation is a particularly dangerous form of development which just allows the wealthy and powerful to capture more wealth and power, leaving the poor even less well off than they were previously. He identifies a series of new fundamental principles upon which, he believes, we can build. The shape of the future, he argues, is one of far greater regionalisation and localisation of markets.

Manfred Max-Neef: The world on a collision course

'Solutions imply new models that, above all else, begin to accept the limits of the carrying capacity of the Earth. We need to move from efficiency to sufficiency and well-being. Also necessary is the solution of the present economic imbalances and inequities. Without equity, peaceful solutions are not possible. We need to replace the dominant values of greed, competition and accumulation, for those of solidarity, cooperation and compassion. The paradigm shift requires turning away from economic growth at any cost. Transition must be towards societies that can adjust to reduced levels of production and consumption, favouring localised systems of economic organisation...

A fundamental change could be an increased re-localisation of the economy at local levels, designing new rules that bring production and consumption closer: a human-scale economy.

A NEW ECONOMY

A possible alternative is a new economy based on five postulates and one fundamental value principle:

Postulate 1: The economy is to serve the people; the people are not to serve the economy.

Postulate 2: Development is about people and not about objects.

Postulate 3: Growth is not the same as development; development does not necessarily require growth.

Postulate 4: No economy is possible in the absence of ecosystem services.

Postulate 5: The economy is a subsystem of a larger and finite system, the biosphere; hence permanent growth is impossible.

Value principle: No economic interest, under any circumstance, can be above the reverence for life.

Going through the list, it is not difficult to conclude that what we have today is, one after the other, exactly the opposite. Yet to assume that an economy based on these postulates is not feasible is absurd. It is already being practised in many countries at local level, since it is obvious that such principles can best work at micro-levels.

The most important contribution of a human-scale economy is that it may allow for the transition from a paradigm based on greed, competition and accumulation, to one based on solidarity, cooperation and compassion. Such a transition would allow for greater happiness not only among those who have been marginalised, but also among those responsible for marginalising them, despite what they may believe. Some of the new rules might include:

- Monetary localisation, so that it flows and circulates as much as possible in its place of origin. It can be shown by economic models that if money circulates at least five times in its place of origin, it may generate a small economic boom.
- Produce locally and regionally everything possible, in order to bring consumption closer to the market.
- Protect local economies through tariffs and quotas.
- Encourage local competition in order to avoid monopolies.
- Levy ecological taxes on energy, pollution and other negatives. At present we are taxed for goods and for bads.
- Make a greater democratic commitment to ensure effectiveness and equity in the transition towards local economies.

THE OBSCENITY OF CONTINUING WITH THE SAME

While 1 billion people suffer from hunger, and nearly 3 billion live on less than US$2 a day, we witness the obscene concentration of monetary wealth. The 400 richest Americans accumulate a fortune of US$1.75 trillion. Each of them has an average of US$3.9 billion. The monetary wealth of these people is more than twice the GDP of sub-Saharan Africa, which hosts 800 million people. Such fortunes continue to expand despite the crisis that affects the immense majority of the world's population.

It should be pointed out that today's rich are not related to the growth of the real economy, as was the case in the days of Carnegie, Rockefeller and Ford. The new fortunes, on the contrary, are based on the destruction of the real economy, as we are witnessing just now. Of the 400 multibillionaires, 65 come from finance, 51 from speculative investments, 36 from entertainment, 35 from real-estate speculation, 30 from computer technologies, 28 from gas and petroleum, 20 from retail. Only 5 of the 400 are related to the production of industrial goods. This alone demonstrates one transcendental characteristic of the dominant paradigm: that it generates capitalists that are social parasites.

A deep change is not only urgent, but inevitable!'

Professor Manfred Max-Neef is a Chilean economist specialising in development; in 1981 he founded the Centre for Development Alternatives (CEPAUR), and he is a former rector of the Universidad Austral de Chile in Valdivia

David Woodward, whose direct experience ranges from the international financial institutions to the United Nations, believes that systemic change is unavoidable, possible and desirable given the challenges ahead. He believes that a clear outline of a new, flexible development model is visible, one that can both eradicate poverty and address climate change and resource scarcity.

David Woodward: More with less – rethinking poverty reduction in a changing climate

'The alternative economic model described here revolves primarily around a revitalisation of rural economies, taking advantage of the synergies arising from consumption patterns at low income levels (raising demand, production and consumption of basic goods, of and by low-income communities in a virtuous cycle). It also looks at the potential for widespread application of micro-renewable energy technologies in rural areas, exploiting the potential for considerable cost reductions and technological improvements from the creation of a mass market...

The association of carbon emissions in developing countries with urbanisation suggests an increased focus on reinvigorating rural economies as a driver of development. Rural-led development would help to slow rural–urban migration, reducing the strain on urban infrastructure, and would be more effective in reducing poverty, which is high in rural areas.

However, the focus of the current model on agriculture, and particularly export agriculture, as the basis of rural development has had limited benefits – partly because of the weakness of many tropical agricultural prices over the last thirty years (which itself largely reflects the increase in their supply owing to widespread promotion). Equally, agriculture is among the sectors most vulnerable to the impacts of climate change; and growing awareness and concern about climate change is already encouraging a shift towards local purchasing – a trend which can be expected to intensify over time. At the same time, as the recent food crisis has demonstrated, increasing use of biofuels in the North has the potential to threaten food security in the developing world through major increases in the world prices of basic foods.

This suggests a need for rural development to be based largely on the diversification of rural economies away from agriculture; and for agriculture itself to be oriented primarily towards local needs rather than exports. It is almost inevitable that such a diversification would entail a substantial increase in energy consumption in rural areas. In fact, it is arguable that the limited availability of energy in rural areas in many low-income countries has been an important constraint to their development and diversification.

While carbon constraints clearly should not be allowed to limit development, it is clearly important to minimise the carbon emissions that result. This suggests an emphasis on renewable energy sources. There is a potentially important synergy here between climate change mitigation and rural development. A major reason for the inadequacy of energy infrastructure in rural areas in many developing countries is that scarcity of population, together with limited public resources and purchasing power, makes conventional centralised electricity generation financially unviable. However, the potential for renewable electricity generation (solar, wind, hydroelectricity, and in some cases wave and tidal power) is often considerable. Renewable generation is also more conducive to decentralised generation systems, producing electricity on a relatively small scale at community level. The widespread application of micro-renewable energy technologies in rural areas could have a trans-formative effect even greater than that of mobile telephony in the field of communications, stimulating the regeneration of rural economies, while limiting carbon emissions (and slowing deforestation by reducing reliance on fuelwood).'

David Woodward is a former economic adviser in the Foreign and Commonwealth Office; technical assistant to the UK executive director to the IMF and the World Bank; development economist in the Strategy Unit of the World Health Organization; and economic policy adviser to Save the Children (UK)

There is increasing evidence that more money, beyond the point that a level of material sufficiency has been reached, does not bring greater happiness or life satisfaction.[14] This is all very well when you've got it, but doesn't help those who haven't and who are yet to achieve a level of sufficiency. Greater attention also needs to be paid to the often hidden costs of superficially affluent societies. Many suffer from high levels of depression, suicide rates, family and community breakdown and addiction – all the symptoms of so-called 'affluenza'. Whilst money can fuel consumption – and generate all the greenhouse gas emissions associated with new cars, new gadgets, overseas holidays and new infrastructure – it is becoming increasingly clear that, beyond a certain level at least, money cannot buy happiness.

Bhutan and Thailand offer alternative views to the obsessive belief that ever increasing wealth and economic output lead to strong sustainable societies. In Thailand, King Bhumbiol Adulyadej has developed the philosophy of the 'Sufficiency Economy' to lead his people to a balanced way of life and to serve as the main sustainable development theory for the country. The philosophy is underpinned by a middle path between local society and the global market. The aim of the approach is to allow the nation to modernise, but to do so in a sustainable manner – one which will not lead to detrimental outcomes arising from rapid economic and cultural transitions.[15] 'By creating a self-supporting economy, Thai citizens will have what they need to survive but not excess, which would turn into waste.' The King goes on to state that sufficiency is about living in moderation and being self-reliant so as to avoid endogenous and exogenous shocks that could destabilise the country. 'The Sufficiency Economy should enable the community to maintain adequate population size, enable proper technology usage, preserve the richness of the ecosystems and survive without the necessity of intervention from external factors.' According to the King, 'If we contain our wants, with less greed, we would be less belligerent towards others. If all countries entertain this – this is not an economic system – the idea that we all should be self-sufficient, which implies moderation, not to the extreme, not blinded with greed, we can all live happily.'[16]

For over thirty years, the Kingdom of Bhutan has followed the words of the former king, Jigme Singye Wangchuck, who stated that 'Gross National Happiness is more important than Gross National Product.' Development in this instance becomes a continuous process towards achieving a balance between the material and non-material needs of individuals and society. The country's philosophy of development recognises that growth should not be an end in itself.[17] Included in Gross National Happiness (GNH) is a middle path in which spiritual and material pursuits are balanced. Gross National Happiness has four main pillars:

1. sustainable and equitable socio-economic development;
2. conservation of the environment;
3. preservation and promotion of culture;
4. promotion of good governance.

The Centre for Bhutan Studies explains the reasoning behind the GNH approach like this:

> Across the world, indicators focus largely on market transactions, covering trade, monetary exchange rates, stockmarket, growth, etc. These dominant, conventional indicators, generally related to Gross Domestic Product (GDP) reflect quantity of physical output of a society. GDP, along with a host of supporting indicators, is the most widely used indicator. Yet GDP is heavily biased towards increased production and consumption, regardless of the necessity or desirability of such outputs, at the expense of other more holistic criterion. It is biased against conservation since it does not register conservation or stocks. Indicators determine policies. The almost universal use of GDP-based indicators to measure progress has helped justify policies around the world that are based on rapid material progress at the expense of environmental preservation, cultures, and community cohesion.[18]

In response to this, the Centre has generated the Gross National Happiness index to reflect the happiness and general well-being of the Bhutanese population more accurately and profoundly than a monetary measure. The measure will inform both Bhutanese people and the wider world about the current levels of human fulfilment in Bhutan and how these vary across districts and across time, and will also inform government policy.

Once we acknowledge that sustainable and happy lives rely on natural resources, including stable levels of atmospheric greenhouse gas concentrations, the question of how to measure this well-being, and find an alternative to traditional measures of 'progress' or 'development', such as gross domestic product, emerges. Clearly we need an indicator to tell us when consuming more actually becomes detrimental to our livelihoods and life satisfaction. The Happy Planet Index (HPI) developed by the new economics foundation provides one such solution.[19] Described as 'an innovative new measure that shows the ecological efficiency with which human well-being is delivered', it allows us to look at development in a very different light. It shows the ecological efficiency with which lives of relative length and satisfaction are enabled. It differs markedly from the indicator of national income usually referred to by commentators to say whether or not the economy is growing, and relied on by governments to measure their success – gross domestic product (GDP).

The HPI shows that 'good lives do not have to cost the earth.' Take Germany and the United States, for instance. People's life expectancy and their 'perceived' and, to some extent, 'measured' sense of life satisfaction are almost identical in both countries. However, Germany's ecological footprint is roughly half that of the United States. Basically Germans are as happy as Americans but use half the resources as Americans to achieve happiness. The opposite is also true: Russia and Japan have roughly the same ecological footprint, but if you are born in Japan you are likely to live seventeen years longer than if you were born in Russia, and you likely to be some 50 per cent more satisfied than the average

Russian.[20] If indicators like the HPI and more detailed national accounts of well-being were used to set meaningful policy goals and measure progress rather than GDP, the world would almost certainly be a happier place.

The United Kingdom has toyed with this idea. In 2010 the prime minister David Cameron launched the Measuring National Well-being programme, operated by the Office for National Statistics. It functions, however, alongside traditional ways to measure progress such as GDP and has done little to date to reform how decisions are made. As in most industrialised countries, achieving growth remains the driving force behind UK policymaking. There are, nevertheless, other doors opening as a way to introduce change following the global financial crisis. With a loss of confidence in the markets and the private sector, people are again looking to governments to secure their well-being. Bold governments therefore have a window of opportunity to rein in and redirect the power of the private sector, and push through policies that could help slow down our seemingly inexorable march to a world that is 4°C warmer and support those struggling with the impacts of global warming. A focus on 'green growth' could potentially see a more integrated approach to economic growth and environmental sustainability.

The Green New Deal

In the UK, the Green New Deal Group – a group of experts from the financial, energy and environmental fields – offers an innovative approach to visioning new development paths. Underpinning their thinking is the recognition that the global economy is facing a triple crunch – 'a combination of a credit-fuelled financial crisis, accelerating climate change and soaring energy prices underpinned by an encroaching peak in oil production'.[21] The Green New Deal entails 're-regulating finance and taxation plus a huge transformational programme aimed at substantially reducing the use of fossil fuels and in the process tackling the unemployment and decline in demand caused by the credit crunch. It involves policies and novel funding mechanisms that will reduce emissions contributing to climate change and allow us to cope better with the coming energy shortages caused by peak oil.' The Group points out that the three linked threats – financial meltdown, climate change and peak oil – have their roots in the current model of globalisation. However, it is not globalisation per se but the model of development that underpins globalisation that is the root cause of the problem.

The Green New Deal consists of two main strands. First, it outlines a structural transformation of the regulation of national and international financial systems, and major changes to taxation systems. Second, it calls for a sustained programme to invest in and deploy energy conservation and renewable energies, coupled with effective demand management. Focusing on the needs of the UK, the Green New Deal involves:

- A bold new vision for low-carbon energy production that will involve making every building a power station. The strategy will involve tens of millions properties with maximised energy efficiency. Alongside this will run a 'maximised' renewable energy programme.
- Creating and training a 'carbon army' of workers to provide the human resources for the vast environmental reconstruction programme that is required if truly sustainable development is ever to be achieved.
- More realistic fossil fuel prices that are high enough to create economic incentives to drive efficiency and bring alternative energy sources to market whilst, at the same time, reflecting the true environmental costs of burning fossil fuels.
- A wide-ranging package of financial innovations and incentives to assemble the tens of billions of pounds that need to be invested in the development of new, efficient energy infrastructure and initiatives to reduce energy demand.
- Re-regulating the domestic financial system to ensure that the creation of money at low rates of interest is consistent with democratic aims, financial stability, social justice and environmental sustainability.
- Breaking up the discredited financial institutions that have needed so much public money to prop them up in the last credit crunch.
- Re-regulating and restricting the international finance sector to transform national economies and the global economy.
- Subjecting all derivative products and other exotic instruments to official inspection.
- Minimising corporate tax evasion by clamping down on tax havens and corporate financial reporting.

This book argues that our chances of triumphing over climate change will rise dramatically if we change the context within which we 'fight its fire'. More than that, it suggests that we are already surrounded by a sleeping architecture of better ways to organise our economies, communities and livelihoods. Indeed, some of these new models for human development are being created and applied right now. Whilst there is no single answer to how the global economy should be reshaped to enable human development in a carbon-constrained future, it is clear that a major reshaping is both unavoidable and desirable. The issue is whether governments and financial institutions continue to support old, failed approaches with their policy frameworks and our financial resources, or whether they will move to encourage and replicate new approaches that take account of our changed economic and environmental circumstances. We have, in fact, much more choice about our collective economic future than we have been led to believe. The challenge, it seems, is clear, and many of the solutions known. The task is now to act.

Notes

PREFACE

1. The International Institute for Environment and Development website, www.iied.org/smoke provides free access to all the Up in Smoke reports, references for which (in the order they were published) are as follows: A. Simms, J. Magrath and H. Reid, *Up in Smoke: Threats from, and Responses to, the Impact of Global Warming on Human Development*, New Economics Foundation, London, 2004; A. Simms and H. Reid, *Africa – Up in Smoke? The Second Report from the Working Group on Climate Change and Development*, New Economics Foundation, London, 2005; A. Simms and H. Reid, *Up in Smoke? Latin America and the Caribbean: The Threat from Climate Change to the Environment and Human Development, The Third Report from the Working Group on Climate Change and Development*, New Economics Foundation, London, 2006; J. Magrath and A. Simms, *Africa – Up in Smoke 2. The Second Report on Africa and Global Warming from the Working Group on Climate Change and Development*, New Economics Foundation, London, 2006; H. Reid and A. Simms, *Up in Smoke? Asia and the Pacific. Fifth Report of the Working Group on Climate Change and Development*, New Economics Foundation, London, 2007; A. Simms, V. Johnson and M. Edwards, *Other Worlds Are Possible: Human Progress in an Age of Climate Change*, New Economics Foundation, London, 2009.

INTRODUCTION

1. See M. Pilson, 'We are evaporating our coal mines into the air', *AMBIO* 35(3) (2006): 130–33. Pilson demonstrates that this phrase was actually written almost a century later in 1983 by Jesse Ausubel, then a US government scientist. In a historical note on the concerns of climate change, Ausubel had drawn on the works of Svante Arrhenius and early-twentieth-century scientist Alfred J. Lokta.
2. J. Jouzel et al., 'Orbital and millennial Antarctic climate variability over the past 800,000 years', *Science* 317 (2007): 793–6.
3. S. Solomon et al., *Climate Change 2007: The Physical Science Basis. Contribution of the Working Group I to the Fourth Assessment Report of the Intergovernmental Panel on Climate Change*, Cambridge University Press, Cambridge, 2007.
4. N. Oreskes, 'The scientific consensus on climate change', *Science* 306(5702) (2004): 1686.

5. J. Cook et al., 'Quantifying the consensus on anthropogenic global warming in the scientific literature', *Environmental Research Letters* 8(2) (2013): 4024.
6. S. Goldenberg, 'Secret funding helped build vast network of climate denial thinktanks', *Guardian*, 14 February 2013.
7. E. Conway and N. Oreskes, *Merchants of Doubt: How a Handful of Scientists Obscured the Truth on Issues from Tobacco Smoke to Global Warming*, Bloomsbury, London and New York, 2010.
8. T. Corcoran, 'The cool down in climate polls', *Financial Post*, 6 January 2010.
9. Based on per capita emissions data from www.carbonplanet.com/country_emissions.
10. UNEP, *The Emissions Gap Report 2012: A UNEP Synthesis Report*, United Nations Environment Programme, Nairobi, 2012.
11. S. Huq and C. Toulmin, *The Three Eras of Climate Change*, IIED sustainable development opinion paper, IIED, London, 2006.
12. C. Hall et al., 'Hydrocarbons and the evolution of human culture', *Nature* 426 (2003): 318–22.
13. R. Ayres and B. Warr, *The Economic Growth Engine: How Energy and Work Drive Material Prosperity*, Edward Elgar, Cheltenham, 2009.
14. D. Woodward and A. Simms, *Growth Isn't Working: The Unbalanced Distribution of Benefits and Costs from Growth*, New Economics Foundation, London, 2006.
15. C.D. Keeling, 'Rewards and penalties of monitoring the earth', *Annual Review of Energy and the Environment* 23 (1998): 25–82
16. See http://co2now.org for the latest carbon dioxide concentrations.
17. G. Peters et al., 'Rapid growth in CO_2 emissions after the 2008–2009 global financial crisis', *Nature Climate Change* 2 (2011): 2–4.
18. D.H. Meadows, D.L. Meadows, J. Randers and W.W. Behrens III, *Limits to Growth*, New American Library, New York, 1972.
19. J. Rockström et al. 'A Safe Operating Space for Humanity', *Nature* 461 (2008): 472–5.
20. L. Mehta (ed.), *The Limits to Scarcity: Contesting the Politics of Allocation*, Routledge, London, 2010.
21. Data for 2010 from the official United Nations site for the MDG indicators: http://mdgs.un.org.
22. A. Costello et al., 'Managing the health effects of climate change', Lancet and University College London Institute for Global Health Commission, *Lancet* 373 (2009): 1693–733.
23. *The World Factbook 2013–14*, Central Intelligence Agency, Washington DC, 2013.
24. Data for 2010 from the official United Nations site for the MDG indicators: http://mdgs.un.org.
25. Quoted in R. Roach, *Dried up, Drowned out: Voices from the Developing World on a Changing Climate*, Tearfund, Teddington, 2005.

CHAPTER 1

1. Adapted from M.L. Parry, O.F. Canziani, J.P. Palutikof, P.J. van der Linden and C.E. Hanson (eds), *Contribution of Working Group II to the Fourth Assessment Report of the Intergovernmental Panel on Climate Change*, Cambridge University Press, Cambridge and New York, 2007.
2. S. Rahmsdorf, 'A semi-empirical approach to projecting future sea-level rise', *Science* 315 (2007): 368–70.

3. W.T. Pfeffer, J.T. Harper and S. O'Neel, 'Kinematic constraints on glacier contributions to 21st century sea-level rise', *Science* 321(2008): 1340–43.
4. Royal Society, *Climate Change: A Summary of the Science*, Royal Society, London, 2010.
5. Adapted from M.L. Parry et al. (eds), *Contribution of Working Group II to the Fourth Assessment Report of the Intergovernmental Panel on Climate Change.*

CHAPTER 2

1. See http://millionsofmouths.com/info.html.
2. M. Parry, A. Evans, M.W. Rosegrant and T. Wheeler, *Climate Change and Hunger: Responding to the Challenge*, World Food Programme, Rome, 2009.
3. J.J. McCarthy, O.F. Canziani, N. Leary, D.J. Dokken and K.S. White (eds), *Climate Change 2001: Impacts, Adaptation and Vulnerability, IPCC Working Group II, Third Assessment Report*, Cambridge University Press, Cambridge, 2001.
4. X. Diao, P. Hazell, D. Resnick and J. Thurlow, *The Role of Agriculture in Development: Implications for Sub-Saharan Africa*, Research Report 153, International Food Policy Research Institute, Washington DC, 2007.
5. International Labour Organization (ILO); www.ilo.org/global/industries-and-sectors/agriculture-plantations-other-rural-sectors/lang--en/index.htm (accessed 25 June 2013).
6. W. Schlenker and D.B. Lobell, 'Robust negative impacts of climate change on African agriculture', *Environmental Research Letters* 5(1) (2010).
7. V.A. Orindi and L.A. Murray, *Adapting to Climate Change in East Africa: A Strategic Approach*, Gatekeeper series no. 117, IIED, London, 2005.
8. Research from the Adaptive research project, part-funded by Oxfam.
9. See www.ethicalteapartnership.org.
10. World Food Programme, *Hunger and Climate Change*, World Food Programme, Rome, 2010.
11. M.L. Parry et al., Effects of climate change on global food production under SRES emissions and socio-economic scenarios, *Global Environmental Change* 14 (2004): 53–67.
12. Cited in DFID, *Climate Change and Poverty: Key Sheets*, Department for International Development, London, 2004.
13. MOST (Ministry of Science and Technology of the People's Republic of China), CASS (Chinese Academy of Science), CMA (China Meteorological Administration), *National Assessment Report on Climate Change*, Science Press, Bejing, 2007.
14. Data from the Ministry of Agriculture in Bangladesh; see www.bangladesh.gov.bd.
15. I.M Faisal and S. Parveen, 'Food security in the face of climate change, population growth and resource constraints: implications for Bangladesh', *Environmental Management* 34 (2004): 487–98.
16. S. Huq and J. Ayers, *Climate Change Impacts and Responses in Bangladesh*, Policy Department Economic and Scientific Policy, European Parliament, Brussels, 2008.
17. R.L. Naylor et al., 'Using El Niño–Southern Oscillation climate data to improve food policy planning in Indonesia', *Bulletin of Indonesian Economic Studies* 38 (2002): 75–91.

18. FAO, *FAO/WTP Crop and Food Supply Assessment Mission to Timor-Leste*, Food and Agriculture Organization of the United Nations, Rome, 2003.
19. C.S. Lobban and M. Schefter, *Tropical Pacific Island Environments*, Island Environments Books, Mangilao, Guam, 1997.
20. R.L. Naylor et al., 'Assessing risks of climate variability and climate change for Indonesian rice agriculture', *Proceedings of the National Academy of Sciences* 104 (2007): 19.
21. L. Kalaughter, *Climate Models Indicate Rice Agriculture in Indonesia Will Suffer*, IOP Publishing, Bristol, 2007.
22. K. Boonprakrob and S. Hattirat, *Crisis or Opportunity: Climate Change and Thailand*, Greenpeace Southeast Asia, Bangkok, 2006.
23. World Food Programme, *Hunger and Climate Change*, World Food Programme, Rome, 2010.
24. G. Xuejie et al., Climate change due to greenhouse effects in China as simulated by a regional climate model, *Advances in Atmospheric Sciences* 18(6) (2001): 1224–30.
25. See www.unep.org/dewa/assessments/ecosystems/iaastd/tabid/105853/ default.aspx.
26. D. Howden, 'Christmas appeal: simple measures that help in extreme temperatures', *Independent*, 17 December 2005.
27. V. Shiva, 'India needs her small farmers for food security, livelihood security, peace and democracy', *ZNET Daily commentaries*, 5 April 2007, www.zmag. org/Sustainers/Content/2007–04/05shiva.cfm.
28. Data from World Bank website: http://web.worldbank.org/wbsite/external/ topics/extpoverty/extpa/0,,contentMDK:20040961~menuPK:435040~pagePK :148956~piPK:216618~theSitePK:430367~isCURL:Y,00.html (accessed 29 May 2013).
29. A.U. Ahmed, R. Vargas Hill, L.C. Smith, D.M. Wiesmann and T. Frankenberger, *The World's Most Deprived: Characteristics and Causes of Extreme Poverty and Hunger*, International Food Policy Research Institute, Washington DC, 2007.
30. OECD statistics quoted in R. Mayne, *Causing Hunger: An Overview of the Food Crisis in Africa*, Oxfam Briefing Paper 91, July 2006, Oxfam International, Oxford.

CHAPTER 3

1. C.J. Vörösmarty et al., 'Global threats to human water security and river biodiversity', *Nature* 467 (2010): 555–61.
2. A. Costello et al., 'Managing the health effects of climate change', Lancet and University College London Institute for Global Health Commission, *Lancet* 373 (2009): 1693–733.
3. N.W. Arnell, 'Climate change and global water resources: SRES emissions and socio-economic scenarios', *Global Environmental Change*, 14(1) (2004): 31–52.
4. J. Rockström et al., 'Future water availability for global food production: the potential of green water for increasing resilience to global change', *Water Resources Research* 45(7) (2009).
5. Cited in DFID, *Addressing the Water Crisis*, UK Department for International Development, London, 2001.
6. R. Dixon, J. Smith and S. Guill, 'Life on the edge: vulnerability and adaptation

of African ecosystems to global climate change', *Mitigation and Adaptation Strategies for Global Change* 8(2) (2003): 93–113.

7. J.J. McCarthy, O.F. Canziani, N. Leary, D.J. Dokken and K.S. White (eds), *Climate Change 2001: Impacts, Adaptation and Vulnerability. IPCC Working Group II, Third Assessment Report*, Cambridge University Press, Cambridge and New York, 2001.

8. National Climate Change Office at the Department of Environment, *National Communication to the UNFCCC*, Tehran, 2003.

9. Z. Jianyun et al., 'Impact of climate change on water security in China', *Advances in Climate Change Research* 5 (suppl.) (2009): 34–40.

10. N. Cencchi, *Impact of Global Change on Large River Basins: Example of the Yellow River Basin*, International Food Policy Research Institute, Washington DC, 2011.

11. Economist Intelligence Unit, *Water for all? A Study of Water Utilities' Preparedness to Meet Supply Challenges in 2030*, Economist Intelligence Unit, Geneva and London, 2012.

12. M. Mirza and Q. Monirul, 'Global warming and changes in the probability of occurrence of floods in Bangladesh and implications', *Global Environmental Change* 12 (2002): 127–38.

13. This project is one of the 2007 winners of the Ashden Awards for Sustainable Energy; see www.ashdenawards.org.

14. P. McCully, *Before the Deluge: Coping with Floods in a Changing Climate*, IRN Dams, Rivers and People Report 2007, International Rivers Network, Berkeley CA.

15. Ibid.

16. E.A.K. Ford, *From Ice to High Seas: Sea level rise and European Coastlines*, The ice2sea Consortium, Cambridge, 2013.

17. S. Dasgupta, B. Laplante, C. Meisner, D. Wheeler and J. Yan, *The Impact of Sea Level Rise on Developing Countries: A Comparative Analysis*, World Bank Policy Research Working Paper (WPS4136), World Bank, Washington DC, 2007.

18. V.L. Tran, D.C. Hoang and T.T. Tran, 'Building of climate change scenario for Red River catchments for sustainable development and environmental protection', Preprints, Science Workshop on Hydrometeorological Change in Vietnam and Sustainable Development, Ministry of Natural Resource and Environment, Hanoi, 2005, pp. 70–82.

19. Dasgupta et al., *The Impact of Sea Level Rise on Developing Countries*.

20. Thanh Nien News, 'Major losses loom as Vietnam sea level rises', 2007, http://talkvietnam.com/2007/05/major-losses-loom-as-vietnam-sea-level-rises-experts.

21. S. Granich, M. Kelly and N.H. Ninh *Global Warming and Vietnam – A Briefing Document*, University of East Anglia, Norwich; IIED, London; Centre for Environment Research Education and Development, Hanoi, 1993.

22. Thanh Nien News, 'Major losses loom as Vietnam sea level rises'.

23. D. Dutta, 'An integrated tool for assessment of flood vulnerability of coastal cities to sea-level rise and potential socio-economic impacts: a case study in Bangkok, Thailand', *Hydrological Sciences Journal* 56(5) (2011): 805–23.

24. PEACE *Indonesia and Climate Change: Current Status and Policies*, World Bank, DFID and PEACE, Jakarta, 2007.

25. State Oceanic Administration, *National Sea Level Bulletin*, China, 2006.

26. UNEP, *Migratory Species and Climate Change – Impacts of a Changing Environment on Wild Animals*, UNEP/CMS Secretariat, Bonn, 2006.
27. M.L. Parry, O.F. Canziani, J.P. Palutikof, P.J. van der Linden and C.E. Hanson (eds), *Contribution of Working Group II to the Fourth Assessment Report of the Intergovernmental Panel on Climate Change*, Cambridge University Press, Cambridge and New York, 2007.
28. H. Harasawa, 'Key vulnerabilities and critical levels of impacts on east and south east Asia', in H.J. Schellnhuber, W. Cramer, N. Nakicenovic, T. Wigley and G. Yohe (eds), *Avoiding Dangerous Climate Change*, Cambridge University Press, Cambridge and New York, 2006, pp. 243–9.
29. S. Agrawala, T. Ota, A.U. Ahmed, J. Smith and M. van Aalst, *Development and Climate Change in Bangladesh: Focus on Coastal Flooding and the Sundarbans*, OECD, Paris, 2003.
30. Parry et al. (eds), *Contribution of Working Group II to the Fourth Assessment Report of the Intergovernmental Panel on Climate Change*.
31. McCarthy et al. (eds), *Climate Change 2001: Impacts, Adaptation and Vulnerability*.
32. UNEP, *Pacific Island Mangroves in a Changing Climate and Rising Seas*, Regional Seas Programme of UNEP, Secretariat of the Pacific Regional Environment Programme, Samoa; UNEP, New York, 2006.
33. S. Bettencourt et al., *Not If, but When: Adapting to NaturalHazards in the Pacific Islands Region*, World Bank, Washington DC, 2006.
34. See www.upi.com/Science_News/2013/02/11/Island-nation-fighting-sea-level-rise/UPI-32581360636139.
35. Ministry of the Environment and Conservation United Nations Development Programme, *Papua New Guinea: Initial National Communication under the UNFCCC*, Government of Papua New Guinea, Port Moresby, 2000.
36. J. Xu et al. 'The melting Himalayas: cascading effects of climate change on water, biodiversity, and livelihoods', *Conservation Biology* 23(3) (2009): 520–30.
37. W.W. Immerzeel, L.P.H. van Beek and M.F.P. Bierkens, 'Climate change will affect the Asian water towers', *Science* 328(5984) (2010): 1382–5.
38. Xu et al., 'The melting Himalayas'.
39. Parry et al. (eds), *Contribution of Working Group II to the Fourth Assessment Report of the Intergovernmental Panel on Climate Change*.
40. S. Piao et al., 'The impacts of climate change on water resources and agriculture in China', *Nature* 467 (2010): 43–51.
41. X. Li et al., 'Cryospheric change in China', *Global and Planetary Change* 62 (2008): 210–18.
42. Piao et al., 'The impacts of climate change on water resources and agriculture in China'.
43. A. Costello et al., 'Managing the health effects of climate change', Lancet and University College London Institute for Global Health Commission, *Lancet* 373 (2009): 1693–733.
44. B. Horstmann, *Glacial Lake Outburst Floods in Nepal and Switzerland: New Threats Due to Climate Change*, Germanwatch, Bonn, 2004.
45. Piao et al., 'The impacts of climate change on water resources and agriculture in China'.
46. The Panos Oral Testimony Programme.
47. R.S. Bradley et al., 'Threats to water supplies in the Tropical Andes', *Science* 312 (2006): 1755–6.

CHAPTER 4

1. A.J. McMichael (ed.), *Climate Change and Human Health: Risk and Responses*, WHO, UNEP and WMO, Geneva, 2003.
2. S. Hales et al., 'Potential effect of population and climate changes on global distribution of dengue fever: an empirical model', *Lancet* 360 (2002): 830–34.
3. S. Bettencourt et al., *Not If, but When: Adapting to Natural Hazards in the Pacific Islands Region*, World Bank, Washington DC, 2006.
4. McMichael (ed.), *Climate Change and Human Health*.
5. A. McSmith, 'The pollution gap', *Independent*, 25 March 2006.
6. P. Martens et al., 'Climate change and future populations at risk of malaria', *Global Environmental Change* 9(1) (1999): S89–S107.
7. UNEP, *Africa Environment Outlook: Past, Present and Future Perspectives. Impacts of the State of the Environment*, UNEP, Washington DC, 2005.
8. G. Zhou et al., 'Association between climate variability and malaria epidemics in the East African highlands', *Proceedings of the National Academy of Sciences* 101(8) (2004): 2375–80.
9. M.L. Parry, O.F. Canziani, J.P. Palutikof, P.J. van der Linden and C.E. Hanson (eds), *Contribution of Working Group II to the Fourth Assessment Report of the Intergovernmental Panel on Climate Change*, Cambridge University Press, Cambridge and New York, 2007.
10. F.C. Tanser, B. Sharp and D. le Sueur, 'Potential effect of climate change on malaria transmission in Africa', *Lancet* 362 (2003): 1792–8.
11. J.J. McCarthy, O.F. Canziani, N. Leary, D.J. Dokken and K.S. White (eds), *Climate Change 2001: Impacts, Adaptation and Vulnerability, IPCC Working Group II, Third Assessment Report*, Cambridge University Press, Cambridge and New York, 2001.
12. J.R. Jovel, *Natural Disasters and Their Economic and Social Impact*, CEPAL Review No. 38, Economic Commissions, Latin America and the Caribbean, Santiago de Chile, 1989.
13. R.S. Kovats, 'El Niño and human health', *Bulletin of the World Health Organization* 78(9) (2000): 1127–35.
14. C. Seas et al., 'New insights on the emergence of cholera in Latin America during 1991: the Peruvian experience', *American Journal of Tropical Medicine and Hygiene* 62(4) (2000): 513–17.
15. McCarthy et al. (eds), *Climate Change 2001: Impacts, Adaptation and Vulnerability*.
16. J. McGhie et al., *The Climate of Poverty: Facts, Fears and Hope*, Christian Aid, London, 2006.

CHAPTER 5

1. Financial Times, 'Colombia holds out for a big oil find', *Financial Times*, 21 February 2002.
2. M. Mark, 'Nigeria's penalty for gas flaring will not curb emissions, say campaigners', *Guardian*, 31 May 2012.
3. Ibid.
4. W. Jobin, 'Health and equity impacts of a large oil project in Africa', *Bulletin of the World Health Organization*, WHO, Geneva, 2003.
5. WWF Brazil, *Powerswitch Study for Brazil*, WWF, Brasilia, 2006.

6. Netherlands Environmental Assessment Agency, *China Now No. 1 in CO2 Emissions; USA in Second Position*, MNP, Bilthoven, The Netherlands, 2007.
7. Data from the US Energy Information Administration website: www.eia.gov/cfapps/ipdbproject/IEDIndex3.cfm?tid=90&pid=44&aid=8.
8. Ibid.
9. UNEP/GRID–Arendal and Development Alternatives, *Climate Change Mitigation in India*, UNEP/GRID–Arendal, Arendal, Norway; Development Alternatives, New Delhi.
10. IMF, *Energy Subsidy Reform: Lessons and Implications*, International Monetary Fund, Washington DC, 28 January 2013.
11. KPMG, *Taxes and Incentives for Renewable Energy*, KPMG International Cooperative, 2012.
12. A. McCrone, *Global Trends in Renewable Energy Investment 2012*, Frankfurt School of Finance and Management, Frankfurt, 2012.
13. See http://web.worldbank.org/wbsite/external/news/0,,contentMDK:232909 74~menuPK:51062077~pagePK:34370~piPK:34424~theSitePK:4607,00.html.
14. Christian Aid. See www.christianaid.org.uk/pressoffice/pressreleases/march-2011/free-fossil-fuels-climate-change-chain-gang-0103.aspx, 2011.
15. Letter from Desmond Tutu and other Nobel laureates to President Wolfensohn, 9 February 2004.
16. A. McCrone, *Global Trends in Renewable Energy Investment 2012*, Frankfurt School of Finance and Management, Frankfurt, 2012.
17. M.Z. Jacobson and M.A. Delucchi, 'Providing all global energy with wind, water, and solar power, Part I: Technologies, energy resources, quantities and areas of infrastructure, and materials', *Energy Policy* 39(3) (2011): 1154–69.
18. International Energy Agency, *The World Energy Outlook*, International Energy Agency, Paris, 2012.
19. Ibid.
20. N. Bruce, R. Perez-Padilla and R. Albalak, *The Health Effects of Indoor Air Pollution Exposure in Developing Countries*, World Health Organization, Geneva, 2002.
21. OECD, 'Exploiting Africa's huge potential as weapon against poverty', OECD, Paris, 2004; www.oecd.org/dataoecd/43/45/32285615.PDF.
22. www.ashdenawards.org.
23. This project is one of the 2007 winners of the Ashden Awards for Sustainable Energy.
24. This project is one of the 2007 winners of the Ashden Awards for Sustainable Energy.
25. This project is one of the 2007 winners of the Ashden Awards for Sustainable Energy.
26. CAN International, *A Viable Global Framework for Preventing Dangerous Climate Change*, CAN Discussion Paper, CAN, Beirut, 2003.
27. See the Carbon Planet website for per capita greenhouse gas emissions by country: www.carbonplanet.com/home/country_emissions.php.
28. UNEP, *The Emissions Gap Report 2012: A UNEP Synthesis Report*, United Nations Environment Programme, Nairobi, 2012.
29. Wetlands International, *Policy Brief on Indirect Land Use Change and Peatlands*, Wetlands International, Wageningen, 2013.
30. A. Hooijer, M. Silvius, H. Wösten and S. Page, *PEAT-CO2, Assessment of CO2 Emissions from Drained Peatlands in SE Asia*, Delft Hydraulics and Wetlands International, The Netherlands, 2006.

31. Ibid.
32. Quoted in L.R. Brown, *Plan B 2.0: Rescuing a Planet under Stress and a Civilization in Trouble*, Norton, London and New York, 2006.
33. S. Schlesinger, *Sugar Cane and Land Use Change in Brazil: Biofuel Crops, Indirect Land Use Change and Emissions*, Friends of the Earth Europe, Brussels, 2010.
34. M. Colchester et al., *Promised Land: Palm Oil and Land Acquisition in Indonesia – Implications for Local Communities and Indigenous Peoples*, Forest People's Programme, Perkumpulan Sawit Watch, HuMA and the World Agroforestry Centre, 2006.
35. See www.biofuelindonesia.com/news/2007/03/business-and-investment-biofuel.html (accessed 13 June 2013).

CHAPTER 6

1. D. Guha-Sapir and P. Hoyois, *Measuring the Human and Economic Impact of Disasters*, Government Office for Science, Foresight, London, 2012.
2. International Federation of Red Cross and Red Crescent Societies, *World Disasters Report 2012: Focus on Forced Migration and Displacement*, International Federation of Red Cross and Red Crescent Societies, Geneva, 2012.
3. C.B. Field (eds), *Managing the Risks of Extreme Events and Disasters to Advance Climate Change Adaptation, A Special Report of Working Groups I and II of the Intergovernmental Panel on Climate Change*, Cambridge University Press, Cambridge and New York, 2012.
4. Guha-Sapir and Hoyois, *Measuring the Human and Economic Impact of Disasters*.
5. M. Whittaker, *CEO briefing: A Document of the UNEP FI Climate Change Working Group*, UNEP Finance Initiatives, UNEP, Nairobi, n.d.
6. M.L. Parry, O.F. Canziani, J.P. Palutikof, P.J. van der Linden and C.E. Hanson (eds), *Contribution of Working Group II to the Fourth Assessment Report of the Intergovernmental Panel on Climate Change*, Cambridge University Press, Cambridge and New York, 2007.
7. Ibid.
8. J.J McCarthy, O.F. Canziani, N. Leary, D.J. Dokken and K.S. White (eds), *Climate Change 2001: Impacts, Adaptation and Vulnerability, IPCC Working Group II, Third Assessment Report*, Cambridge University Press, Cambridge, 2001.
9. A. Dupont, 'The strategic implications of climate change', *Survival: Global Politics and Strategy* 50(3) (2008): 29–54.
10. International Federation of Red Cross and Red Crescent Societies, *World Disasters Report Focus on Recovery*, International Federation of Red Cross and Red Crescent Societies, Geneva, 2001.
11. Parry et al. (eds), *Contribution of Working Group II to the Fourth Assessment Report of the Intergovernmental Panel on Climate Change*.
12. E.J. Burke, S.J. Brown and N. Christidi, 'Modelling the recent evolution of global drought and projections for the twenty-first century with the Hadley Centre climate model', *Journal of Hydrometeorology* 7 (2006): 1113–25.
13. M. de Wit and J. Stankiewicz 'Changes in surface water supply across Africa with predicted climate change', *Science* 311(5769) (2006): 1917–21.
14. Parry et al. (eds), *Contribution of Working Group II to the Fourth Assessment Report of the Intergovernmental Panel on Climate Change*.

15. IPCC (Intergovernmental Panel on Climate Change; R.T. Watson and the Core Writing Team, eds), *Climate Change 2001: Synthesis Report. A Contribution of Working Groups I, II, and III to the Third Assessment Report of the Intergovernmental Panel on Climate Change*, Cambridge University Press, Cambridge, 2001.
16. See www.grida.no/publications/vg/africa/page/3102.aspx (accessed 14 June 2013).
17. R.T. Watson, M.C. Zinyowera and R.H. Moss (eds), *The Regional Impacts of Climate Change: An Assessment of Vulnerability*, IPCC, Cambridge University Press, Cambridge 1997.
18. N. Brooks, *Drought in the African Sahel: Long Term Perspectives and Future Prospects*, Tyndall Centre for Climate Change Research, Norwich, 2004.
19. M. Kirkbride, *Delivering the Agenda: Addressing Chronic Under-development in Kenya's Arid Lands*, Oxfam Briefing Paper 88, Oxfam International, Oxford, 2006.
20. Data from www.unicef.org/wcaro/overview_4570.html (accessed 15 June 2013).
21. See www.oecdobserver.org/news/archivestory.php/aid/181/Shifting_sands_of_Sahel_aid.html (accessed 15 June 2013).
22. Data from the World Bank; see http://data.worldbank.org/indicator/DT.ODA.ODAT.PC.ZS?page=1 (accessed 15 June 2013).
23. S. Lautze, E. Stites, N. Nojumi and F. Najimi () *Qaht -E-Pool – 'A Cash Famine'. Food Insecurity in Afghanistan 1999–2002*, Feinstein International Famine Centre, Tufts University, Massachusetts, 2002.
24. Oxfam–Vietnam and the Graduate School of Global Environmental Studies of Kyoto University, Japan, *Drought Management Considerations for Climate Change Adaptation: Focus on the Mekong Region (Report Vietnam)*, Oxfam in Vietnam, Hanoi, 2007.
25. Pauline was interviewed as part of a Panos Oral Testimony Project on Climate Change in Mocho, Jamaica, in December 2005.
26. See www.guardian.co.uk/world/2013/feb/17/filipino-super-typhoon-climate-change (accessed 17 June 2013).
27. Parry et al. (eds), *Contribution of Working Group II to the Fourth Assessment Report of the Intergovernmental Panel on Climate Change*.
28. P.J. Webster et al., 'Changes in tropical cyclone number, duration and intensity in a warming environment', *Science* 309 (2005): 1844–6.
29. B. Sercombe and A. Albanese, *Our Drowning Neighbours: Labor's Policy Discussion Paper on Climate Change in the Pacific*, Australian Labor Party, Canberra, 2006.
30. S. Bettencourt et al., *Not If, but When: Adapting to Natural Hazards in the Pacific Islands Region*, World Bank, Washington DC, 2006.
31. International Federation of Red Cross and Red Crescent Societies, *World Disasters Report Focus on Recovery*, International Federation of Red Cross and Red Crescent Societies, Geneva, 2001.
32. Ibid.
33. World Food Programme, *2009 Food Aid Flows*, World Food Programme, Rome, 2009.
34. R. Mayne, *Causing Hunger: An Overview of the Food Crisis in Africa*, Oxfam Briefing Paper 91, Oxfam International, Oxford, July 2006.
35. K. Watkins, *Fighting Climate Change: Human Solidarity in a Divided World*.

Human Development Report 2007/2008, UNDP, Palgrave Macmillan, New York, 2007.

36. S. La Trobe and P. Venton, *Natural Disaster Risk Reduction: The Policy and Practice of Selected Institutional Donors*, Tearfund, London, 2003.

37. DFID, *Disaster Risk Reduction: A Development Concern*, DFID, London, 2005.

38. UN, *Plan of Implementation of the World Summit on Sustainable Development*, Report of the World Summit on Sustainable Development, Johannesburg, 2002. A/CONF.199/20.

CHAPTER 7

1. C.D. Thomas et al., 'Extinction risk from climate change', *Nature* 427 (2004): 145–8.

2. Millennium Ecosystem Assessment, *Ecosystems and Human Well-Being: Biodiversity Synthesis. A Report of the Millennium Ecosystem Assessment*, World Resources Institute, Washington DC, 2005, p. 10.

3. J. Pounds, M.P.L. Fogden and J.H. Campbell, 'Biological response to climate change on a tropical mountain', *Nature* 398 (1999): 611–15.

4. See www.rspb.org.uk/climate/wildlife/seabirds/ (accessed 18 June 2013).

5. K. Boonprakrob and S. Hattirat, *Crisis or Opportunity: Climate Change and Thailand*, Greenpeace Southeast Asia, Bangkok, 2006.

6. M. Case, *The Impacts of Climate Change on Hawksbill Turtles*, WWF Climate Change Programme, Washington DC, 2008.

7. See wwf.panda.org/what_we_do/where_we_work/amazon/about_the_amazon/wildlife_amazon (accessed 19 June 2013).

8. T.M. Lenton et al., 'Tipping elements in the Earth's climate system', *Proceedings of the National Academy of Sciences of the United States of America* 105(6) (2008): 1786–93.

9. A. Khalik, 'Climate change already hitting RI's poorest', *Jakarta Post*, 11 June 2007.

10. M.L. Parry, O.F. Canziani, J.P. Palutikof, P.J. van der Linden and C.E. Hanson (eds), *Contribution of Working Group II to the Fourth Assessment Report of the Intergovernmental Panel on Climate Change*, Cambridge University Press, Cambridge and New York, 2007.

11. A.K. Bhatnagar and M. Koul, 'Impact of climate change on medicinal plants: an assessment', in S.K. Dash and P. Rao (eds), *Assessment of Climate Change in India and Mitigation Policies*, WWF, New Delhi, 2004.

12. DEFRA, *Keysheet 7: Climate Change Impacts on Forestry in India*, DEFRA, London, n.d.

13. See www.who.int/mediacentre/factsheets/fs134/en (accessed 19 June 2013).

14. T. De Silva, *Industrial Utilization of Medicinal Plants in Developing Countries*, United Nations Industrial Development Organization, Vienna, n.d.

15. G.F. Midgley et al., 'Assessing the vulnerability of species richness to anthropogenic climate change in a biodiversity hotspot', *Global Ecology and Biogeography* 11(6) (2002): 445–51.

16. B. Brown et al., 'Bleaching patterns in coral reefs', *Nature* 404 (2000): 142–3.

17. R.W. Buddemeier, J.A. Kleypas and R.B. Aronson, *Coral Reefs and Global Climate Change: Potential Contributions of Climate Change to Stresses on Coral Reef Ecosystems*, Pew Center on Global Climate Change, Arlington VA, 2004.

18. M.D. McField, 'Coral response during and after mass bleaching in Belize', *Bulletin of Marine Science* 64(1) (1999): 155–72.

19. M.D. McField, 'Influence and disturbance on coral reef community structure in Belize', *Proceedings of the Ninth International Coral Reef Symposium*, Bali, October 2000, pp. 6–68.
20. See http://worldwildlife.org/places/mesoamerican-reef (accessed 19 June 2013).
21. H. Jeans et al., 'The role of ecosystems in climate change adaptation: Lessons for scaling up', in E.L.F. Schipper et al. (eds), *Community Based Adaptation to Climate Change: Scaling It up*, Routledge, London, 2014.
22. H. Reid, M. Chambwera and L. Murray, *Tried and Tested: Learning from Farmers on Adaptation to Climate Change*, IIED Gatekeeper series no. 153, IIED, London, 2013.
23. H. Reid, 'Climate change – biodiversity and livelihood impacts', in D. Roe (ed.), *The Millennium Development Goals and Conservation*, IIED, London, 2004, pp. 37–54.
24. S. Dasgupta et al., *The Impact of Sea Level Rise on Developing Countries: A Comparative Analysis*, World Bank Policy Research Working Paper (WPS4136), World Bank, Washington DC, 2007.
25. Data from www.aidflows.org (accessed 19 June 2013).
26. S. Agrawala et al., *Development and Climate in Fiji: Focus on Coastal Mangroves*, OECD, Paris, 2003.
27. Ibid.
28. K. Swiderska et al., *Adapting Agriculture with Traditional Knowledge*, IIED briefing paper, October 2011, IIED, London.
29. N. Stern, *Stern Review: The Economics of Climate Change*, HM Treasury, London, 2006.
30. Y. Pan et al. 'A large and persistent carbon sink in the world's forests', *Science* 333 (2011): 988–93.
31. Data from The World Resources Institute's Forest Landscapes Initiative, 2009; see www.wri.org/project/global-forest-watch (accessed 19 June 2013).
32. See www.nature.org/ourinitiatives/urgentissues/rainforests/rainforests-facts. xml (accessed 19 June 2013).
33. A. Krishnaswamy and A. Hanson, *Our Forests Our Future: Summary Report of the World Commission on Forests and Sustainable Development*, World Commission on Forests and Sustainable Development, Winnipeg, Manitoba, 1999.
34. Conservation International, *The World's Ten Most Threatened Forest Hotspots*, 2011; see www.conservation.org/newsroom/pressreleases/Pages/The-Worlds-10-Most-Threatened-Forest-Hotspots.aspx (accessed 19 June 2013).
35. FAO, *Global Forest Land-use Change from 1990 to 2005: Initial Results from a Global Remote Sensing Survey*, FAO, Rome, 2011.
36. K.S. Walter and H.J. Gillett (eds) *1997 IUCN Red List of Threatened Plants*, IUCN, The World Conservation Union, Gland and Cambridge, 1998.
37. IUCN, *1996 IUCN Red List of Threatened Plants*, IUCN, Gland, 1996.
38. WWF, *Palm Oil, Soy and Tropical Forests: A Strategy for Life*, WWF Forest Conversion Programme, Gland, 2008.
39. H. Burley, *What's Feeding Our Food? The Environmental and Social Impacts of the Livestock Sector*, Friends of the Earth, London, 2008.
40. S. Murphy, D. Burch and J. Clapp, *Cereal Secrets: The World's largest Grain Traders and Global Agriculture*, Oxfam research report, Oxfam, Oxford, 2012.
41. See www.greenpeace.org.uk/forests/climate-change (accessed 20 June 2013).
42. See www.foeeurope.org/press/2011/

Jan25_Europes_overconsumption_driving_destruction_Amazon.html (accessed 20 June 2013).
43. See www.greenpeace.org.uk/forests/climate-change (accessed 20 June 2013).
44. See www.fao.org/regional/honduras/pbcc (accessed 20 June 2013).
45. M.V. Larios, A.C. Guerrero, M.R. Mendieta and A. Alejandro, *Honduras frente al cambio climático*, PBBC-FAO, Tegucigalpa, 2003.
46. Environmental Investigation Agency, *The Illegal Logging Crisis in Honduras: How U.S. and E.U. Imports of Illegal Honduran Wood Increase Poverty, Fuel Corruption and Devastate Forest and Communities*, Center for International Policy, Washington DC, 2005.
47. V. Vidal, 'Impactos de la Aplicación de Políticas sobre cambio climatico en la Forestacion del Paramo del Ecuador', Programa de Doctorado en Ciencias ambientales, Universidad Autónoma de Barcelona, 2000, in J. Recharte, J. Torres and G. Medina, II Conferencia Electrónica sobre usos Sostenibles y Conservación del Ecosistema Páramo en los Andes, 22 May–30 June 2000, CONDESAN, Lima, pp. 47–51.
48. See www.virginearth.com (accessed February 2014).
49. W.F. Laurance, 'The Value of Trees', *New Scientist* 2547 (2006): 24.
50. I. Nhantumbo and L. Rolington, *Talking REDD+: Beyond Forestry – Joining up and Moving Forward*, IIED, London, 2011.

CHAPTER 8

1. UN, *World Urbanization Prospects, the 2011 Revision: Highlights*, Department of Economic and Social Affairs, Population Division, United Nations, New York, 2012.
2. Data from the World Population Prospects database of the United Nations Department of Economic and Social Affairs; see http://esa.un.org/unpd/wup/Analytical-Figures/Fig_1.htm.
3. See www.unhabitat.org/list.asp?typeid=44&catid=140 (accessed 20 June 2013).
4. See www.unhabitat.org/content.asp?typeid=19&catid=10&cid=928 (accessed 20 June 2013).
5. UNFPA, *State of World Population 2007: Unleashing the Potential of Urban Growth*, United Nations Population Fund, New York, 2007.
6. See www.citiesalliance.org/node/420 (accessed 20 June 2013).
7. M. Alam and M.D.G. Rabbani, 'Vulnerabilities and responses to climate change for Dhaka', *Environment and Urbanisation* 19 (2007): 81–97.
8. BPS, *Social-Economic Indicators of Indonesia*, Badna Pusat Statistik, Jakarta, 2006.
9. R. Indriyanti and B. Pedrique, *Access to Primary Healthcare for the population of the Precarious Areas of North Jakarta (Indonesia): Annual Report 2006*, Médecins du Monde (MDM)/Dokter Dunia, Indonesia, 2006.
10. PEACE, *Indonesia and Climate Change: Current Status and Policies*, World Bank, DFID and PEACE, Jakarta, 2007.
11. Asian Development Bank, *Socioeconomic Impacts of Climate Change and a National Response Strategy. A Report of the Regional Study on Global Environmental Issues: Country Case Study of Indonesia*, State Ministry for the Environment, Indonesian Forum for the Environment, Jakarta, 2003.
12. The Climate Group, *Low Carbon Leader: Cities*, The Climate Group, London, 2005.

13. NYCGP, *Best Practice: Comprehensive Climate Change Plan. City: Mexico City.* New York City Global Partners, New York, 2012.
14. National Adaptation Programmes of Action submitted to the UNFCCC to date are available at http://unfccc.int/national_reports/napa/items/2719.php.

CHAPTER 9

1. See www.unifem.org/gender_issues/women_poverty_economics (accessed 20 June 2013).
2. Karat Coalition, *Climate Change: Women in Developing Countries, the Hardest Hit*, Karat Coalition, Warsaw, 2011.
3. A.G. Patt, A. Dazé and P. Suarez, 'Gender and climate change vulnerability: what's the problem? What's the solution?', in M. Ruth and M.E. Ibarrarán (eds), *Distributional Impacts of Climate Change and Disasters: Concepts and Cases*, Edward Elgar, Cheltenham, 2009, p. 82.
4. A. Swarup, I. Dankelman, K. Ahluwalia and K. Hawrylyshyn, *Weathering the Storm: Adolescent Girls and Climate Change*, Plan UK, London, 2011.
5. M. Kimani, 'Women struggle to secure land rights: hard fight for access and decision-making power', *Africa Renewal: Special Edition on Women*, 2012, p. 37.
6. Africa Partnership Forum Support Unit, *Gender and Economic Empowerment of Women*, Africa Partnership Forum Support Unit (OECD), Paris, 2007.
7. Kimani, 'Women struggle to secure land rights', p. 37.
8. FAO, *Women, Agriculture and Food Security*, FAO, Rome, n.d.
9. See http://web.worldbank.org/wbsite/external/topics/extgender/0,,content MDK:22386117~pagePK:210058~piPK:210062~theSitePK:336868,00.html (accessed 21 June 2013).
10. Karat Coalition, *Climate Change*. GenderCC – Women for Climate Justice, *In Retrospect: Gender in COP15*, Gender CC, Berlin, n.d.
11. Data from the CIA *World Fact Book*; see www.cia.gov/library/publications//the-world-factbook/fields/2103.html (accessed 21 June 2013).

CHAPTER 10

1. L. Tamiotti et al., *Trade and Climate Change: WTO–UNEP Report*, World Trade Organization, Geneva, 2009.
2. Greenpeace International, *Equity and Climate Action: Greenpeace Position*, Greenpeace International, Amsterdam, 2009.
3. A. Simms, *Collision Course: Free Trade's Free Ride on the Global Climate*, New Economics Foundation, London, 2000.
4. Tamiotti et al., *Trade and Climate Change*.
5. Fairtrade Africa, *Fighting Back Climate Change: How Fairtrade Helps Producers in Africa Cope*, Fairtrade Africa, Nairobi, n.d.
6. UNEP, *Trade Liberalisation and the Environment – Lessons Learned from Bangladesh, Chile, India, Philippines, Romania and Uganda: A Synthesis Report*, United Nations Environment Programme, Geneva, 1999.
7. M. Davis, *Late Victorian Holocausts: El Niño Famines and the Making of the Third World*, Verso, London and New York, 2002.

CHAPTER 11

1. N. Myers, *Environmental Refugees: An Emergent Security Issue*, 13th Economic Forum, Prague, 23–27 May 2005.

2. M. Conisbee and A. Simms, *Environmental Refugees: The Case for Recognition*, New Economics Foundation, London, 2003.
3. Arab Republic of Egypt, *Egypt National Environmental, Economic and Development Study (NEEDS) for Climate Change. Under the UNFCCC*, Arab Republic of Egypt, Cabinet of Ministries, Ministry of State for Environmental Affairs, Egyptian Environmental Affairs Agency, Climate Change Central Department, Cairo, 2010.
4. J.-L.E. Cartron, G. Ceballos and S. Felger, *Biodiversity, Ecosystems and Conservation in Northern Mexico*, Oxford University Press, Oxford, 2005.
5. US Department of Homeland Security, *Estimates of the Unauthorized Immigrant Population Residing in the United States: 1990 to 2000*, US Department of Homeland Security, Washington DC, 31 January 2003.
6. Asociación Mexicana de Transformación Rural y Urbana (AMEXTRA), Mexico, quoted in R. Roach, *Dried up, Drowned out: Voices from the Developing World on a Changing Climate*, Tearfund, Teddington, 2005.
7. R. Ramesh, 'Paradise Almost Lost: Maldives Seek to Buy a New Homeland', *Guardian*, 10 November 2008.
8. M. Conisbee and A. Simms, *Environmental Refugees: The Case for Recognition*. New Economics Foundation, London, 2003.
9. Ibid.
10. Ibid.

CHAPTER 12

1. J. Lind, M. Ibrahim and K. Harris, *Climate Change and Conflict: Moving Beyond the Impasse*, IDS In Focus Briefing, issue 15, Institute of Development Studies, Brighton, May 2010.
2. J. Barnett and W.N. Adger, 'Climate change, human security and violent conflict', *Political Geography* 26(6) (2007): 639–55.
3. UNEP, *Sudan Post-Conflict Environment Assessment*, UNEP, Nairobi, 2007.
4. J. Sachs, 'Land, water and conflict', *Newsweek*, 7–14 July 2008.
5. Lind, Ibrahim and Harris, *Climate Change and Conflict*.
6. I. Salehyan, 'From climate change to conflict? No consensus yet', *Journal of Peace Research* 45(3) (2008): 315–26.

CHAPTER 13

1. R. Roach, *Two Degrees, One Chance: The Urgent Need to Curb Global Warming*, Tearfund, Oxfam, Practical Action, Christian Aid, London, 2007.
2. See Article 4.8 and 4.9 of the United Nations Framework Convention on Climate Change.
3. World Bank, *The Economics of Adaptation to Climate Change*, World Bank, Washington DC, 2010.
4. C. Crabbe, 'France caught cold by heatwave', *Bulletin of the World Health Organisation* 81(10) (2003): 773–4.
5. GEA, *Global Energy Assessment: Toward a Sustainable Future*, Cambridge University Press, Cambridge, 2012.
6. K. Pender, 'Government bailout hits $8.5 trillion', *San Francisco Chronicle*, 26 November 2008.
7. H.E. Daly, *Steady-State Economics*, W.H. Freeman, San Francisco, 1977.
8. H.E. Daly, *Beyond Growth: Economics of Sustainable Development*, Beacon Press, Boston MA, 1997.

9. A. Turner, 'Dethroning growth', in A. Simms and J. Smith (eds), *Do Good Lives Have to Cost the Earth?* Constable & Robinson, London, 2008.

10. A. Simms, V. Johnson, J. Smith and S. Mitchell, *Consumption Explosion: The Third UK Interdependence Day Report*, New Economics Foundation, London, 2009.

11. D. Woodward and A. Simms, *Growth Isn't Working: The Unbalanced Distribution of Benefits and Costs from Growth*, New Economics Foundation, London, 2006.

13. W. Maathai, *The Challenge for Africa*, Pantheon, New York, 2009.

12. Woodward and Simms, *Growth Isn't Working*.

14. S. Abdallah et al., *The (un)Happy Planet Index 2.0: Why Good Lives Don't Have to Cost the Earth*, New Economics Foundation, London, 2009.

15. UN ESCAP, *Green Growth at a Glance: The Way Forward for Asia and the Pacific*, United Nations Economic and Social Commission for Asia and the Pacific, Bangkok, 2006.

16. United Nations Environmental Programme, Regional Resource Centre for Asia and the Pacific (UNEP RRCAP) resources; see www.rrcap.ait.asia/nsds/pub/sustainable%20development%20pathways.pdf (accessed 25 June 2013).

17. See www.grossnationalhappiness.com (accessed 25 June 2013).

18. See https://sites.google.com/site/thekingdomofbhutan/nhi (accessed 23 June 2013).

19. See www.happyplanetindex.org (accessed 23 June 2013).

20. N. Marks, A. Simms, S. Thompson and S. Aballah, *The Happy Planet Index: An Index of Human Well-being and Environmental Impact*, New Economics Foundation, London, 2006.

21. Green New Deal Group, *A Green New Deal: Joined-up Policies to Solve the Triple Crunch of the Credit Crisis, Climate Change and High Oil Prices*, New Economics Foundation, London, 2008.

Bibliography

Abdallah S. et al. (2009) *The (un)Happy Planet Index 2.0: Why Good Lives Don't Have to Cost the Earth.* New Economics Foundation, London.

Africa Partnership Forum Support Unit (2007) *Gender and Economic Empowerment of Women.* Africa Partnership Forum Support Unit (OECD), Paris.

Agrawala, S., et al. (2003) *Development and Climate Change in Bangladesh: Focus on Coastal Flooding and the Sundarbans.* OECD, Paris.

Agrawala, S., et al. (2003) *Development and Climate in Fiji: Focus on Coastal Mangroves.* OECD, Paris.

Ahmed, A.U., et al. (2007) *The World's Most Deprived: Characteristics and Causes of Extreme Poverty and Hunger.* International Food Policy Research Institute, Washington DC.

Alam, M., and M.D.G. Rabbani (2007) 'Vulnerabilities and responses to climate change for Dhaka'. *Environment and Urbanisation* 19: 81–97.

Arab Republic of Egypt (2010) *Egypt National Environmental, Economic and Development Study (NEEDS) for Climate Change. Under the UNFCCC.* Arab Republic of Egypt, Cabinet of Ministries, Ministry of State for Environmental Affairs, Egyptian Environmental Affairs Agency, Climate Change Central Department, Cairo.

Arnell, N.W. (2004) 'Climate change and global water resources: SRES emissions and socio-economic scenarios'. *Global Environmental Change* 14(1): 31–52.

Asian Development Bank (2003) *Socioeconomic Impacts of Climate Change and a National Response Strategy: A Report of the Regional Study on Global Environmental Issues: Country Case Study of Indonesia.* State Ministry for the Environment, Indonesian Forum for the Environment, Jakarta.

Asociación Mexicana de Transformación Rural y Urbana (AMEXTRA), Mexico. Quoted in R. Roach (2005), *Dried up, Drowned out: Voices from the Developing World on a Changing Climate.* Tearfund, Teddington.

Ayres R., and B. Warr (2009) *The Economic Growth Engine: How Energy and Work Drive Material Prosperity.* Edward Elgar, Cheltenham.

Barnett, J., and W.N. Adger (2007) 'Climate change, human security and violent conflict'. *Political Geography* 26(6): 639–55.

Bettencourt, S., et al. (2006) *Not If, But When: Adapting to Natural Hazards in the Pacific Islands Region.* World Bank, Washington DC.

Bhatnagar, A.K., and M. Koul (2004) 'Impact of climate change on medicinal plants: an assessment'. In S.K. Dash and P. Rao (eds), *Assessment of climate change in India and mitigation policies.* WWF, New Delhi.

Boonprakrob, K., and S. Hattirat (2006) *Crisis or Opportunity: Climate Change and Thailand.* Greenpeace Southeast Asia, Bangkok.

BPS (2006) *Social-Economic Indicators of Indonesia.* Badna Pusat Statistik, Jakarta.

Bradley, R.S., et al. (2006) 'Threats to water supplies in the Tropical Andes'. *Science* 312: 1755–6.

Brooks, N. (2004) *Drought in the African Sahel: Long Term Perspectives and Future Prospects.* Tyndall Centre for Climate Change Research, Norwich.

Brown, B., et al. (2000) 'Bleaching patterns in coral reefs'. *Nature* 404: 142–3.

Brown, L.R. (2006) *Plan B 2.0: Rescuing a Planet under Stress and a Civilization in Trouble.* Norton, London and New York.

Bruce, N., R. Perez-Padilla and R. Albalak (2002) *The Health Effects of Indoor Air Pollution Exposure in Developing Countries.* World Health Organization, Geneva.

Buddemeier, R.W., J.A. Kleypas and R.B. Aronson. (2004) *Coral Reefs and Global Climate Change: Potential Contributions of Climate Change to Stresses on Coral Reef Ecosystems.* Pew Center on Global Climate Change, Arlington VA.

Burke, E.J., S.J. Brown and N. Christidis (2006) 'Modelling the recent evolution of global drought and projections for the twenty-first century with the Hadley Centre climate model'. *Journal of Hydrometeorology* 7: 1113–25.

Burley, H. (2008) *What's Feeding Our Food? The Environmental and Social Impacts of the Livestock Sector.* Friends of the Earth, London.

CAN International (2003) *A Viable Global Framework for Preventing Dangerous Climate Change.* CAN Discussion Paper. CAN, Beirut.

Cartron, J.-L.E., G. Ceballos and S. Felger (2005) *Biodiversity, Ecosystems and Conservation in Northern Mexico.* Oxford University Press, Oxford.

Case, M. (2008) *The Impacts of Climate Change on Hawksbill Turtles.* WWF Climate Change Programme, Washington DC.

Cencchi, N. (2011) *Impact of Global Change on Large River Basins: Example of the Yellow River Basin.* International Food Policy Research Institute, Washington DC.

CIA (2013–14) *The World Factbook.* Directorate of Intelligence, USA, Alexandria VA.

The Climate Group (2005) *Low Carbon Leader: Cities.* The Climate Group, London.

Colchester, M., et al. (2006) *Promised Land: Palm Oil and Land Acquisition in Indonesia – Implications for Local Communities and Indigenous Peoples.* Forest People's Programme, Perkumpulan Sawit Watch, Bogor, HuMA and the World Agroforestry Centre.

Conisbee, M., and A. Simms (2003) *Environmental Refugees: The Case for Recognition.* New Economics Foundation, London.

Conway, E., and N. Oreskes (2010) *Merchants of Doubt: How a Handful of Scientists Obscured the Truth on Issues from Tobacco Smoke to Global Warming.* Bloomsbury, London and New York.

Cook, J., et al. (2013) 'Quantifying the consensus on anthropogenic global warming in the scientific literature'. *Environmental Research Letters* 8(2): 4024.

Corcoran, T. (2010) 'The cool down in climate polls'. *Financial Post,* 6 January.

Costello, A., et al. (2009) 'Managing the health effects of climate change'. Lancet and University College London Institute for Global Health Commission. *Lancet* 373: 1693–733.

Crabbe, C. (2003) 'France caught cold by heatwave'. *Bulletin of the World Health Organization* 81(10): 773–4.

Daly, H.E. (1977) *Steady-State Economics.* W.H. Freeman, San Francisco.

Daly, H.E. (1997) *Beyond Growth: Economics of sustainable Development.* Beacon Press, Boston MA.

Dasgupta, S., et al. (2007) *The Impact of Sea Level Rise on Developing Countries: A*

Comparative Analysis. World Bank Policy Research Working Paper (WPS4136). World Bank, Washington DC.

Davis, M. (2002) *Late Victorian Holocausts: El Niño Famines and the Making of the Third World*. Verso, London and New York.

De Silva, T. (n.d.) *Industrial Utilization of Medicinal Plants in Developing Countries*. United Nations Industrial Development Organization, Vienna.

de Wit, M., and J. Stankiewicz (2006) 'Changes in surface water supply across Africa with predicted climate change.' *Science* 311(5769): 1917–21

DEFRA (n.d.) *Keysheet 7: Climate Change Impacts on Forestry in India*. DEFRA, London.

DFID (2001) *Addressing the Water Crisis*. UK Department for International Development, London.

DFID (2004) *Climate Change and Poverty: Key Sheets*. Department for International Development, London.

DFID (2005) *Disaster Risk Reduction: A Development Concern*. DFID, London.

Diao, X., et al. (2007) *The Role of Agriculture in Development: Implications for Sub-Saharan Africa*. Research Report 153. International Food Policy Research Institute, Washington DC.

Dixon, R., J. Smith and S. Guill (2003) 'Life on the edge: vulnerability and adaptation of African ecosystems to global climate change'. *Mitigation and Adaptation Strategies for Global Change* 8(2):93–113

Dupont, A. (2008) 'The Strategic Implications of Climate Change'. *Survival: Global Politics and Strategy* 50(3): 29–54.

Dutta, D. (2011) 'An integrated tool for assessment of flood vulnerability of coastal cities to sea-level rise and potential socio-economic impacts: a case study in Bangkok, Thailand'. *Hydrological Sciences Journal* 56(5): 805–23.

Economist Intelligence Unit (2012) *Water for All? A Study of Water Utilities' Preparedness to Meet Supply Challenges in 2030*. Economist Intelligence Unit, Geneva and London.

Environmental Investigation Agency (2005) *The Illegal Logging Crisis in Honduras: How U.S. and E.U. Imports of Illegal Honduran Wood Increase Poverty, Fuel Corruption and Devastate Forest and Communities*. Center for International Policy, Washington DC.

Fairtrade Africa (n.d.) *Fighting Back Climate Change: How Fairtrade Helps Producers in Africa Cope*. Fairtrade Africa, Nairobi.

Faisal, I.M., and S. Parveen (2004) 'Food security in the face of climate change, population growth and resource constraints: implications for Bangladesh'. *Environmental Management* 34: 487–98.

FAO (2003) *FAO/WTP Crop and Food Supply Assessment Mission to Timor-Leste*. Food and Agriculture Organization of the United Nations, Rome.

FAO (2011) *Global Forest Land-use Change from 1990 to 2005: Initial Results from a Global Remote Sensing Survey*. FAO, Rome.

FAO (n.d.) *Women, Agriculture and Food Security*. FAO, Rome.

Field, C.B., et al. (eds) (2012) *Managing the Risks of Extreme Events and Disasters to Advance Climate Change Adaptation*. A Special Report of Working Groups I and II of the Intergovernmental Panel on Climate Change. Cambridge University Press, Cambridge.

Financial Times (2002) 'Colombia holds out for a big oil find'. *Financial Times*, 21 February 2002.

Ford, E.A.K. (2013) *From Ice to High Seas: Sea Level Rise and European Coastlines*. The ice2sea Consortium, Cambridge.

GEA (2012) *Global Energy Assessment: Toward a Sustainable Future*. Cambridge University Press, Cambridge.

Goldenberg, S. (2013) 'Secret funding helped build vast network of climate denial thinktanks'. *Guardian*, 14 February 2013.

Granich, S., M. Kelly and N.H. Ninh (1993) *Global Warming and Vietnam – A Briefing Document*. University of East Anglia, Norwich; IIED, London; Centre for Environment Research Education and Development, Hanoi.

Green New Deal Group (2008) *A Green New Deal: Joined-up Policies to Solve the Triple Crunch of the Credit Crisis, Climate Change and High Oil Prices*. New Economics Foundation, London.

Greenpeace International (2009) *Equity and Climate Action: Greenpeace Position*. Greenpeace International, Amsterdam.

Guha-Sapir, D., and P. Hoyois (2012) *Measuring the Human and Economic Impact of Disasters*. Government Office for Science, Foresight, London.

Hales, S., et al. (2002) 'Potential effect of population and climate changes on global distribution of dengue fever: an empirical model'. *Lancet* 360: 830–34.

Hall C., et al. (2003) 'Hydrocarbons and the evolution of human culture'. *Nature* 426: 318–22.

Harasawa, H. (2006) 'Key vulnerabilities and critical levels of impacts on east and south east Asia'. In H.J. Schellnhuber et al. (eds) (2006) *Avoiding Dangerous Climate Change*, pp. 243–9. Cambridge University Press, Cambridge.

Hooijer, A., et al. (2006) *PEAT-CO2, Assessment of CO2 Emissions from Drained Peatlands in SE Asia*. Delft Hydraulics and Wetlands International, The Netherlands.

Horstmann, B. (2004) *Glacial Lake Outburst Floods in Nepal and Switzerland: New Threats Due to Climate Change*. Germanwatch, Bonn.

Howden, D. (2005) 'Christmas appeal: simple measures that help in extreme temperatures'. *Independent*, 17 December 2005.

Huq, S., and J. Ayers (2008) *Climate Change Impacts and Responses in Bangladesh*. Policy Department Economic and Scientific Policy, European Parliament, Brussels.

Huq, S., and C. Toulmin (2006) *The Three Eras of Climate Change*. IIED Sustainable Development Opinion Paper. IIED, London.

IMF (2013) *Energy Subsidy Reform: Lessons and Implications*. International Monetary Fund, Washington DC.

Immerzeel, W.W., L.P.H. van Beek and M.F.P. Bierkens (2010) 'Climate change will affect the Asian water towers'. *Science* 328(5984): 1382–5.

Indriyanti, R., and B. Pedrique (2006) *Access to Primary Healthcare for the Population of the Precarious Areas of North Jakarta (Indonesia): Annual Report 2006*. Medecins du Monde (MDM)/Dokter Dunia, Indonesia.

International Energy Agency (2010) *The World Energy Outlook*. International Energy Agency, Paris.

International Energy Agency (2012) *The World Energy Outlook*. International Energy Agency, Paris.

International Federation of Red Cross and Red Crescent Societies (2001) *World Disasters Report Focus on Recovery*. International Federation of Red Cross and Red Crescent Societies, Geneva.

International Federation of Red Cross and Red Crescent Societies (2012) *World Disasters Report 2012: Focus on Forced Migration and Displacement*. International Federation of Red Cross and Red Crescent Societies, Geneva.

IPCC (2001) *Climate Change 2001: Synthesis Report. A Contribution of Working Groups I, II, and III to the Third Assessment Report of the Intergovernmental*

Panel on Climate Change, ed. R.T. Watson and the Core Writing Team. Cambridge University Press, Cambridge.

IUCN (1996) *1996 IUCN Red List of Threatened Animals*. IUCN, Gland.

Jacobson, M.Z., and M.A. Delucchi (2011) 'Providing all global energy with wind, water, and solar power, Part I: Technologies, energy resources, quantities and areas of infrastructure, and materials'. *Energy Policy* 39(3): 1154–69.

Jeans, H., et al. (2014) 'The role of ecosystems in climate change adaptation: Lessons for scaling up'. In E.L.F. Schipper et al., *Community Based Adaptation to Climate Change: Scaling it up*. Routledge, London.

Jianyun, Z., et al. (2009) 'Impact of climate change on water security in China'. *Advances in Climate Change Research* 5(suppl.): 34–40.

Jobin, W. (2003) 'Health and equity impacts of a large oil project in Africa'. *Bulletin of the World Health Organization*. WHO, Geneva.

Jouzel, J., et al. (2007) 'Orbital and millennial Antarctic climate variability over the past 800,000 years'. *Science* 317: 793–6.

Jovel, J.R. (1989) *Natural Disasters and Their Economic and Social Impact*. CEPAL Review No. 38. Economic Commissions, Latin America and the Caribbean, Santiago de Chile.

Kalaughter, L. (2007) *Climate Models Indicate Rice Agriculture in Indonesia Will Suffer*. IOP Publishing, Bristol.

Karat Coalition (2011) *Climate Change: Women in Developing Countries, the Hardest Hit*. Karat Coalition, Warsaw.

Keeling, C.D. (1998) 'Rewards and penalties of monitoring the earth'. *Annual Review of Energy and the Environment* 23: 25–82.

Khalik, A. (2007) 'Climate change already hitting RI's poorest'. *Jakarta Post*, 11 June 2007.

Kimani, M. (2012) 'Women struggle to secure land rights: hard fight for access and decision-making power'. *Africa Renewal: Special Edition on Women 2012*.

Kirkbride, M. (2006) *Delivering the Agenda: Addressing Chronic Under-development in Kenya's Arid Lands*. Oxfam Briefing Paper 88. Oxfam International, Oxford.

Kovats, R.S. (2000) 'El Niño and human health'. *Bulletin of the World Health Organization* 78(9): 1127–35.

KPMG (2012) *Taxes and Incentives for Renewable Energy*. KPMG International Cooperative, Amsterdam.

Krishnaswamy, A., and A. Hanson (1999) *Our Forests, Our Future: Summary Report of the World Commission on Forests and Sustainable Development*. World Commission on Forests and Sustainable Development, Winnipeg, Manitoba.

La Trobe, S., and P. Venton (2003) *Natural Disaster Risk Reduction: The Policy and Practice of Selected Institutional Donors*. Tearfund, Teddington.

Larios, M.V., et al. (2003) *Honduras frente al cambio climático*. PBBC–FAO, Tegucigalpa.

Laurance, W.F. (2006) 'The value of trees'. *New Scientist* 2547: 24.

Lautze, S., et al. (2002) *Qaht -E-Pool – 'A Cash Famine'. Food Insecurity in Afghanistan 1999–2002*. Feinstein International Famine Centre, Tufts University, Massachusetts.

Lenton, T.M., et al. (2008) 'Tipping elements in the Earth's climate system'. *Proceedings of the National Academy of Sciences of the United States of America* 105(6): 1786–93.

Leslie, J. (2007) *Before the Deluge: Coping with Floods in a Changing Climate*. International Rivers Network, Berkeley CA.

Li, X., et al. (2008) 'Cryospheric change in China. *Global and Planetary Change* 62: 210–18.

Lind, J., M. Ibrahim and K. Harris (2010) *Climate Change and Conflict: Moving Beyond the Impasse*. IDS In Focus Briefing, issue 15, May 2010. Institute of Development Studies, Brighton.

Lobban, C.S., and M. Schefter (1997) *Tropical Pacific Island Environments*. Island Environments Books, Mangilao, Guam.

Maathai, W. (2009) *The Challenge for Africa*. Pantheon, New York.

Magrath, J., and A. Simms (2006) *Africa – Up in Smoke 2. The Second Report on Africa and Global Warming from the Working Group on Climate Change and Development*. New Economics Foundation, London.

Mark, M. (2012) 'Nigeria's penalty for gas flaring will not curb emissions, say campaigners'. *Guardian*, 31 May 2012.

Marks, N., et al. (2006) *The Happy Planet Index: An Index of Human Well-being and Environmental Impact*. New Economics Foundation, London.

Martens, P., et al. (1999) 'Climate change and future populations at risk of malaria'. *Global Environmental Change* 9(1): S89–S107.

Mayne, R. (2006) *Causing Hunger: An Overview of the Food Crisis in Africa*. Oxfam Briefing Paper 91, July 2006. Oxfam International, Oxford.

McCarthy, J.J., et al. (eds) (2001) *Climate Change 2001: Impacts, Adaptation and Vulnerability, IPCC Working Group II, Third Assessment Report*. Cambridge University Press, Cambridge.

McCrone, A. (2012) *Global Trends in Renewable Energy Investment 2012*. Frankfurt School of Finance and Management, Frankfurt.

McCully, P. (2007) *Before the Deluge: Coping with Floods in a Changing Climate*. IRN Dams, Rivers and People Report 2007. International Rivers Network, Berkeley CA.

McField, M.D. (1999) 'Coral response during and after mass bleaching in Belize'. *Bulletin of Marine Science* 64(1): 155–72.

McField, M.D. (2002) 'Influence and disturbance of coral reef community structure in Belize'. *Proceedings of the Ninth International Coral Reef Symposium*, Bali, October 2000, pp. 6–68.

McGhie, J., et al. (2006) *The Climate of Poverty: Facts, Fears and Hope*. Christian Aid, London.

McMichael, A.J. (ed.) (2003) *Climate Change and Human Health: Risk and Responses*. WHO, UNEP, WMO, Geneva.

McSmith, A. (2006) 'The pollution gap'. *Independent*, 25 March 2006.

Meadows, D.H., et al. (1972) *Limits to Growth*. New American Library, New York.

Mehta, L. (ed.) (2010) *The Limits to Scarcity: Contesting the Politics of Allocation*. Routledge, London.

Midgley, G.F., et al. (2002) 'Assessing the vulnerability of species richness to anthropogenic climate change in a biodiversity hotspot'. *Global Ecology and Biogeography* 11(6): 445–51.

Millennium Ecosystem Assessment (2005) *Ecosystems and Human Well-Being: Biodiversity Synthesis: A Report of the Millennium Ecosystem Assessment*. World Resources Institute, Washington DC.

Ministry of the Environment and Conservation United Nations Development Programme (2000) *Papua New Guinea: Initial National Communication under the UNFCCC*. Government of Papua New Guinea, Port Moresby.

Mirza, M., and Q. Monirul (2002) 'Global warming and changes in the probability of occurrence of floods in Bangladesh and implications'. *Global Environmental Change* 12: 127–38.

MOST (Ministry of Science and Technology of the People's Republic of China), CASS (Chinese Academy of Science), CMA (China Meteorological

Administration) (2007) *National Assessment Report on Climate Change*, Science Press, Bejing.

Murphy, S., D. Burch and J. Clapp (2012) *Cereal Secrets: The World's Largest Grain Traders and Global Agriculture*. Oxfam research report. Oxfam, Oxford.

Myers, N. (2005) 'Environmental Refugees: An Emergent Security Issue'. 13th Economic Forum, Prague, 23–27 May.

National Climate Change Office at the Department of Environment (2003) *National Communication to the UNFCCC*, Tehran.

Naylor, R.L., et al. (2002) 'Using El Niño-Southern Oscillation climate data to improve food policy planning in Indonesia'. *Bulletin of Indonesian Economic Studies* 38: 75–91.

Naylor, R.L., et al. (2007) 'Assessing risks of climate variability and climate change for Indonesian rice agriculture'. *Proceedings of the National Academy of Sciences* 104: 19.

Netherlands Environmental Assessment Agency (2007) *China Now No. 1 in CO_2 Emissions; USA in Second Position*. MNP, Bilthoven, The Netherlands.

Nhantumbo, I., and L. Rolington (2011) *Talking REDD+: Beyond Forestry – Joining up and Moving Forward*. IIED, London.

NYCGP (2012) *Best Practice: Comprehensive Climate Change Plan. City: Mexico City*. New York City Global Partners, New York.

OECD (2004) 'Exploiting Africa's huge potential as weapon against poverty'. OECD, Paris; www.oecd.org/dataoecd/43/45/32285615.pdf.

Oreskes, N. (2004) 'The Scientific Consensus on Climate Change'. *Science* 306(5702): 1686.

Orindi, V.A., and L.A. Murray (2005) *Adapting to Climate Change in East Africa: A Strategic Approach*. Gatekeeper series no. 117. IIED, London.

Oxfam–Vietnam and the Graduate School of Global Environmental Studies of Kyoto University, Japan (2007) *Drought Management Considerations for Climate Change Adaptation: Focus on the Mekong Region (Report Vietnam)*. Oxfam in Vietnam, Hanoi.

Pan, Y., et al. (2011) 'A large and persistent carbon sink in the world's forests'. *Science* 333: 988–93.

Parry, M.L., et al. (2004) 'Effects of climate change on global food production under SRES emissions and socio-economic scenarios. *Global Environmental Change* 14: 53–67.

Parry, M.L., et al. (eds) (2007) *Contribution of Working Group II to the Fourth Assessment Report of the Intergovernmental Panel on Climate Change*. Cambridge University Press, Cambridge and New York.

Parry, M., et al. (2009) *Climate Change and Hunger: Responding to the Challenge*. World Food Programme, Rome.

Patt, A.G., A. Dazé and P. Suarez (2009) 'Gender and climate change vulnerability: what's the problem? What's the solution?' In M. Ruth and M.E. Ibarrarán (eds), *Distributional Impacts of Climate Change and Disasters: Concepts and Cases*, p. 82. Edward Elgar, Cheltenham.

PEACE (2007) *Indonesia and Climate Change: Current Status and Policies*. World Bank, DFID and PEACE, Jakarta.

Pender, K. (2008) 'Government bailout hits $8.5 trillion'. *San Francisco Chronicle*, 26 November.

Peters, G.P., et al. (2011) 'Rapid growth in CO_2 emissions after the 2008–2009 global financial crisis'. *Nature Climate Change* 2: 2–4.

Pfeffer W.T., J.T. Harper and S. O'Neel (2008) 'Kinematic constraints on glacier contributions to 21st century sea-level rise'. *Science* 321: 1340–43.

Piao, S., et al. (2010) 'The impacts of climate change on water resources and agriculture in China'. *Nature* 467: 43–51.

Pilson, M. (2006) 'We are evaporating our coal mines into the air'. *AMBIO* 35(3): 130–33.

Pounds, J., M.P.L. Fogden and J.H. Campbell (1999) 'Biological response to climate change on a tropical mountain'. *Nature* 398: 611–15.

Rahmsdorf, S. (2007) 'A semi-empirical approach to projecting future sea-level rise'. *Science* 315: 368–70.

Ramesh, R. (2008) 'Paradise almost lost: Maldives seek to buy a new homeland'. *Guardian*, 10 November.

Reid, H. (2004) 'Climate change – biodiversity and livelihood impacts'. In D. Roe (ed.), *The Millennium Development Goals and Conservation*, pp. 37–54. IIED, London.

Reid, H., M. Chambwera and L. Murray (2013) *Tried and tested: Learning from farmers on adaptation to climate change*. IIED Gatekeeper series no. 153. IIED, London

Reid, H., and A. Simms (2007) *Up in Smoke? Asia and the Pacific. Fifth Report of the Working Group on Climate Change and Development*. New Economics Foundation, London.

Roach, R. (2005) *Dried up, Drowned out: Voices from the Developing World on a Changing Climate*. Tearfund, London.

Roach, R. (2007) *Two Degrees, One Chance: The Urgent Need to Curb Global Warming*. Tearfund, Oxfam, Practical Action, Christian Aid.

Rockström, J., et al. (2008) 'A safe operating space for humanity'. *Nature* 461: 472–5.

Rockström, J., et al. (2009) 'Future water availability for global food production: the potential of green water for increasing resilience to global change'. *Water Resources Research* 45(7).

Royal Society (2010) *Climate Change: A Summary of the Science*. Royal Society, London.

Sachs, J. (2008) 'Land, water and conflict'. *Newsweek*, 7–14 July 2008.

Salehyan, I. (2008) 'From climate change to conflict? No consensus yet'. *Journal of Peace Research* 45(3): 315–26.

Schlenker, W., and D.B. Lobell (2010) 'Robust negative impacts of climate change on African agriculture'. *Environmental Research Letters* 5(1).

Schlesinger, S. (2010) *Sugar Cane and Land Use Change in Brazil: Biofuel Crops, Indirect Land Use Change and Emissions*. Friends of the Earth Europe, Brussels.

Seas, C., et al. (2000) 'New insights on the emergence of cholera in Latin America during 1991: the Peruvian experience'. *American Journal of Tropical Medicine and Hygiene* 62(4): 513–17.

Sercombe, B., and A. Albanese (2006) *Our Drowning Neighbours: Labor's Policy Discussion Paper on Climate Change in the Pacific*. Australian Labor Party, Canberra.

Shiva, V. (2007) 'India needs her small farmers for food security, livelihood security, peace and democracy'. *ZNET Daily commentaries*, 5 April.

Simms, A. (2000) *Collision Course: Free Trade's Free Ride on the Global Climate*. New Economics Foundation, London.

Simms, A., (2009) *Consumption Explosion: The Third UK Interdependence Day Report*. New Economics Foundation, London.

Simms, A., V. Johnson and M. Edwards (2009) *Other Worlds are Possible: Human Progress in an Age of Climate Change*. New Economics Foundation, London.

Simms, A., J. Magrath and H. Reid (2004) *Up in Smoke. Threats From, and*

Responses to, the Impact of Global Warming on Human Development. New Economics Foundation, London.

Simms, A., and H. Reid (2005) *Africa – Up in Smoke? The Second Report from the Working Group on Climate Change and Development.* New Economics Foundation, London.

Simms, A., and H. Reid (2006) *Up in smoke? Latin America and the Caribbean. The threat from Climate Change to the Environment and Human Development. The third report from the Working Group on Climate Change and Development.* New economics foundation, London.

Simms A., and J. Smith (eds) (2008) *Do Good Lives Have to Cost the Earth?* Constable & Robinson, London.

Solomon S., (2007) *Climate Change 2007: The Physical Science Basis. Contribution of the Working Group I to the Fourth Assessment Report of the Intergovernmental Panel on Climate Change.* Cambridge University Press, Cambridge.

State Oceanic Administration (2006) *National Sea Level Bulletin.* State Oceanic Administration, China.

Stern, N. (2006) *Stern Review: The Economics of Climate Change.* HM Treasury, London.

Swarup, A., et al. (2011) *Weathering the Storm: Adolescent Girls and Climate Change.* Plan UK, London

Swiderska, K., et al. (2011) *Adapting Agriculture with Traditional Knowledge.* IIED briefing paper, October. IIED, London.

Tamiotti, L., et al. (2009) *Trade and Climate Change. WTO–UNEP Report.* World Trade Organization, Geneva.

Tanser, F.C., B. Sharp and D. le Sueur (2003) 'Potential effect of climate change on malaria transmission in Africa'. *Lancet* (362): 1792–8.

Thanh Nien News (2007) 'Major losses loom as Vietnam sea level rises'. http://talkvietnam.com/2007/05/major-losses-loom-as-vietnam-sea-level-rises-experts.

Thomas, C.D., et al.(2004) 'Extinction risk from climate change'. *Nature* 427: 145–8.

Tran, V.L., D.C. Hoang and T.T. Tran (2005) *Building of Climate Change Scenario for Red River Catchments for Sustainable Development and Environmental Protection.* Preprints, Science Workshop on Hydrometeorological Change in Vietnam and Sustainable Development, Hanoi, Vietnam, Ministry of Natural Resource and Environment, Hanoi, pp. 70–82.

UN (2002) *Plan of Implementation of the World Summit on Sustainable Development.* United Nations, New York.

UN (2012) *World Urbanization Prospects: The 2011 Revision. Highlights.* Department of Economic and Social Affairs, Population Division, United Nations, New York.

UN ESCAP (2006) *Green Growth at a Glance: The Way Forward for Asia and the Pacific.* United Nations Economic and Social Commission for Asia and the Pacific, Bangkok.

UNEP (1999) *Trade Liberalisation and the Environment – Lessons Learned from Bangladesh, Chile, India, Philippines, Romania and Uganda: A Synthesis Report.* United Nations Environment Programme, Geneva.

UNEP (2005) *Africa Environment Outlook: Past, Present and Future Perspectives. Impacts of the State of the Environment.* UNEP, Washington DC.

UNEP (2006) *Migratory Species and Climate Change – Impacts of a Changing Environment on Wild Animals.* UNEP/CMS Secretariat, Bonn.

UNEP (2006) *Pacific Island Mangroves in a Changing Climate and Rising Seas.*

Regional Seas Programme of UNEP, Secretariat of the Pacific Regional Environment Programme, Samoa. UNEP, New York.

UNEP (2007) *Sudan Post-Conflict Environment Assessment*. UNEP, Nairobi.

UNEP (2012) *The Emissions Gap Report 2012: A UNEP Synthesis Report*. United Nations Environment Programme, Nairobi, Kenya.

UNEP/GRID–Arendal and Development Alternatives (2011) *Climate Change Mitigation in India*. UNEP/GRID–Arendal, Norway; Development Alternatives, New Delhi.

UNFPA (2007) *State of World Population 2007: Unleashing the Potential of Urban Growth*. United Nations Population Fund, New York.

US Department of Homeland Security (2003) *Estimates of the Unauthorized Immigrant Population Residing in the United States: 1990 to 2000*. 31 January. US Department of Homeland Security, Washington DC.

Vidal, V. (2000) 'Impactos de la Aplicación de Políticas sobre cambio climatico en la Forestacion del Paramo del Ecuador'. Programa de Doctorado en Ciencias ambientales, Universitad Autónoma de Barcelona. In J. Recharte, J. Torres and G. Medina, II Conferencia Electrónica sobre usos Sostenibles y Conservación del Ecosistema Páramo en los Andes, 22 May–30 June, pp. 47–51. CONDESAN, Lima.

Vörösmarty, C.J., et al. (2010) 'Global threats to human water security and river biodiversity'. *Nature* 467: 555–61.

Watkins, K. (2007) *Fighting Climate Change: Human Solidarity in a Divided World. Human Development Report 2007/2008*. UNDP. Palgrave Macmillan, New York.

Watson, R.T., M.C. Zinyowera and R.H. Moss (eds) (1997) *The Regional Impacts of Climate Change: An Assessment of Vulnerability*. Intergovernmental Panel on Climate Change. Cambridge University Press, Cambridge.

Webster, P.J., et al. (2005) 'Changes in tropical cyclone number, duration and intensity in a warming environment'. *Science* 309: 1844–6.

Wetlands International (2013) *Policy Brief on Indirect Land Use Change and Peatlands*. Wetlands International, Wageningen.

Whittaker, M. (n.d.) *CEObriefing: A Document of the UNEP FI Climate Change-Working Group*. UNEP Finance Initiatives. UNEP, Nairobi.

Woodward D., and A. Simms (2006) *Growth Isn't Working: The Unbalanced Distribution of Benefits and Costs from Growth*. New Economics Foundation, London.

World Bank (2010) *The Economics of Adaptation to Climate Change*. World Bank, Washington DC.

World Food Programme (2009) *2009 Food Aid Flows*. World Food Programme, Rome.

World Food Programme (2010) *Hunger and Climate Change*. World Food Programme, Rome.

WWF (2008) *Palm Oil, Soy and Tropical Forests: A Strategy for Life*. WWF Forest conversion Programme, Gland.

WWF Brazil (2006) *Powerswitch Study for Brazil*. WWF, Brasilia.

Xu, J., et al. (2009) 'The melting Himalayas: cascading effects of climate change on water, biodiversity, and livelihoods'. *Conservation Biology* 23(3): 520–30.

Xuejie, G., et al. (2001) 'Climate change due to greenhouse effects in China as simulated by a regional climate model', *Advances in Atmospheric Sciences* 18(6): 1224–30.

Zhou, G., et al. (2004) 'Association between climate variability and malaria epidemics in the East African highlands'. *Proceedings of the National Academy of Sciences* 101(8): 2375–80.

Index